Dictionary
of
Special Education
and
Rehabilitation

Fourth Edition

Edited by

Glenn A. Vergason
Georgia State University

M. L. Anderegg
Kennesaw State College (Georgia)

Published by Love Publishing Company
Denver, Colorado 80222

Library of Congress Catalog Card Number 95-82151

Copyright © 1997, 1990, 1985, 1978
Love Publishing Company
Printed in the United States of America
ISBN 0-89108-243-3

Contents

Preface to Fourth Edition

This reference work is offered in response to a need we have observed during years of work in special education and rehabilitation. That need is still there, as testified to by the many people who are continuing to use this resource. One of the first problems encountered by new recruits in college is the vocabulary specific to the field. Anyone, in fact, who is not experienced in or directly involved in special education and rehabilitation is likely to be confused by the terminology and jargon. Through this resource, we hope to give more meaning to the language of special education and rehabilitation.

We have sought to provide an understandable explanation of the terminology most commonly used by educators and by rehabilitation workers. This work is not categorical but tries to cover the specialties with equal attention to all. The terms were selected after perusing the pages and indexes of nearly 100 currently used texts and professional books, and some are continual with updates from the 1971 publication titled *A Dictionary of Exceptional Children*.

An attempt was made to compose the definitions in the clearest, most practical manner possible, and key terms within a single definition are cross-referenced by use of italics. Pronunciations, where needed, are included in a phonetic style. The word-by-word method is used for alphabetization. In this style, *acoustic neuroma* precedes *acoustically handicapped,* for example.

We are indebted to Stan Love for his belief in and support of this project. The current edition represents the fifth form in which this dictionary has appeared since its publication as the first *Dictionary of Exceptional Children* by Dr. Leo Kelly in 1971. Subsequent editions were authored by Dr. Kelly and Dr. Vergason. In the fourth edition, Dr. M. L. Anderegg has joined Dr. Vergason as coauthor.

The present edition represents a major expansion, improvement, and updating. The listings of resources at the back of the book have undergone extensive revisions. Associations and journals that have changed names or ceased to exist are noted. New associations and journals have been added. The current list represents the best that can be obtained at this point in time. Every effort was made to verify accuracy. Canadian, European, and Australian entries are included.

Because terminology changes, the same terms in this edition may express different meanings than those written in 1990. We have tried to indicate for the user of this dictionary the preferability of one term's use over that of another.

We hope the more experienced professionals in the field will recognize the value of this work, especially for those they are helping to learn about the field and those with whom they are interacting to further the knowledge of special education and rehabilitation—students, parents, paraprofessionals, aides, laypersons, general educators, and other professionals. It is for them that this source was primarily compiled.

Previous editions contained acknowledgments to many individuals. By the time of this edition, the teachers, colleagues, typists, and graduate assistants have become too numerous to list. Many thanks to all of you who have assisted in any way in this edition, and a special thanks to Elaine Bogan.

A

a- A prefix meaning without, or absent, as in *agenesis* (absence of organ or tissue).

ABA design The most common form of behavior treatment design, in which *baseline* data are collected and then the treatment is conducted, after which there is a return to no treatment and a second baseline is derived.

ABAB design A behavioral treatment design in which *baseline* data are collected and then the *intervention* is introduced, after which there is a reinstatement of baseline, then a reinstatement of the intervention, and then a return to baseline. Sometimes referred to as repeated baseline procedures.

abacus (ab'-uh-kus) A device used in counting and performing calculations by sliding counters along rods or in grooves; often useful as an aid in teaching basic arithmetic, especially to students with *mental retardation* and *visual impairment*.

abbreviated speech The use of incomplete *language* units; may be the result of shyness, the failure to develop a sufficient command of language, underlying speech problems, or a style of communication that the speaker's environment has forced him/her to adopt. (See also *holophrastic speech*.)

abduction (ab-duck'-shun) Movement of a limb outward and away from the center of the body, as in raising an arm laterally. May also refer to movement of the vocal folds during *phonation*. Opposite of *adduction*.

aberration Physical or mental deviation from normal. "Abnormality" and "deviation" can be used synonymously with "aberration."

ability grouping The gathering of students into separate sections according to their basic competence or achievement in a specific area of study; often determined on the basis of *academic achievement* or performance on *standardized tests*.

ability profile A graphic representation of *grade-level* or age-level equivalents for a child, showing strengths and weaknesses on various ability dimensions.

abiotrophy (ab-ee-ot'-roe-fee) *Degeneration* or failure of tissues resulting in a loss of vitality and resistance to infection.

ablation Removal of a body part by surgery.

ablutomania (ab-loo-toe-may'-nee-ah) A psychologically abnormal *compulsion* to clean or wash one's body.

abrachia (ah-brak'-ee-ah) A *congenital* absence of the arms.

absence seizures See *petit mal*.

absolute threshold See *threshold*.

absolutely profoundly disabled A term that came into use in the late 1980s to describe persons who are so *severely retarded* or *multiply handicapped* that no program or training methodology is likely to produce change. (See also *relatively profoundly disabled*.)

abstract concept 1. An idea or image of a situation, a symbol, or an object that can be selected from any specific attributes in the environment; e.g., shape (squareness) is an abstraction (abstract *concept*) from a physical object, which has many aspects in addition to shape. 2. Sometimes used to refer to complex ideas, generally of symbolic origin, that tend to be difficult to understand.

abstract intelligence An *intellectual* capacity to comprehend from symbolic, intangible situations and *language*.

abstract reasoning The ability to understand relationships, ideas, images, and symbols, which are more intangible than objects. The inability to reason abstractly generally is associated with *mental retardation* or *neurological impairment*.

abulia (ah-byew'-lee-ah) Loss of willpower and the ability to make decisions. An individual affected by this condition has little initiative.

abuse *Overt* action resulting in harm without regard for damage done.

academic achievement A student's level of performance in one or more of the basic school subjects; generally measured by *standardized (achievement) tests* or by less formal instruments in the classroom. An *achievement level* of 2.2 in math would indicate that in most math skills the student performs as might be expected of someone in the second month of second grade.

academic aptitude The combination of abilities and potential necessary to achieve in schoolwork. Also called "scholastic aptitude" and "academic potential."

academic inventory A series of *test items*, arranged in order of difficulty, that is administered to a pupil to determine level of academic functioning. Results of the *inventory* become a basis for planning future learning activities.

academic learning time (ALT) The amount of time in which students are engaged in academic activities in which they have high success rates. ALT has the added advantage over *engaged time* and *allocated time* of specifying a high success rate.

acalculia (ay-kal-kyew'-lee-ah) A condition in which an individual has severe problems with, or a total inability to do, simple arithmetic calculations. (See also *dyscalculia*.)

acampsia (ah-kamp'-see-ah) Inflexibility or *rigidity* of a limb or joint; limits *mobility*.

acataphasia (ah-kat-ah-fay'-zee-ah) The inability to phrase words into connected, meaningful sentences.

acceleration 1. The process by which a student completes the work of school grades at a rate of more than one grade each year, thus reducing the time needed to complete a course of study. Practices such as early admission, grade skipping, *advanced placement, telescoping* of *grade levels* in upgraded situations, and credit by examination are some of the approaches used in acceleration. 2. In *behavior modification*, acceleration refers to an increase in the rate of occurrence of a behavior.

accent The syllable(s) in a word that receive(s) more force than the other syllables when the word is spoken. If an individual does not learn the correct accent in a word, the resulting *vocalization* may be distorted.

access time The time required to move to or from a point; may be an important aspect in planning building evacuation procedures for individuals with *disabilities*.

accessible (n., **accessibility**) A term often used to denote building facilities that are *barrier-free*, which enhances use by persons with *physical disabilities*.

accommodation (v., **accommodate**) 1. Involuntary adjustment of the eye by a change in the shape of the *lens*, enabling a person to see clearly at different *focal lengths*. 2. Adjusting teaching methods and modes of response or *evaluation* to a student's *disabilities*.

acculturation (ah-kul-tur-ray'-shun) The process whereby one group absorbs certain features of the culture of a second group.

accuracy The extent to which vision and hearing organs transmit *stimuli* to the brain without distortion or error. Related to *sensory* capability.

acedia (ah-see'-dee-ah) A mental disorder in which the individual is *depressed, apathetic,* and generally in a state of *melancholy.*

acetone (ass'-eh-tone) A liquid *ketone* found in abnormally large quantities in the urine of a person with *diabetes.*

achievement level The degree of success a student has in an academic subject area as determined by *formal* or *informal testing* methods. Thus, a child with an achievement level of 3.2 in math would be achieving as might be expected of someone in the second month of third grade.

achievement test An instrument designed to measure a person's knowledge, skills, and understanding in a subject matter area. Typically, an achievement test consists of measures of more than one type (e.g., reading, math, spelling).

Achilles (ah-kill'-eez) **tendon** The strong, fibrous tissue that joins the muscle in the calf of the leg to the heel bone; often affected by physical conditions involving the feet, such as *clubfoot* and *cerebral palsy.*

achondrogenesis (ah-kahn-droe-jen'-eh-sis A *hereditary* form of *dwarfism* characterized by markedly shortened limbs, with normal head and trunk size. The resulting condition is referred to as *achondroplasia* or achondroplasia dwarfism.

achondroplasia (ah-kahn-droe-play'-zee-ah) A rare defect in the formation of *cartilage* and the skeleton that results in a form of *dwarfism* in which the limbs are short, the trunk size is normal, and the face is small.

achromatopsia (ah-crow-mat-op'-see-ah) A *congenital* eye condition resulting from absence or abnormality of the *retinal* cones used for color differentiation. Vision is generally improved in reduced illumination. In more severe cases, color vision is completely lacking.

acid (vernacular) A term widely used for the *hallucinogen* LSD-25.

acoria (ah-core'-ee-ah) A condition in which a person cannot satisfy his/her hunger and as a result feels he/she never has enough to eat.

acoustic (uh-koo'-stik) Related to the sense of hearing or to the science of sound.

acoustic method 1. A way of teaching persons who are *deaf* to speak properly and to understand speech through stimulation and training of their *auditory* and *tactile* sense organs with sound vibrations produced by the voice or by sonorous instruments; utilizes *residual hearing* to the fullest possible extent. 2. An approach to teaching the production of a new sound or altering the improper production of an old one during speech training or *speech correction* lessons; this method was developed by Max Goldstein.

acoustic neuroma A tumor of the eighth *cranial (auditory)* nerve.

acoustically handicapped Describes a condition of *hearing impairment* great enough that the person requires special services. (See also *hearing loss.*)

acquired immune deficiency syndrome (AIDS) A disease complex that affects the body's disease-fighting capacity so that the afflicted person is susceptible to a number of diseases that the body would otherwise be able to fight off.

acquisition The initial learning of information or skills.

acrocephaly See *oxycephaly.*

acromegaly (ak-roe-meg'-ah-lee)   A condition wherein a mature person develops an enlarged nose, jaw, fingers, toes, or other skeletal *extremities*. This enlargement is caused by the hypersecretion of *pituitary gland* growth *hormones*.

acronym (ak'-roe-nim) A word formed by the initial letters of the principal components of a compound name or term (e.g., CEC for Council for Exceptional Children).

acroparesthesia (ak-roe-pare-es-the'-zee-ah) A condition characterized by a tingling, numbness, or stiffness in the fingers, hands, forearms, or other body *extremities*.

acting-out behavior Inappropriate actions that involve more than usual activity; may be destructive or *aggressive* in nature.

active assisted motion A technique in which a *physical therapist* helps an individual in carrying out prescribed motions in an attempt to strengthen muscles that are too weak to carry out the motion unaided.

active listening A technique in counseling whereby the counselor is able to convey to the client, through his/her appearance, reflective statements, and gestures, an understanding of and interest in what the client is saying. This technique is important in teaching *exceptional children*.

active participation A term used largely in the 1990s by those involved in the education of students with *severe disabilities* in general education settings using *peer tutoring, cooperative learning*, circles of friends, specific support, and other activities that might assist their educational placement.

activities of daily living (ADL) Refers to the practical skills needed to function in society—e.g., dressing, eating, using money. Also termed *independent living skills*.

activity program services A group of professionally recognized *disciplines* (including art, dance, music, *occupational therapy*, and *therapeutic recreation*) whose roles in *special education* and *rehabilitation* treatment programs have been time-proven.

activity time-out The removal of a disruptive student from a specified activity for a specified period of time. (See also *time-out*.)

actometer (ack-tah'-meh-turr) A self-winding calendar wristwatch that has been modified so that one's movement of the *extremity* to which it is attached produces a quantitative reading of activity level by changes in seconds, hours, or days; used to determine how active individuals are.

acuity (ah-kyew'-ih-tee) Ability to note the occurrence of a *sensory stimulus*. Commonly used to refer to how well a person can see, hear, or feel, as in *visual acuity*.

acute Manifesting rapid development of *symptoms* in an illness.

acute otitis media A severe but usually brief case of *otitis media* (*inflammation* of the middle ear), usually accompanied by pain.

AD See *assistive device*.

ADA See *average daily attendance*.

adapted physical education See *adaptive physical education*.

adaptive behavior The effectiveness and degree to which an individual meets standards of self-sufficiency and social responsibility for his/her age-related cultural group. Included in all definitions of *mental retardation*, it involves noncognitive skills, or "street sense"— the ability to cope with the environment.

Usually measured on *adaptive behavior scales.*

adaptive behavior scales Measures developed to *assess* an individual's functioning in nonacademic, nonintellectual skill areas such as social living and maturation.

adaptive physical education A specially designed program of physical activities that takes into account the limitations of a person with a *disability.*

adaptive skills The skills necessary for dealing with the environment; their absence is detrimental to independence. The adaptive skills areas are communicating, *self-care,* home living, social skills, community use, self-direction, health and safety, *functional* academics, leisure, and work. (See also *activities of daily living.*)

ADD See *attention deficit disorder* and *attention deficit hyperactivity disorder.*

addict One who becomes habituated to the use of, or has a *compulsive* need for, something, such as alcohol or drugs. The condition is termed an **addiction.**

additions 1. An *articulatory* disorder in which an individual adds sounds to words, as in "buhrown" for brown. 2. A reading error in which sounds are added to words as they are read.

adduction The movement of a limb inward toward the center of the body, as in lowering an arm from a lateral position. Opposite of *abduction.*

adenoid A mass of lymph-like tissue located between the mouth and the *esophagus,* which, when infected, may become enlarged and obstruct breathing.

adenomia subaceum (add-eh-no'-mee-uh suh-bay'-shum) A butterfly-shaped collection of fibrous tumors on the face around the nose; found in certain forms of *mental retardation* (e.g., *tuberous sclerosis*).

adequacy Relates to *sensory* capability, the extent to which the sensory capability of an individual is sufficient to meet the demands of the task being performed.

ADHD See *attention deficit hyperactivity disorder* and *neurobiological brain disorder.*

adiadochokinesis (ah-dee-ah-doe-koe-kin-ee'-sis) A *"soft" sign* of *minimal brain dysfunction* in which the child being tested has difficulty executing rapid alternating movements, such as synchronizing quick turns of the hands over and over. Children with minimal brain dysfunction display uncoordinated movements.

adipose (add'-ih-poce) Pertaining to fat or the state of being fat. Adipose tissue stores fat.

adjunctive services Special programs that support the child with *disabilities* in general education. Also referred to as *support services.*

ADL See *activities of daily living.*

Adlerian disciplinary approach One of several conceptional approaches to *discipline,* based on the work of Adler and proponents such as Dreikers and Dinkmeyer, emphasizing common-sense responses to behavior problems in which logical behavior consequences are used to deal with the four most common disruptive behaviors of attention seeking, power struggling, revenge seeking, and assumed *inadequacy.*

ADM See *average daily membership.*

administrative remedies An internal set of procedures in an agency or a school system that does not involve judicial action. The agency or system provides a nonlegal series of appeals that a parent can pursue regarding a child's placement, *diagnosis,* etc.

adrenalin (ah-dren'-ah-lin) 1. Secretion of the adrenal glands of the body. 2. Trademark for a crystalline compound prepared as an extract from the adrenal glands; used as a heart *stimulant* and for arresting *hemorrhages*.

adult education An important societal movement aimed at teaching adults the knowledge and skills required to meet needs throughout life; offers opportunities for training and retraining persons with *disabilities* after they have left public school.

adult training center A facility for adults with *disabilities* that offers *work experiences* and recreation under community supervision.

advanced placement (AP) Refers to *acceleration* of courses offered to *gifted* students, which yields grades toward graduation and also college credit if exam grades exceed a certain *criterion* level.

adventitious (add-ven-tish'-us) Acquired after birth through accident or illness. (Compare *congenital*.)

adventitious deafness A condition in which a person born with normal hearing sensitivity loses hearing as a result of an accident or a disease. The loss may be in varying degrees and may be classified according to the nature of the disorder, such as *perception deafness*, *toxic deafness*, or *conductive hearing loss*.

adverse reaction An unwanted reaction or side effect caused by medication.

advisory committee A group of knowledgeable individuals, including parents and consumers, chosen from outside the staff of the program involved, who counsel in the development of services offered by the program. The use of advisory committees has grown in recent years as a result of the nature and extent of legislation and program guidelines.

advocacy (add'-voe-kah-see) Full support for, and representation of, the interests of an individual or a group as if these were self-interests, in a manner free from conflict of interest. A person or group involved in this activity is called an **advocate**.

adynamia (ah-die-nah'-mee-ah) The absence of normal vitality and strength; some forms of this condition culminate in *paralysis*.

afebrile (ah-feb'-ril) **convulsion** Involuntary muscle contractions that occur without fever, usually in young children.

affective Pertaining to the emotions, feelings, or attitudes of an organism. Affective education refers to school *objectives* that deal with *motivation* and the development of self-image.

afferent (af'-er-ent) **nerves** The nerves of the body that convey impulses inward from the *sensory* endings toward the nerve centers or the *central nervous system*.

affirmative action A plan for greater involvement of minorities in employment, enrollment, etc., which may in some instances amount to quotas even though this intent may not be clear. Under *Section 504* of the *Rehabilitation Act of 1973*, the term "voluntary action" has been used instead of "affirmative action"; however, the latter is sometimes viewed as a weaker term.

affirmative industries Nonprofit businesses that employ those with and without *disabilities*. The nondisabled workers set the production standards, *modeling* for the *disabled* workers. Affirmative industries differ from *sheltered workshops* and training centers by the former's emphasis on private enterprise.

AFI See *amaurotic family (familial) idiocy*.

aftercare Provision of medical, educational, or treatment services following an individual's release from a hospital or an *institution*.

age equivalent A *raw score* or *standard score* expressed in years and months, corresponding to the average score for that age-group. For example, if a score of 52 on a *standardized test* is the score achieved by average seventh-grade students, it may be expressed as 7.2. (See also *grade equivalent*.) The first digit (7) refers to the general *grade level*, while the digit following the decimal indicates the number of months completed in that grade. Based on the premise of a 9-month school year, 7.9, for example would indicate the last month in seventh grade.

age norms Numerical values indicative of the average performance on a given instrument or in an activity for individuals of stated age-groups.

age of onset The age at which an individual's *disability* or disease first occurred or became apparent (e.g., the age at which an individual became *blind*).

agenesis (ah-jen'-eh-sis) Absence of an organ or a tissue.

ageusia (ahg-yew'-zee-ah) Absence or *impairment* of the sense of taste.

aggression (adj., **aggressive**) Hostile and attacking behaviors often displayed by individuals with *behavior disorders*; may be destructive or injurious.

aggression replacement training (ART) A social skills training system, developed by Arnold Goldstein, that combines *behavior modification* with *cognitive behavior modification* and moral development training.

agitation Restlessness as a result of *anxiety* and tension.

agitographia (aj-ih-toe-graf-ee-ah) Poor writing ability that may show the qualities of rapid writing movements, distortion of words, or the *omission* of letters or entire words.

agitolalia (aj-ih-toe-lay'-lee-ah) A *speech disorder* in which speech is produced with such great rapidity that it is incoherent or nearly incoherent. Sometimes called **agitophasia**, or *cluttering*.

agnosia (ag-noe'-zee-ah) The inability to recognize familiar objects through *sensory stimuli*, especially with a particular sense organ. Examples are *auditory agnosia*, color agnosia, and *tactile agnosia*.

agoraphobia (ag-oh-rah-foe'-bee-ah) A fear of becoming panic-stricken in public places. Persons who are severely afflicted may fear leaving their homes.

agrammatism (ah-gram'-uh-tizm) A secondary condition evoked by *hearing loss*, in which the child is impaired in the ability to sequence words, omits prefixes and suffixes, and has difficulty mastering quality speech.

agraphia (ah-graf'-ee-ah) A form of *aphasia* characterized by the loss of ability, or the inability, to write, because of a *lesion* in the *central nervous system*. Individuals with agraphia do not seem to be able to relate the mental images of words to the *motor* movements needed to write them.

aide A person who assists another, as in a classroom aide to a teacher; may be paid or unpaid. (See also *teacher aide*.)

AIDS See *acquired immune deficiency syndrome*.

AIDS dementia A mental condition associated with *AIDS* in which rational thought and purpose remain intact but the individual uses fear of contagion to intimidate other individuals.

AIDS-related complex (ARC) A precursor stage to *AIDS*, which may or may not develop into AIDS itself.

air conduction In normal hearing and measurement of hearing, the transmission of sound waves (vibrations in air) through the external canal of the ear to the *eardrum*, causing it to vibrate, which starts the chain reaction resulting in hearing.

akathisia (ack-ah-thee'-zee-ah) *Motor* restlessness that may be manifested in an inability to sit, lie quietly, or sleep. Often seen in *toxic* reactions to drugs administered for the treatment of *psychotic* conditions.

akinesia (ay-kih-nee'-zee-ah) **(akinesis)** Loss of movement in a body part without permanent physical or neurological *impairment*, as in the temporary *paralysis* of a muscle when injected with certain drugs.

akinetic (ay-kih-net'-ik) An *epileptic* activity characterized by temporary loss of consciousness and falling in a passive manner.

alalia (ah-lay'-lee-ah) Loss or absence of the ability to talk.

alaryngeal (ay-lare-en'-jee-ahl) **speech** Speech produced without the use of one's *larynx*.

albinism (al'-bih-niz-um) **(albino)** An inherited condition that results in a deficiency of pigment in the skin, hair, and *iris* of the eye. The condition causes the eyes to appear pinkish and in most cases is accompanied by impaired vision and *photophobia* (sensitivity to light).

alcohol embryopathy See *fetal alcohol syndrome.*

alexia (ah-lek'-see-ah) A *cerebral* disorder that results in the inability to associate meaning with printed or written words. (See also *dyslexia.*)

alkalosis (al-kah-loe'-siss) A condition of the blood or tissue characterized by above-average alkalinity.

allergen Any substance that causes an **allergic** reaction when it comes in contact with the body. An **allergy** is an exaggerated reaction to a substance that does not cause a similar reaction in the average person.

allesthesia (al-ess-thee'-zee-ah) A condition in which one senses being touched at a point other than that at which he/she is actually touched.

allocated time In *effective instruction*, used to describe the time period scheduled for an activity; does not necessarily imply the time the child is on task or paying attention.

alpha-fetoprotein (alpha fetal protein) screening A test used for identifying *neural tube defects* in children while the *fetus* is still in the womb. When combined with *ultrasonography*, this test offers 90% correct *diagnosis* of these defects.

ALT See *academic learning time.*

alternative assessment Refers to one of the sets of *assessment* approaches developed in the 1990s that moves away from *standardized tests* and instead relies on *performance assessment, authentic assessment,* or *portfolio assessment.* All of these terms represent nonstandardized approaches to assessment.

alternative curriculum Any of a variety of curricula that differ from the general education *curriculum.* Such curricula may serve the needs of students who have high *cognitive* ability or lower *functional* levels. Alternative curricula may also address areas such as vocational and life skills.

alternative health care Nontraditional health care utilizing such practices as acupuncture, chiropractic care, and homeopathic medicine.

alternative living Community-based living arrangement as a substitute for *institutionalization.* Individuals with various mental and *physical disabilities* live in apartments or *group homes* under some level of supervision.

alternative schools Any administrative arrangement that differs remarkably from the usual public school. In actual usage, this term is most associated with schools for students who are *aggressive* and/or hostile. Alternative schools are sometimes created for pregnant teenagers or for those who had dropped out of school but are now returning.

Alzheimer's (all'-sie-murz) **disease** A *degenerative* condition affecting older individuals (usually over age 60) that involves neural transmitters and results in *memory* loss, *depression*, and, in the latter stages, violent personality outbursts. Much of the present treatment consists of reducing *stress* for the person and family members.

amaurosis (am-aw-roe'-sis) *Blindness* occurring as a result of a disease of the *optic nerve*, spine, or brain without any change in the structure of the eye.

amaurotic (am-uh-rot'-ik) **family (familial) idiocy (AFI)** A *hereditary* disease producing *mental retardation*, marked changes in the *macula* of the *retina*, increasing failure of vision, *seizures*, and death. AFI is a *degenerative* disease resulting from faulty lipid (fat) *metabolism*. The early *infantile* variety is also known as *Tay-Sachs disease*.

ambidextrous (am-bih-dek'-strus) The ability to use both hands with equal ease and skill.

ambivalence The simultaneous existence of conflicting attitudes (e.g., love-hate) toward a person, object, activity, idea, etc.; may cause frustration that interferes with activity.

amblyopia (am-blee-oh'-pea-ah) A *visual* condition in which the two eyes do not see on the same plane, thus causing

one eye to *mask* the image of the other eye to prevent double vision.

ambulatory Commonly used to refer to an individual who is able to walk or move about independently; not bedridden.

amelia (ah-mee'-lee-ah) A condition in which an individual has no limbs.

ameliorate (ah-mee'-lee-oh-rate) To improve, as in the condition of a sick person or in a specific skill.

amenorrhea (ah-men-oh-ree'-ah) The absence of a female's menstrual cycle.

amentia (ah-men'-chuh) Nondevelopment of the mind, as contrasted with *dementia*, the loss or deterioration of the mind; used with reference to *severe* or *profound mental retardation*.

American Sign Language (ASL) A system of communication among *deaf* persons employing the arms, hands, and other parts of the body to represent thought units. The structure of this *language* tends to be *concept*-based rather than word-based. Also called *Ameslan*.

Ameslan Same as *American Sign Language*.

ametropia (am-eh-troe'-pea-ah) A condition of the eye in which images are not properly *focused* on the *retina*; may produce *myopia*, *astigmatism*, or *hyperopia*.

amicus curiae A Latin term meaning, literally, "friend of the court." Used in discussions of a case to indicate an individual or organization that is neither *plaintiff* nor *defendant* in a *civil case* but, because of special expertise or interest, is allowed by a court to become involved in the case. The involvement usually consists of submitting a "brief" (written presentation) containing supporting legal arguments and special facts to the court.

amimia (ah-mih'-mee-ah) Inability to express oneself through the use of gestures or signs.

aminia (ah-mih'-nee-ah) A behavioral characteristic manifested by an individual not showing expression or changes in facial expression, appearing indifferent.

amino acids A group of complex *organic* nitrogen compounds that combine in a variety of ways to form proteins. Abnormalities of amino acid *metabolism* can cause a number of anomalies, such as *phenylketonuria* and *albinism*.

amnesia (am-nee'-zhah) Loss of the ability to remember or identify past experiences. Amnesia may be either *organic* or *functional*. Causal factors include fatigue, shock, fever, injury to the brain, and extreme *depression*.

amniocentesis (am-nee-oh-sen-tee'-sis) A procedure for analyzing factors in the *amniotic fluid* to determine certain aspects of *fetus* development. Tests of amniotic fluid can aid in identifying *Down syndrome*, *spina bifida*, and other *congenital* defects.

amniotic fluid The liquid in which the developing *fetus* is immersed during pregnancy. Chemical components of this fluid can be analyzed in a procedure called *amniocentesis* to determine if the developing fetus has certain disabling disorders.

amorphous (ah-more'-fuss) Having no definite form (in pharmacy, not crystallized).

amphetamine (am-fet'-uh-meen) A drug with *stimulant* properties that is used legally in diet pills but also may be used for other reasons as a body stimulant. In slang, called "uppers" or "speed."

amplification device See *hearing aid*.

amputee One who has had a limb surgically removed from the body. The process is called **amputation**. The term *congenital amputee* is used when a limb is missing or mostly missing at birth as a result of developmental problems.

amusia (ah-mew'-zee-ah) The inability to recognize or produce musical tones. (See also *tone deafness*.)

amyotonia congenita (ah-my-oh-toe'-nee-uh kon-jen'-ih-tuh) Muscular weakness, as is usually experienced in neuromuscular diseases such as *muscular dystrophy*.

anaclitic (an-ah-klit'-ik) Characterized by a *dependence* on someone or something, as in a newborn baby's developing relationship with the mother. In anaclitic *depression*, a young child's physical, social, or *intellectual* development is slowed by a sudden separation from the mother figure. This condition may become more serious as the period of separation lengthens.

anakusis (anacusis) (an-ah-kyew'-sis) A complete loss of hearing resulting in total deafness.

analgesic (an-uhl-jee'-zik) Any drug used to relieve pain without loss of consciousness.

analysis of variance (ANOVA) A parametric statistical treatment.

analytic touch A *concept* pertaining to *blind* persons, it involves experiencing *tactile* impressions of parts of an object, such as a building, and integrating those impressions to understand a total *concept*. Because blind people do not see the entire object but experience only parts of it, the *perception* that is pieced together is based on analytic touch. (See also *synthetic touch*.)

anaphia (an-ah'-fee-ah) The absence of, or loss of, the sense of touch.

anaplasty (an'-ah-plas-tee) Restorative (plastic) surgery. **Anaplastic** (an-ah-plas'-tik) Describes the restoration of a lost or absent part of the body. A specialist who constructs artificial portions of the body to replace areas that have been destroyed, removed, or were absent is an **anaplastologist**.

anarthria (an-ar'-three-ah) A severe defect in the *central nervous system* that causes an inability to articulate words, resulting in speechlessness.

ancillary Refers to supplementary support or assistance, as in "ancillary personnel" or "ancillary services." *Speech therapy* and *physical therapy* are examples.

anecdotal (an'-ek-dote-ul) **method** A means of recording and analyzing child behavior by observing and reporting, in narrative form, separate occurrences of the child's activities.

anechoic (an-ek-oh'-ik) **chamber** A specially built room designed with soft surfaces to provide maximum sound absorption, which helps keep sound reverberations (echoes) to a minimum. Optimum measurement of *hearing acuity* can be obtained in such a room, which usually is found in a research setting; may be referred to as a "dead room."

anemia (ah-nee'-mee-ah) A condition of the blood in which the red corpuscles are reduced in number or a deficiency in *hemoglobin* exists. Anemia may result in skin pallor, loss of vitality, shortness of breath, and palpitations of the heart.

anencephalus (an-en-cef'-ah-lus) A condition in which the brain of a *fetus* fails to develop and may be almost totally absent. At birth, *severe mental retardation* is present. Life expectancy is limited.

anenesis (ah-nen'-eh-siss) Failure of a body to develop.

anesthesiologist (an-es-thee-zee-ahl'-oh-gist) A physician certified by the American Board of Anesthesiology or having the equivalent education and experience; administers the *anesthetic* during surgery.

anesthetic (an-es-thet'-ik) A drug used to cause the loss of sensation or consciousness; usually administered in conjunction with surgery.

anesthetist (an-es'-thu-tist) A *generic* term used to identify *anesthesiologists*, other physicians or dentists in that role, or qualified nurses who administer *anesthetics*.

aneurysm (an'-you-rizm) An abnormal bulge or sac in the wall of an artery, a vein, or the heart.

angiocardiography (an-jee-oh-kar-dee-ah'-gruh-fee) Radiographic use of *X-ray* technology for examination of the heart and its vessels.

aniridia (an-ih-rid'-ee-ah) A *visual* condition resulting from failure of the *iris* to develop fully; produces hypersensitivity to light.

aniseikonia (an-ih-sih-koe'-nee-ah) A *visual* disorder in which images produced by the two eyes are of unequal size. If the discrepancy in size is large, *fusion* of the image through *binocular vision* is not accomplished. Both images may be seen, or one eye may *mask* the image of the other.

anisometropia (an-ih-so-meh-troe'-pea-ah) A *visual impairment* caused by a considerable inequality in refractive power of the two eyes.

ankylosis (ang-kill-oh'-sis) Stiffening or fixation of a joint, often caused by fibrous or bony tissues growing into joint spaces.

annual goals One of the stipulations of *PL 94–142*; requires written statements of what a child is targeted to accomplish within a year's time.

annual review One of the stipulations of *PL 94–142*; requires an *evaluation* at least once a year of how the instructional program has worked for the child.

anomaly (ah-nom'-ah-lee) Deviation from the standard, or an irregularity in development. Often used to refer to disabling conditions without naming specific conditions.

anomia (ah-no'-mee-ah) A condition of not recalling or remembering words or the names of objects well.

anophthalmia (an-of'-thal-mee-ah) A birth defect in which a child's eyes fail to develop in utero; requires multiple plastic surgery to create openings for artificial eyes that serve cosmetic purposes only. A newly founded parent group exists to provide support to parents of children with anophthalmia.

anopia (an-oh'-pea-uh) Absence or imperfect development of the eye, resulting in *visual impairment*.

anorectic (an-oh-rek'-tik) Describes a substance that reduces the appetite.

anorexia (an-oh-rek'-see-uh) Partial or complete loss or lack of appetite; self-imposed food deprivation.

anorexia nervosa (an-oh-rek'-see-ah ner-voe'-sah) A serious condition in which an individual refuses to eat; results in a loss of weight, vitality, and, if untreated, death. Occurs most often in teenage girls who have emotional problems related to their physical image. One of the classifications of the *DSM*-IV System; refers to those who have intense fears of becoming obese. A similar condition is *bulimia*.

anosmics (an-oz'-mix) Lack of the sense of smell, thus preventing the use of *olfactory stimuli* to aid in learning and reacting to danger. The condition, although rare, is observed most often in individuals who have *albinism*.

ANOVA See *analysis of variance*.

anoxemia (an-ok-see'-mee-ah) A condition in which the oxygen content of the blood is lowered to a level below that needed to sustain the life of cells.

anoxia (ah-nock'-see-ah) An inadequate supply of oxygen to the body. If severe, it may result in *brain injury* or other *organic* damage.

antagonistic Struggling against, as in a muscle acting in opposition to another muscle. In *spastic cerebral palsy* antagonistic muscles that should be relaxed remain contracted.

antecedent (an-teh-see'-dent) A condition or event that precedes a response and is observed to be associated with its occurrence.

anterior Toward the front or face side, as in the anterior of the body. Opposite of *posterior*.

anti- A prefix meaning against or opposed to, as in *anticonvulsant* (an agent that works against *convulsions*).

antibody A substance in the circulatory system that serves to combat germs or nullify the disease-causing effects of germs.

anticonvulsant Any of a group of medications administered to help control *seizures*. With these medications, about 50% of *epileptic* individuals achieve complete control and about another 30%, partial control.

antidepressant Any drug taken for the purpose of relieving *depression* or elevating the mood of an individual.

antidote Any drug or substance used to combat or remedy the harmful effects of poisons.

antigen An agent that, when introduced into the body, promotes the formation of *antibodies*.

antimetropia (an-tie-meh-troe'-pea-ah) A *visual* condition in which one eye is *nearsighted* and the other is *farsighted*;

suppression of vision in one eye frequently occurs.

antipyresis (an-tie-pie-ree'-sis) The administration of remedies to combat fever.

anxiety Emotional tension or confusion coupled with a feeling of generalized threat based upon unknown conditions or sources. (If the sources were known, the condition would be called fear.) Children who are helped to understand or deal with their anxiety may show remarkable improvement in school adjustment or achievement.

AP See *advanced placement*.

apathy (ap'-ah-thee) (adj., **apathetic**) Indifference, or a lack of feeling and emotion.

Apert's syndrome An inherited disorder manifested by a high, narrow *cranial* cavity and often early closure of the skull sutures; associated *mental retardation* may be reduced through early surgical *intervention*.

Apgar test The most used *screening* instrument for determining the health status of a newborn. Babies are rated on a 0–2 scale for five vital signs: *a*ppearance or coloring, *p*ulse, *g*rimace, *a*ctivity, and *r*espiration. (The first letter in each word combines to make the *acronym* APGAR.)

aphakia (ah-fay'-kee-ah) Absence of the *lens of the eye*.

aphasia (ah-fay'-zyuh) (adj., **aphasic**) A disorder caused by disease or injury to brain centers resulting in the loss or *impairment* of the ability to produce or comprehend *language*. The condition may affect either written or spoken language. (See also *sensory aphasia*.)

aphonia (ah-foe'-nee-ah) A loss of voice or the absence of voice resulting from *paralysis* of the vocal cords; may have either *organic* or psychological causes.

aplasia (ah-play'-zee-ah) Lack of development, as in a body organ.

apoplexy (ap'-uh-pleck-see) A sudden loss of consciousness, sensation, and/or voluntary motion caused by the rupture or obstruction of a *cerebral* artery, as in a *stroke*.

apperception (ap-er-sep'-shun) The process of assimilating new events and their relation to previously acquired knowledge, and of *evaluating* these current experiences in the light of past experiences.

applied behavioral analysis See *behavioral analysis*.

appropriate education See *free appropriate public education*.

apraxia (ah-prak'-see-ah) The inability to produce purposeful speech in the absence of *paralysis* or other *motor impairment*. May result in the loss of the ability to express elementary *language* units. The manifesting condition is an *expressive language disorder* associated with interneurosensory *processing* that seems to be related to *memory* of the *motor* act of speech. (See also *learning disability*.)

aptitude test A device or measure administered to determine an individual's potential ability to perform a certain type of activity or *readiness* to learn in a specific area. Examples are a musical aptitude test and a mechanical aptitude test.

aqueous (ah'-kwee-us) **humor** The fluid that fills the front chamber of the eye, in front of the crystalline *lens*.

ARC See *AIDS-related complex*. Also stands for Association for Retarded Citizens, which was formerly the National Association for Mentally Retarded Citizens.

architectural barrier Any part of the physical, constructed environment or the arrangement of structures within an environment or a building that can inhibit or prevent persons with *disabilities* from using facilities or moving about. When such barriers are removed, the resulting environment may be described as *barrier-free*. The Architectural Barriers Act of 1968, as amended, requires that all public buildings receiving federal financing must be barrier-free and *accessible* to those with *physical disabilities*.

arithmetic (air-ith-met'-ik) **processes** The basic computations of addition, subtraction, multiplication, and division.

arithmetic reasoning The use of basic mathematical processes in problem-solving situations in the everyday environment.

arrested development Incomplete growth of an individual or a part of an individual that takes place sometime in the life cycle prior to total maturation.

arrhythmia (arhythmia) (ah-rith'-mee-ah) Any change from the normal rhythm of the heartbeat.

ART See *aggression replacement training*.

art therapy Designates widely varying practices in education, *rehabilitation*, and *psychotherapy* in which the materials and activities of *visual* arts are used for *therapeutic* purposes, particularly with children who have *emotional disturbances*. Allows *nonverbal* self-expression through the manipulation of art media.

arteriosclerosis (ar-teer-ee-oh-skler-oh'-sis) Hardening or thickening of the walls of the arteries.

arthritis A disease condition of the skeletal joints that causes *inflammation* and *motor impairment*. Arthritis has several forms and is usually associated with severe pain and medication needs.

arthrodosis (ar-throw-doe'-sis) The surgical fixation or immobilization of a joint

by removing *cartilaginous* substances so the bones grow solidly together.

arthrogryposis (ar-throw-gri-poh'-sis) A severe crippling disease of children in which the joints become fixed or bend only partially.

arthroplasty (ar'-throw-plas-tee) The surgical rebuilding or formation of new joints.

articulation (adj., **articulatory**) Speech sound production by modification of the stream of voiced and unvoiced breath, usually through movements of the jaws, lips, tongue, and *soft palate*; can also refer to speech sound *discrimination*.

articulators The parts of the body's speech mechanism responsible for the formation of speech sounds, including the lips, teeth, gum ridge, *hard palate*, *soft palate*, and tongue.

articulatory defect Poor or indistinct speech resulting from the failure, or inability, to properly *vocalize* essential speech sounds. Articulatory defects usually are characterized as *omissions*, *substitutions*, or *distortions*. The preferred term is now *phonological disorder*.

artificial environments Instructional environments used to train students with *severe disabilities* how to perform or interact in real-life settings. For example, includes the use of pictures of stores, pictures of money, etc., as a precursor to *community-based instruction* in shopping behaviors.

ASL See *American Sign Language*.

asphyxia (az-fix'-ee-ah) Deprivation of oxygen, as occurs in smoke suffocation or drowning. If the deprivation is prolonged, the person may go into a *coma* with accompanying *brain injury* or death.

aspiration 1. A desire to succeed in what is above one's current level of functioning. The **level of aspiration** is the maximum goal that an individual or a group desires to reach in a specific activity at any given moment. 2. The expulsion of breath during speech.

assault An intentional *tort* in which the aggressor creates a circumstance in which the party being accosted feels a fear of imminent peril without actually being touched (e.g., by shaking a threatening fist or threatening to strike with an object). (See also the related term *battery*.)

assessment (v., **assess**) Special *diagnosis* that may include mental, social, psychological, and educational *evaluations*, used to determine assignment to programs or services; a process employing observation, testing, and *task analysis* to determine an individual's strengths and weaknesses for educational and social purposes.

assimilation (v., **assimilate**) 1. The incorporation of newly learned knowledge, or that to be learned, into one's thought patterns for use in solving problems. 2. The process by which the body absorbs food for constructive *metabolism*. 3. The *inclusion* of new members as an integral part of a group, as contrasted to *parallelism*.

assistive device (AD) Any tool that can aid a person with a *disability* in becoming more independent.

assistive technological device (ATD) An item or piece of equipment that increases, maintains, or improves the *functional* capabilities of a student or person with *disabilities* and that, under *IDEA*, must be provided as part of the *IEP* as a *related service*; includes such functions as *augmentative communication*, assistive listening, computer access, environmental control, *self-care*, and vision.

assistive technology According to *IDEA*, any item, piece of equipment, or product system, whether acquired commercially or otherwise, that is modified or customized to increase, maintain, or improve the *functional* capabilities of individuals with *disabilities*. Such items include, among others, high-tech wheelchairs, *sensory* devices, communication devices, computers, and environmental controls.

associated method A *multisensory* training approach developed by Margaret McGinnis at the Central Institute for the Deaf in St. Louis to teach speech and a total *language* program to *deaf, aphasic*, and other language-deficient children.

associative prompts One or more *concrete* or representational displays (i.e., a picture) presented with a target *concept* (i.e., a word) to promote correct responding for students with *severe disabilities*. The concrete or representational display is subsequently *faded* so that only the target concept remains.

astereognosis (as-tare-ee-ahg-no'-sis) The inability to identify objects by touch. A type of *agnosia*.

asthenia (az-thee'-nee-ah) Weakness or loss of strength.

asthenopia (az-thee-no'-pea-ah) Weakness or fatigue of the *visual* organs, usually accompanied by headaches, eye pain, and poor vision.

asthma (adj., **asthmatic**) A *chronic respiratory* condition in which the individual has episodes of difficulty in breathing. Emotional factors can contribute to asthmatic conditions.

astigmatism (ah-stig'-muh-tizm) An eye condition involving a refractive error, in which the rays from one point of an object are not brought to a single *focus* because of a difference in the degree of *refraction* in the different meridians of the eye; causes blurred *visual* images.

asymbolia (ay-sim-boe'-lee-ah) The inability, or loss of ability, to comprehend symbols such as words, figures, signs, and gestures. (See also *strephosymbolia*.)

asymmetrical (ay-sih-meh'-trih-kal) Describes a condition in which the sides of the body (that normally are alike) are different, or lack symmetry. This imbalance may cause poor body functioning.

ataxia (ah-tack'-see-ah) (adj., **ataxic**) A type of *cerebral palsy* in which a lack of muscle coordination results in a loss of precision movement and, sometimes, balance. Ataxia is attributed to injury to the *cerebellum*; the high *incidence* of *visual* problems associated with ataxia relates to the proximity of the injury to the visual centers.

ATD See *assistive technological device*.

athetosis (ath-eh-toe'-sis) (adj., **athetoid**) A form of *cerebral palsy* in which involuntary motions cause purposeless, repetitive movements of the *extremities*, head, and tongue. Speech becomes difficult to master, and all willed movements must be superimposed on the involuntary motions.

atlantoaxial (at-lan'-toe-ax-ee-al) **instability** A physical disorder associated with *Down syndrome* in which there is greater than normal *mobility* of the two upper cervical vertebrae—C1 and C2, at the top of the neck. It is estimated that this condition is present in 50% of those with moderate and severe mental *disabilities* in the United States and in 12% to 15% of all individuals with Down syndrome. Individuals with this condition may be exposed to serious injury if they forcibly *flex* the neck because the vertebrae may shift and squeeze or sever the spinal cord.

atonia (atony) Loss of normal muscle tone; *flaccid*.

atresia (ah-tree'-zee-ah) A *congenital* closure of a natural body opening (e.g., the ear).

at-risk A term applied to children or adolescents who appear to have a higher than usual probability of expressing some social, psychological, or physical deviation in the future. In *special education* the term has been applied most often to preschool children who are potentially *disabled* but for whom one wishes to avoid a *categorical label*. (See also *high risk*.)

atrophy (ah'-troe-fee) The *degeneration* or wasting away of an organ or muscular portion of the body because of disease, disuse, or lack of nourishment.

attendant A title given to one who aids in the care of persons with *disabilities* within an *institution* or *residential* facility.

attending *Cognitively processing* the presence of a *stimulus*.

attention (v., **attend**) Selectivity in *perception*; the direction of perception to certain *stimuli* rather than others.

attention deficit disorder (ADD) A generalized term referring to individuals with *neurological* conditions resulting in behavior and learning that may be different from the *norm*. Individuals with *attention deficit disorder* express clinically significant *impairment* in social, educational, and occupational functioning that results from *attention deficits*, *hyperactivity deficits*, or a combination of inattention and *hyperactivity*. See also *neurobiological brain disorder*.

attention deficit hyperactivity disorder (ADHD) One of the classifications of the *DSM*-IV System; inattention, *impulsivity*, and *hyperactivity* are present before age 7. Attention Deficit Hyperactivity Disorder is the same as *attention deficit disorder* except in the former emphasis is placed on the hyperactivity. Either *ADD* or *ADHD* is acceptable *language*. The American Psychiatric Association's 1994 classification manual lists three types of attention disorders: ADD, predominantly in attention; ADHD, predominantly hyperactive; and ADD, combined types.

attention span The length of time an individual can concentrate on a specific subject or activity without thinking of or *attending* to something else.

attenuate (ah-ten'-you-ate) To reduce in *intensity*.

Attorney's Fee Act Slang term for the Handicapped Children's Protection Act of 1986, the federal act that made it possible for parents to receive assistance in paying lawyers when they prevail in legal actions against schools.

attribution theory A *concept* in which a child's perseverance in the face of failure is viewed as being related to whether he/she perceives success and/or failure to occur as a result of his/her own efforts and ability, the whims of fate, or the influence of powerful others. Those with *disabilities* often attribute their failures or lack of success to others or to their disabilities.

atypical Having characteristics that differ to some degree from the *norm*; describes a person who in some way differs to a marked degree from others of a specific type, class, or category.

auding Hearing, recognizing, and interpreting a spoken *language*.

audiogram A graph of *hearing threshold* levels as measured with an *audiometer* and plotted for different pure-tone *frequencies* for each ear.

audiologist A professional trained in the use of an *audiometer*, who studies *auditory* function based on behavioral observations. The audiologist *diagnoses hearing losses* and selects and fits *hearing aids*.

audiology The science of hearing. In *special education* and *rehabilitation*, refers to the *discipline* that researches hearing and *assesses* and trains individuals with hearing disorders.

audiometer (au-dee-om'-eh-ter) An instrument that measures hearing sensitivity and *acuity*. The amount of *hearing loss* is recorded in terms of *decibels*, units of *hearing loss*, or as a percentage of normal hearing sensitivity. Sometimes called a *pure-tone audiometer*.

audiometric zero The level of sound just perceivable by the average hearing human; the level of zero *decibels* on an *audiometer*.

audiometry The measurement of hearing through the use of an *audiometer*.

audiovisual Describes any mode of presentation directed to both sight and hearing. Television, for example, is audiovisual.

audition The process of hearing.

auditory Pertaining to the sense of hearing.

auditory acuity One's ability to hear sounds as a result of the sensitivity of the *auditory* mechanism (i.e., how well one hears).

auditory agnosia (ag-noe'-zee-ah) The inability to relate sounds to their meanings; a form of *aphasia*.

auditory association The ability to understand the meaning and relationship of words as they are being spoken.

auditory blending The ability to combine *vocally* the *phonemes* of a word that has been pronounced with separations between phonemes in a way that demonstrates that the word is accurately recognized as a whole.

auditory canal The passageway from the outer ear to the middle ear.

auditory closure The ability of an individual to complete a whole word, phrase, or sound based upon the presentation of only a part (e.g., hearing several musical notes and being able to recognize the song they represent). Auditory closure is a skill most children possess; if lacking or impaired, *language processing* problems occur.

auditory decoding One's ability to understand the meaning of spoken words and environmental sounds.

auditory discrimination The ability to hear differences and similarities among and between sounds. Poor *discrimination* can lead to problems in the use of spoken *language*.

auditory feedback See *feedback*.

auditory integration training Technique employed in the United States since 1991, in which music is electronically filtered for the *frequencies* specific to children with *autism* who are *hyperacoustically* sensitive. Use of this technique results in reduced *agitation* and responses to these frequencies when the person is later exposed to the same music and frequencies.

auditory learner 1. An individual whose optimal learning vehicle is through sound. 2. A child with *learning disorders* who has the ability to learn auditorially while other modalities may not be successful.

auditory memory The ability to retain and recall information that has been heard.

auditory modality The hearing mechanism or system that is used to receive an *auditory* signal and process the signal for meaning.

auditory motor function Movement in response to *stimuli* or cues that have been heard; carrying out an activity in response to spoken directions.

auditory nerve The eighth *cranial* nerve; carries nerve impulses of sound from the inner ear to the brain.

auditory perception The ability to identify sounds; the assignment of meaning to a sound (e.g., relating barking to a dog.)

auditory sequential memory The ability to hear and remember a sequence of *auditory* materials. Also called *auditory* sequencing.

auditory training Instruction and practice in the development and use of *auditory* skills to enable a person with an *acoustic disability* to make maximum use of *residual hearing*. Auditory training is helpful in an individual's adjustment to a recently fitted *hearing aid*.

augmentative communication Any form of communication that is used in place of or in addition to customary forms of communications. May include signing, *communication boards*, gestures, object cues, and signals.

augmentative communication devices A variety of aids offering communication to nonoral children through the use of *communication boards*, mechanical means, or computer-assisted means. These devices allow children without *oral language* to make their desires known. (See also *nonoral communication*.)

aura (or'-ah) A condition that occurs in some individuals with *epilepsy* just prior to a *seizure*. The person may see unusual colors, hear ringing sounds, smell peculiar odors, or experience other phenomena during this time. Knowledge of the aura can be useful as a warning, giving the person time to arrange for privacy and other optimum conditions.

aural (adv., **aurally**) Pertaining to the ear or the sense of hearing.

auricle (or'-ih-kull) The external cartilagenous portion of the ear. Also known as outer ear or *pinna*.

authentic assessment A form of *alternative assessment* that requires realistic demands and is set in real-life *contexts*. The *performance assessment* is tied to something practical (i.e., community-based performance becomes authentic assessment).

authoritarianism An approach to child management or administration in which the person in charge is very directive and autocratic and makes most of the decisions that arise.

autism (adj., **autistic**) A severe disorder of communication and behavior that begins in early childhood, usually prior to 30 months of age but up to 42 months. Almost half of the children with this disorder lack meaningful speech, and all are generally described as withdrawn into themselves, uninterested in others, and/or affectionless. They sometimes have an interest in or attachment to animals or inanimate objects. The condition is also *labeled infantile autism, Kanner's syndrome*, and *autistic syndrome.*

autistic syndrome See *autism.*

autoerotic Sexual gratification or arousal resulting from one's own ideas or actions.

autoid Behaviors that, in the absence of *autism*, nevertheless appear very similar to *stereotypes* typical of the behaviors of individuals with autism.

automatic level functions *Psycholinguistic* functions assumed to occur without the involvement of higher *language* processes. If someone says, "Johnny has an apple and Mary has two apples; how many apples do they have?" the child should make an automatic response of "three" without higher level thought.

automatism A *manneristic behavior* seen in some individuals with *severe disabilities, blindness*, and *emotional/behavior disorders*. May be expressed as rocking or other *self-stimulatory* movements or sounds, including subtle and inappropriate repetitive movements such as lip smacking, chewing, and swallowing. (See also *blindism, stereotypic behavior.*)

autonomic nervous system The part of the nervous system that regulates involuntary muscles and glandular tissues.

autosomal dominant inheritance A form of inheritance in which a defective *gene* from one parent causes a disorder to be expressed in an offspring.

autosomal recessive inheritance A form of inheritance in which *genes* must come from both parents in order to be expressed in the offspring.

autotelic Describes a system developed by O. K. Moore that uses typewriters and computers to teach academic skills.

autotopagnosia (aw-toe-top-ag-noe'-zee-ah) The inability to correctly recognize or orient various parts of the body.

average daily attendance (ADA) A figure arrived at by dividing the total number of days of school attendance (of students) by the actual number of days school has been in session.

average daily membership (ADM) A figure arrived at by totaling the number of attendees on all days of a session and dividing by the number of days in the session.

average intelligence The *range* of *IQs* from 90 to 110, in which the largest number of individuals occur.

aversion therapy A technique in which the escape from and avoidance of shock or another unpleasant *stimulus* are used to increase social interaction in *autistic* children.

aversive stimulus An agent or a situation that a person typically avoids because it produces discomfort. Aversive *stimuli* cause the strength of a behavior to decrease when they are presented immediately after the behavior occurs. In recent years educators have been less likely to employ aversive stimuli, and caution has been exerted to not do anything that would be hurtful to the individual.

aversives Noxious consequences employed contingently to decrease an unwanted behavior, usually resulting in temporary pain or illness and generally reserved for *self-injurious behaviors* that have resisted *positive reinforcement* for incompatible behaviors.

avoidance learning A term describing an individual's behavior when trying to avoid or escape consequences that are unpleasant.

B

babbling A stage of *language development* that occurs very early in childhood and is characterized by the repetition of sounds. Babbling is sometimes used as a technique in *speech therapy* in cases in which repetition will help strengthen certain muscles or the development of certain sounds.

Babinski reflex A muscular reaction that causes extension of the "big toe" when the sole of the foot is tickled or stimulated. Considered to be physiological or natural in infants but *pathological* in adults.

baby talk Speech characterized by patterns of pronunciation imitating or carried over from earliest speech. The speech may involve *substitutions* of one sound for another, as in "witta" for "little"; it also may involve sound *distortions*, *omissions*, and *inflectional* patterns characteristic of a young child's speech.

backward (reverse) chaining A process used in systematic teaching and *reinforcement* wherein the behavior just before the terminal behavior in performing an act is used as the starting point for teaching that act, and each future step involves backing up in the sequence. In the example of teaching a child to put on a jacket, the sequence would be started just before the final pulling up of the zipper. The teacher would back up to the behavior just before pulling the zipper. For the opposite approach, see *forward chaining.*

backward child A term of British origin that refers to a level of *intellectual* functioning comparable to the educational classification previously used in the United States of *trainable mentally retarded*. The child's intellectual level, when *assessed* with an individual *intelligence* test, would involve *IQ* scores ranging from 20 to 50.

ballistic movement A fast, easy motion of a limb caused by a single contraction of a muscle group with no *antagonistic* muscle group contracting to oppose it.

ballistograph (baa-lis'-toe-graf) An instrument for measuring activity that incorporates a chair suspended by cables from a supporting superstructure (known as a stabilmetric chair). Movement causes a pattern to be recorded on a sheet of paper. The ballistograph has been used to study *hyperactivity* in children.

barbiturate (bar-bich'-er-ut) Any of a group of drugs derived from barbituric acid that acts to depress the *central nervous system*. Barbiturates are used medically for relieving tension and *anxiety*, as an *anticonvulsant* in treating *epilepsy*, and for pain relief.

barotrauma (bare-oh-traw'-muh) Injury to the ear as a result of a change in barometric (air) pressure.

barrier-free See *architectural barrier*, *accessibility*.

barylalia (bar-ih-lay'-lee-ah) Poor *articulation* that produces thick, indistinct speech.

basal (bay'-zul) 1. Denotes the highest level of a test on which an individual can pass all items. 2. A program or *curriculum* for beginners that provides learning *fundamentals*, as in a *basal reading series*.

basal ganglia (bay'-zul gang'-lee-ah) The collection or mass of nerve cells at the base of the brain comprising the thalamus, corpus striata, and other structures. This area is affected in *athetoid cerebral palsy*.

basal reading series (basal reader) The main or primary reading series that a school system adopts for use in all elementary and middle grades.

base rate The percentage, or frequency, of occurrence of any behavior within a certain amount of time (e.g., number of times out of seat per 10-minute interval).

baseline Beginning observations as a foundation for measurement prior to *intervention* or treatment; a beginning point for comparison of treatment effects. In some research designs, a second baseline is collected after treatment has been stopped to analyze the effectiveness of the treatment.

BASIC See *Beginners All-purpose Symbolic Instruction Code.*

battered child syndrome (BCS) Any set of circumstances or *symptoms* indicating *child abuse*. The *abuse* may be physical, sexual, moral, emotional, medical, environmental, or educational. The battered child may be left with residual problems, such as *physical* or mental *disabilities*.

battery 1. An intentional *tort* in which the aggressor makes physical contact in wronging a person—e.g., by grabbing, pushing, or striking. (See also the related term *assault*.) 2. A group of tests administered to an individual to determine the various characteristics as *assessed* by each test. May be used to refer to a group of tests standardized on the same population to allow comparison of results.

BCS See *battered child syndrome.*

BD See *behavior disorder.*

Beginners All-purpose Symbolic Instruction Code (BASIC) An easy-to-learn computer *language*. It is the basic introductory *language* of most microcomputers used in schools.

BEH See *Bureau of Education for the Handicapped.*

behavior coding A system for examiners or trainers to code subjects' behavior into defined categories. The examiner records observations by type of response using the coded system.

behavior disorder (BD) A condition in which a person's actions are so inappropriate, disruptive, and possibly destructive that they may interfere with education and may require special services. This term has replaced emotionally disturbed in most government programs, but it is presently in the process of being replaced by *emotional/behavior disorder*.

behavior management A collection of techniques and methodologies, one of which is *behavior modification*, used to change or control human behavior.

behavior modeling A procedure in which an individual is presented with a simulated or actual demonstration of a desired behavior and is expected to learn the behavior by copying or imitation.

behavior modification The *shaping* of an individual's behavior to minimize or eliminate negative behaviors and to emphasize and *reinforce* positive behaviors through control of a learning environment with planned and systematic application of the principles of learning.

behavior rating scales Any of a number of measures or instruments that list specific observable behaviors and provide a means of ranking their severity or importance. Rating scales are one approach to identifying and *assessing* children with emotional or behavior problems.

behavior rehearsal An activity designed to influence behavior through practice of a desired behavior under simulated or highly structured conditions. As the desired behavior gains in strength, the rehearsal setting may gradually take on characteristics similar to the natural situations in which the problem behavior occurred.

behavior therapy An approach to treating emotional and behavioral problems that is based on learning theory or principles of *conditioning*, in which the primary *objective* is to modify the problem behaviors that brought the individual to treatment. Behavior therapy is based on the premise that undesirable behaviors are *maladaptive* habits, and if those habits are changed, the problems are removed because the undesirable behaviors have been unlearned or more appropriate behaviors have been learned.

behavioral analysis The science employing the principles of behavior to facilitate improvement of behavior or learning.

behavioral assessment A method of observing and recording behaviors over a specified time. Also referred to as *direct measurement*.

behavioral contract An agreement, written or *oral*, between two persons, usually a student and a teacher. It includes a statement that if the student behaves in a certain way the teacher will provide a specific reward.

behavioral objective A statement of expected learning accomplishment for a child. Behavioral *objectives* must meet four *criteria*: (1) state what the learner will be expected to do; (2) state this in measurable terms; (3) state under what conditions the performance will be demonstrated; and (4) include the criteria for judging the quality of the student's performance. For example, the student will recite the letters of the alphabet in correct order with no more than two errors in one minute.

behavioral repertoire The *range* of behaviors that a student is capable of performing.

behavioral rigidity Inability or difficulty in developing new, appropriate responses when introduced to unfamiliar situations. Behavioral *rigidity* often causes difficulty for individuals with *disabilities* when coping with new circumstances or learning new skills.

behaviorism A psychological theory based on the principle that behavior is the result of one's past experiences, through which one has learned or been *conditioned*.

Bell's palsy A condition involving the peripheral branch of the facial nerve that results in *paralysis* of facial muscles. The condition usually disappears in 3 to 5 weeks.

benign (bee-nine') Not tending to cause death; not recurrent or fatal. Opposite of *malignant*.

bi- A prefix denoting two, as in "bi-monthly."

bibliotherapy The use of reading (especially of materials that include characters with whom an individual identifies) for *therapeutic* purposes.

bifurcate (by'-fer-kate) To divide into two branches (v.); forked (adj.)

bilabial (by-lay'-bee-ul) Describes a *consonant* sound formed using both lips, as in *p, b,* and *m.*

bilateral When used in reference to the body, means involvement of both sides.

bilingual education A *concept* addressing the needs of students for whom English is not the primary *language.*

bilingualism (by-ling'-wuh-liz-um) The capability of speaking more than one *language.* The percentage of **bilingual** children in *special education* has consistently been higher than their *prevalence* in the larger population. Some believe that bilingualism complicates the *language development* process; others believe that in some cases bilingualism can have a facilitative effect on language skills.

bilirubin (bil-ih-roo'-bin) A compound formed by the breakdown of free *hemoglobin,* which is released through the destruction of red blood cells. A high content of bilirubin in the brain of a *fetus* is *toxic* and causes *kernicterus,* which results in *spasticity* of certain muscle groups and *mental retardation.*

bimanual Refers to a skill or activity requiring the use of both hands; sometimes used in reference to the ability to use both hands.

binaural (by-nor'-ul) **amplification** Magnification of sound in both ears simultaneously through the use of *hearing aids.*

binocular vision The ability to *focus* both eyes simultaneously on the same object so that the two images fuse into a single shape. The inability to do this is termed *amblyopia.*

biofeedback The process of measuring involuntary (*autonomic nervous system*) body functions such as blood pressure and brain waves and employing techniques to exert control over selected functions for *therapeutic* value.

biogenic (adj.) Refers to biological and *hereditary* factors; used in conjunction with *behavior disorders.*

biopsy (by'-op-see) The removal of live body tissue and examination of the sample obtained, usually under a microscope, to establish the *diagnosis* of disease conditions.

biosocial Describes something possessing characteristics that stem from both biological and social processes or forces.

bipolar disorder A serious mental disorder that is biological in origin and psychological in expression. Characterized by excessive periods of *mania* and *depression.* Also called *manic-depressive psychosis.*

birth trauma Describes a condition of injury to the brain that occurs at the time of birth or is due to the birth process. Birth trauma may leave a residual effect of physical or mental injury. (See also *brain injury.*)

blend A word or sound produced by combining other words, parts of words, or letters.

blind (blindness) Refers to a lack of sufficient vision for the daily activities of life. Legally defined in most states as having central *visual acuity* of 20/200 or less in the better eye with correction or having *peripheral vision* contracted to the extent that the widest diameter of the *visual field* covers an angular distance of no greater than 20 degrees.

blindism A behavior pattern, such as swaying the body back and forth or moving the head from side to side, that is a characteristic motion of *blind* persons. Such behavior patterns are interpreted to be acts of involuntary *self-stimulatory behavior* resulting from a lack of meaningful activity. Because the *symptoms* are also observed in children with *emotional disturbance, brain injury*, and *mental retardation,* the terminology is changing to *stereotypic behavior* or *manneristic behavior.*

Bliss method A means of *nonoral communication* that requires one to point to abstract symbols that are associated with actual experiences or written words. These symbols are combined and modified to replicate the English *language.* The method is used primarily with individuals who have *severe disabilities.*

Bliss symbol scanner A device for teaching the Bliss symbol system to individuals with *severe disabilities.*

blocking Interference or stopping of the flow of thought or associations, which may affect communication or problem-solving ability. Blocking is often a temporary behavior and is usually caused by unconscious conflicts that cause *anxiety* and tension. Blocking is closely related to *stuttering* behavior.

Bloom's taxonomy A *conceptualization* to explain the ways children learn. Emphasizes knowledge, *comprehension*, analysis, *synthesis*, and *evaluation*. The latter levels, considered to be the highest levels of *cognition*, are more appropriate for *gifted* students.

Bobath therapy A form of physical treatment emphasizing *reflex inhibition* as a basic form of treatment for *cerebral palsy.* Treatment evolved in England, emphasizing *positioning*, stimulation of muscle groups, and *physical therapy.*

body concept How one thinks he/she looks; one's opinion of his/her physical self.

body image One's recognition of his/her body and consciousness of one's position in space and time.

body language An extension of oneself through physical movements and gestures in place of or in addition to speech; represents a form of communication.

bone conduction Transference of sound waves to the inner ear by vibration of the bones of the skull. Bone conduction *audiometry* is especially useful in differentiating conductive from *sensorineural hearing loss.*

bone conduction hearing aid An *amplification device* worn behind the ear to assist the conduction of sound waves by vibration through the skull bones.

borderline intelligence The level of *intellectual* ability that falls between normal and *mildly retarded.* An equivalent term is *slow learner.* This level has been removed from the American Association on Mental Retardation's classification manual.

brachycephalous (brack-ee-sef'-uh-lus) (adj., **brachycephalic**) Having a short, broad head.

bradycardia (bray-dee-kar'-dee-ah) A condition in which the pulse rate is less than 60 beats per minute; may be of either physiological or *psychological etiology.*

braille (brayl) A *tactile* (touch) approach to reading and writing for *blind* persons, in which the letters are formed by combinations of raised dots in a cell two dots wide by three dots high. This approach was developed in France by Louis Braille (1809–1852). Braille may be written by hand with a *slate and stylus* or mechanically with a *brailler*, braillewriter, or computer printer. In *Grade I braille*, every letter is spelled out; in *Grade II braille*, contractions are substituted for words according to certain definitive rules. The latter is the most widely used braille form in English-speaking areas.

brailler See *Perkins brailler.*

brailler, pocket See *pocket brailler.*

brain damage See *brain injury, closed head injury.*

brain disorder A loosely used term for a *neurological* disorder or *syndrome* indicating *impairment* or injury to brain tissue.

brain injury Any damage to tissues of the brain that leads to *impairment* of the function of the *central nervous system.* This terminology has largely given way to the term *specific learning disability.*

brain-injured approach Methodology applied to the education of children who display characteristics typical of *brain injury.* The philosophy is predicated on the belief that uninjured portions of the brain can be trained to perform functions of the injured portion.

brain-injured child A term used in the 1940s and 1950s by Alfred Strauss and others to indicate a child with learning and behavioral problems that were postulated to result from injury to the brain. The terminology has largely given way to the terms *specific learning disability* or *learning disability.*

brainstorming A problem-solving technique in which the members of a group contribute spontaneous ideas to a discussion. This technique can be used to stimulate *creativity* and problem-solving activities, especially with *gifted* children.

breathiness (breathy) A quality of speech characterized by an excessive air flow or expiration of air that results in the excess air being unvocalized and wasted for speech purposes.

breech birth A *natal* condition in which the baby is in an *atypical* position, with the buttocks or feet appearing first, rather than in the usual headfirst *vertex* position.

Bright's disease A *chronic* disease of the kidneys; same as *nephritis.*

Broca's (broe'-kuz) **area** The portion of the brain designated as the center for articulated or *motor* speech. This area is located in the *posterior* portion of the left third frontal convolution of the *cerebrum.* Damage in Broca's area is believed to be a contributing factor in the speech and *language disorder* called *aphasia.*

bronchial asthma An *asthmatic* condition characterized by wheezing but no infection.

bronchography (brahn-kahg'-ruh-fee) Radiographic examination of the bronchial passages of the lungs.

bruxism (bruk'-sizm) Nonfunctional gnashing and grinding of teeth occurring during the day and/or night. The adverse effects have been noted in severe dental wear and damage to tissue, bone, and joints. In some *institutions* this condition has been recorded in over half of the individuals.

Buckley Amendment See *Family Education Rights and Privacy Act.*

bulimia (boo-lee'-mee-ah) A condition akin to *anorexia nervosa* that is characterized by eating to excess (binge eating), then vomiting or use of laxatives, and repeating the process. Associated with poor *body image* and self-concept.

Bureau of Education for the Handicapped (BEH) Now called *Office of Special Education Programs* and is part of the U.S. Department of Education.

burnout A term increasingly used to indicate the disillusionment experienced by teachers, human service workers, and others who have perceived their work situations as being harmful, threatening, or unfulfilling over a period of time. Such individuals become fatigued and may express a variety of physical *symptoms*. A change in employment is often sought.

bursa A fluid-filled sac or pouch located in an area of the body at which friction would otherwise exist (e.g., the knee joint). **Bursitis**, or *inflammation* of the bursa, results in muscle pain and limited movement of the affected area.

C

CA See *chronological age*.

caesarean (suh-sare'-ee-an) **section** A surgical procedure for delivering a baby that involves incision through the abdominal and *uterine* walls, as contrasted with the usual vaginal delivery; sometimes necessary to protect the health of the mother or prevent ill effects (including *mental retardation* resulting from oxygen deficiency at birth) in the baby.

CAI See *computer-assisted instruction*.

Canterbury aid An electronic device used by individuals who are *blind* to aid in *mobility*. It is worn on the head and emits sounds so that the individual can react to the echoes, which signify tangible objects.

captioned Refers to a film that has been adapted for movies or television in which the narrative or dialogue appears in print at the bottom of the screen or can be seen on a television screen using a special electronic device. An aid to individuals who are *deaf* or *hearing impaired*.

carcinogen (kar-sin'-oh-jen) Any substance capable of producing cancer.

carcinoma (kar-sin-oh'-mah) A growth of *malignant* cells; cancer.

cardiac Pertaining to the heart.

cardiac distress A situation in which an individual experiences what appears to be a heart attack. Whether real or imagined, treatment should be undertaken.

cardiopulmonary resuscitation (CPR) A technique used to supply oxygen to another person's body and circulate his/her blood when that person's heart and lungs have stopped functioning properly. The administration of CPR requires the helper to compress the chest of the stricken person and breathe into his/her *respiratory* tract.

cardiovascular (kar-dee-oh-vas'-cue-lar) Refers to the circulatory system and its parts, including the heart and blood vessels.

career education An educational emphasis stressing teaching of the work ethic and job familiarity early in life, to be followed up throughout the child's schooling by training for some type of occupation(s). In *special education*, because of the considerable emphasis already placed on vocational training and *habilitation*, this movement has facilitated stronger programs and preparation of *prevocational teachers* and job placement coordinators.

carrel (care'-ul) A booth or cubicle designed to keep external distractions to a minimum, where a child will experience the least possible interference.

carrier A person with a *covert* disease condition that can be transmitted to offspring; for example, in *muscular dystrophy* neither parent may have the condition but it may appear in their children if either parent is a carrier.

cartilage (adj., **cartilaginous**) The tough, elastic substance between bones and joints; provides a slippery surface that permits the joints to *flex* smoothly. Injury to the cartilage may result in stiffening of the joint.

cascade of services Schematic representation of the various administrative *delivery systems* in *special education*. The most often used schematic representation is pyramid-shaped and is credited to Maynard Reynolds and Evelyn Deno of the University of Minnesota.

case conference A meeting of representatives of the professional *disciplines* working with a child with a *disability*, at which *diagnostic* findings are shared and future plans for education and treatment are made. Also referred to as a *staffing*. A case conference with the parents is required by *PL 94-142* and later federal statutes to plan educational placement and develop an *individualized education program*.

case finding costs Those *rehabilitation* costs incurred as a counselor works up a case—e.g., costs for the *diagnostician* and for medical treatment.

case history An accumulation of pertinent data about an individual, such as family background, personal history, physical development, medical history, test results, and anecdotal records of behavior. The case history often is used in making decisions on treatment services.

caseload The number of individuals assigned for treatment to a given professional or agency during a specific time period.

casework The use of comprehensive studies of individual cases by *social*

workers **(caseworkers)** in their professional practice of assisting individuals or families to make better personal, social, or economic adjustments.

catalogia (kat-uh-log'-ee-uh) Constant repetition of words, as displayed in some mental disorders. (See also *idiolalia*; *echolalia*.)

cataract A condition causing opacity of the *lens of the eye*, resulting in *visual* limitation or *blindness*. Surgical replacement of the lens is the most frequently used method of restoring or improving sight. Cataracts occur much more often among adults than among children; in children the condition may occur as a result of *rubella* (one form of *measles*).

catarrh (kuh-tar') An *inflammatory* condition of any mucous membrane of the body that causes irritation of tissues and a fluid discharge. Inflammation of the *nasal* and air passages may be accompanied by a cough.

catatonia (kat-uh-tahn'-ee-ah) (adj., **catatonic**) A form of *mental illness* characterized by a trance-like *stupor* that at times causes *rigidity* of muscles; may alternate with restless activity lacking in purpose and at times resulting in unwarranted excitement.

catchment area The geographical region designated to be served by specified *mental health* or related programs.

categorical *Labeling* by specific classifications such as *"mental retardation"* and *"learning disabilities"* instead of more *generic*, or general, terms.

catharsis (kah-thar'-sis) A *therapeutic* approach toward relieving *anxieties* by encouraging an individual to tell anything he/she associates with his/her problem, freeing the mind of *repressed memories* that are causing the emotional conflict.

catheter (kath'-eh-ter) A narrow tube of rubber, plastic, metal, or glass that can be inserted into the body to introduce fluids or to empty the bladder or kidneys by a method known as **catheterization**.

cauterize To treat a condition by searing a body part with a special device, such as an electric needle.

CBA *Acronym* for *curriculum-based assessment*. See *curriculum-based measurement*; the two terms are used interchangeably, but some professionals differentiate between the two.

CBI See *competency-based instruction*.

CBM See *curriculum-based measurement*.

ceiling The upper limit of ability that can be measured by a test. If a test is too easy, it will not have enough "top"; the ceiling will be too low to allow proper measurement.

ceiling age The age level on a test at which an individual cannot pass any of the items.

ceiling effect A limitation of an *assessment* device resulting from there not being enough difficult questions; prevents the *gifted* from showing their true levels of performance.

central deafness *Impairment* of hearing resulting from damage to the *auditory nerve* pathways or in the centers of hearing in the brain *cortex*.

central nervous system (CNS) The portion of an individual's nervous system that includes the brain and spinal cord. *Sensory* images are transmitted to the CNS, and *motor* impulses are given in response.

cerebellum (ser-eh-bel'-um) A part of the brain located at the lower rear; has the appearance of a walnut. Its function is to control *fine motor* coordination. In-

jury to this area may result in *ataxic cerebral palsy*, causing difficulty in walking.

cerebral (ser-ee'-brul or sare'-eh-brul) Pertaining to the brain or the main *hemisphere* of the brain.

cerebral dominance The primary control of one *hemisphere* of the brain over the other in initiating or controlling bodily movements. Normally, this dominance resides in the left *hemisphere* in a right-handed person and in the right *hemisphere* in a left-handed person.

cerebral hemisphere The left or the right side of the brain; the largest portion of the brain in higher mammals.

cerebral palsy (CP) A condition resulting in an abnormal alteration of human movement or *motor* function; arises from defect, injury, or disease of the tissues of the *central nervous system*. Three main types are usually described—*spastic*, *athetoid*, and *ataxic*.

cerebrospinal fluid The body liquid that surrounds and lubricates the brain and spinal cord.

cerebrum (ser-ee'-bruhm) The two *hemispheres* of the main part of the brain, located in the upper and forepart of the *cranium*; the organ of voluntary control, conscious sensations, and learning processes.

cert. den. An abbreviation for *certiorari* denied. In a citation to a case, indicates that a higher court (usually the Supreme Court) has declined to order a lower court to send the case to it for review. By contrast, *cert. granted* means the higher court has ordered a lower court to send a case to it for review.

cert. granted An abbreviation for *"certiorari granted,"* which indicates that a higher court agrees to review a case; *"cert. den."* means that it will not. If *certiorari* is denied, the lower court ruling stands and continues to apply in the U.S. Circuit in which it was issued. In practice, other courts often use such rulings as a *precedent*.

certified occupational disability assistant (CODA) A certified *aide* trained in *occupational therapy* who is licensed to assist an *occupational therapist*. The individual must work under the supervision of an *occupational therapist*.

certiorari A Latin term (abbreviated **cert.**) that indicates in a citation to a case that an order from an appeals court (usually the Supreme Court) to a lower court has been entered to either require or decline to require the lower court to send up a case for review. The right-to-education cases decided by the U.S. Supreme Court usually go to that court on a petition (request) for certiorari by one of the parties (and the court sometimes grants the request and orders the lower court to send the case to it for review).

cerumen (seh-roo'-men) Ear wax.

CF See *cystic fibrosis*.

CFR See *Code of Federal Regulations*.

chaining Refers to two or more performances linked by common *stimuli*. The *stimulus* linking two performances serves both as the *conditioned reinforcer* maintaining the frequency of the first performance and as a *stimulus* for the second. (See *forward chaining* and *backward [reverse] chaining*.)

chancre (shang'-ker) An initial sore or ulcer associated with a disease, particularly a *venereal disease* such as *syphilis*.

character disorder A disturbance in one's personality manifested by destructive, acting out, or *aggressive* behavior without apparent conscience or guilt. (See *conduct disorder*.)

character neurosis A deterioration or disturbance in a person's nature that causes or may cause adjustment problems.

checkmark system A *reinforcement* program employed in *behavior management* programs in which the individual receives checkmarks on a special card for working on task, for completing work, and for several other contingencies. (See *engineered classroom*; *token*.)

chemotherapy (kee-moe-thair'-uh-pea) Treatment for a disease or a means of preventing the disease through the use of drugs to destroy the disease agent.

CHI See *closed head injury*.

child abuse and neglect The physical or mental injury, sexual abuse, *negligence*, or maltreatment of an individual under age 18 by a person who is responsible for that individual's welfare.

child advocate A person (or group) who actively pursues and seeks support for a child's rights and entitlements. (See *advocacy*.)

Child Find An organized effort to identify children with *disabilities*; particularly active in regard to younger, preschool children. In the 1980s the terminology changed to "Child Serve."

Child Serve See *Child Find*.

child welfare Components or divisions of community agencies that plan and organize services for the physical, mental, and social well-being of children. New terminology includes Health Service Agencies, Life Service Agencies, and Human Resource Agencies.

child-centered curriculum A school *curriculum* in which the pupil's maturity, interests, experiences, and needs in general are the main considerations in selecting materials and activities for that student's educational program.

childhood schizophrenia A psychological disorder generally occurring before *puberty* that is manifested in *atypical* body movements, *emotional disturbance*, *perceptual disorders*, and *hallucinations*.

children with special health care needs A term denoting children with medically related conditions in which either the medical problem is a threat to the child's survival or the medical condition causes extraordinary restrictions on the child's education. Sometimes called *medically fragile* children.

Chisanbop (chiz'-an-bop) A method of using the fingers for math calculations; employed by *blind* persons and other children with *disabilities* who may have difficulty with computation.

choice responding The study of factors affecting choices; schedule strain which occurs when the *schedule of reinforcement* is so lean as to incur avoidance and escape responses, thus having the same effect as an *aversive stimulus*.

cholecystography (koe-leh-sis-tahg'-ruh-fee) A medical procedure for examining the gall bladder. Involves injecting into the patient or having the patient swallow certain opaque substances that enter the bile and allow the gall bladder to be visible on *X rays*.

chorea (koe-ree'-uh) A nervous disorder characterized by spasmodic twitching of muscles; commonly referred to as "St. Vitus Dance."

choreiform (koe-ree'-ih-form) **movements** Characterized by difficulty in keeping the arms outstretched while the eyes are closed. A test for choreiform movements is used in the *diagnosis* of *minimal brain dysfunction*; these movements are considered to be a *"soft" sign* of minimal brain dysfunction.

chorioretinitis (koe-ree-oh-ret-ih-ny'-tis) *Inflammation* of two of the layers of the eye, the *choroid* and *retinal* layers.

choroid The layer of the eye between the *sclera* and *retina*; contains blood vessels that provide nourishment to the *retina*.

chromatin (krow'-muh-tin) The *genetic* material in the nucleus of body cells. The chromatin of every cell is controlled by principles of organization that determine inherited characteristics.

chromosomal anomaly (krow-moe-so'-muhl ah-nom'-uh-lee) Irregularity in *chromosome* material, which may result in the birth of a child with *disabilities*. *Down syndrome* is an example.

chromosomal The basic unit in the nucleus of body cells that carries the *genes* or *hereditary* factors.

chronic Pertaining to a disease, condition, habit, or situation that is continuous or recurring and of relatively long duration.

chronically ill A condition in which an illness has persisted for an extended period of time and is not *acute* or life threatening.

chronological age (CA) The amount of time, usually expressed in years and months, that has elapsed since an individual's birth.

chronological peer(s) Used to denote students of like *chronological age* as opposed to comparisons of *mental age*. Would refer to students with *disabilities* and nondisabled students who have each lived the same number of years.

CIC See *clean intermittent catheterization*.

cineplasty (sin'-eh-plas-tee) The fitting of an *amputee* with a *prosthetic device* that allows the person to activate the *extremity* by a *motor* within the muscles of the stump itself.

cirrhosis (sir-oh'-sis) A *pathological* wasting away of connective tissues of a body organ, generally the liver.

citizens advocacy Interceding for the rights and entitlements of persons with *disabilities* by individuals not related to those for whom they are interceding. (See also *advocacy*.)

civil case A lawsuit brought by one or more individuals to seek redress of some legal injury (or aspect of an injury) for which there are civil (noncriminal) remedies. In right-to-education cases, these remedies are based on the federal or state constitutions, federal or state statutes, or federal or state agency regulations, or a combination of federal and state constitutions, statutes, and regulations. Right-to-education cases are always civil suits.

class action A *civil case* brought on behalf of the *plaintiffs* who are named in the suit as well as on behalf of all other persons similarly situated to vindicate their legally protected interests. *Mills v. Board of Education* was brought on behalf of 12-year-old Peter Mills and six other school-age children who were named in the complaint, as well as on behalf of all other *exceptional children* in the District of Columbia. By contrast, *Board v. Rowley* was not a class action lawsuit because it was brought on behalf of only one person, who sued to protect only her rights, not the rights of other people.

class size The number of children allowed by state statutes to be assigned to given types of classes. As an example, in some states the class size for a *self-contained class* is a minimum of 10 and a maximum of 15.

classes One of J. P. Guilford's *products of thinking*, in which *units* of thought are grouped into categories. (See *structure of the intellect*.)

classroom unit A measure used to determine support to schools under state-aid plans. The school verifies the number of classroom *units* in operation by reporting the number of pupils in *average daily attendance* and the state reim- burses a fixed amount of money to the district per unit verified.

classwide peer tutoring (CWPT) A version of *peer tutoring* that combines peer-mediated instruction, teacher-orchestrated procedures, and whole-class participation. Usually involves the pairing off of all students in the class. In a subject area one student serves as the tutor and reads to the other student for 10 minutes, followed by 5 minutes of comprehensive questioning. Then the roles are reversed with the other student taking the role of reading and questioning.

claustrophobia The fear of being in enclosed or narrow spaces.

clavicle The collarbone.

clean intermittent catheterization (CIC) A procedure used with *paraplegics* to drain urine from the bladder on a regular schedule. The procedure involves inserting a clean but not sterile tube through the urethra and into the bladder. Regular use may prevent infections and kidney damage.

clear type Denotes the 18- to 24-point type size in which textbooks and other educational materials are printed for use by students with *visual impairments*. The larger than usual print is more easily seen and enhances readability. Also termed *large type*.

cleft lip A split or opening of the upper lip, which is *congenital* and often associated with *cleft palate*. The condition is surgically correctable, especially if undertaken at an early age. "Cleft palate" is used if the cleft also involves the hard and soft palate.

cleft palate A condition characterized by an opening in the roof of the mouth, involving the hard or soft *palate*, or both; often extends through the upper lip. Usually attributed to faulty development before birth, but may occur as a result of injury or disease. The condition causes *nasal* speech, *articulation* problems, and sometimes additional physical problems. Cleft palate usually is treated by surgery and *speech therapy*.

client-centered therapy Counseling wherein the counselor serves as a catalyst or facilitator in helping a client arrive at his/her own solutions to problems. Also referred to as the *nondirective approach*.

clinic An agency or organization of *interdisciplinary* workers qualified to *evaluate* and *diagnose* more than one aspect of an individual or family in need of assistance and service. Clinics may be classified in many different ways, including various kinds of medical clinics, speech clinics, *mental health* clinics, and reading clinics.

clinical An approach for analyzing learning difficulties through the use of a variety of tests, instruments, and technical aids in an attempt to detect specific needs and plan an educational program directed at remediating deficiencies.

clinical type Any of a number of disabling conditions (especially pertaining to *mental retardation*) in which the physical traits and features are readily recognizable as being characteristic of the specific condition. Examples are *Down syndrome*, *cretinism*, *microcephaly*, and *hydrocephaly*.

clonic (klah'-nik) **block** 1. The involuntary jerking of speech muscles; produces a repetition of parts of words or speech sounds. (See also *stuttering*.) 2. Refers to the movements a person has during a *grand mal seizure*.

cloning The process of asexually producing *genetically* identical cells from a single cell.

clonus (kloe'-nus) Any form of *seizure* characterized by rapid contraction and relaxation of muscles.

closed caption Procedure for producing written text that is visible with an electronic decoder on the lower part of television screens. The text allows *deaf* individuals to know the *auditory* portion of the program.

closed head injury (CHI) Documented *traumatic* head injury resulting in *neurological* damage that is most reliably detected by medical *diagnostic* methods. Characteristics include alterations in *cognitive* functions ranging from subtle to obvious. Medical history usually includes loss of consciousness and delayed behavioral residuals that occur up to several years after the original injury. *Special education* placement is usually in *learning disabilities* or other health-impaired programs.

closure 1. Achieving completion of a behavior or mental act. 2. Achieving a whole even though parts of the whole may be left out (e.g., as in *visual closure* or *auditory closure*).

cloze (close) procedure A teaching method in which words or other *language* units are systematically deleted from reading material and the student is asked to fill in the missing parts. The teacher also may tape-record a reading lesson and then have the child listen and respond to pauses on the tape, as in, "The man drove his car into the _____."

clubfoot A *congenital* abnormality in which one or both feet are turned downward and inward at the ankle. If the condition is recognized early in a child's life and prompt corrective action is taken, the *prognosis* for minimizing any disabling condition is good.

clumsiness A characteristic of many children who have *minimal brain dysfunc-*

tion; involves a lack of neuromotor co-ordination in activities such as walking, running, throwing, climbing stairs, and dressing.

cluster grouping Assigning groups of *gifted* children to a single teacher at each level.

clustering A *learning strategy* that involves teaching students with *learning disabilities* to group or categorize material to be learned. Clustering allows larger amounts of material to be remembered. See also *learning disabled*.

cluttering A *speech disorder* characterized by rapid or excessive speech that is difficult to understand. Also termed *agitolalia*.

CMV See *cytomegalovirus*.

coccyx (kok'-six) The small, triangular bone at the bottom of the vertebral column. It is formed by the union of the four rudimentary vertebrae that terminate the tail end of the spinal column.

cochlea (kah'-klee-uh) The snail-like coil of the organ of hearing located in the inner ear.

cochlea implant A surgical procedure in which an electronic *prosthetic device* is implanted in the inner ear to stimulate the *auditory nerve* and improve hearing. Such bionic devices do not restore normal hearing but may improve *auditory discrimination*.

CODA See *certified occupational disability assistant*.

code learning Responding to systematically occurring events so that rules can be established. Employed with *deaf* people in teaching *language*.

code of ethics A set of written and approved moral standards intended to guide the conduct of a given group. The Code of Ethics for teachers is a statement of ideals, principles, and standards for pro-fessional conduct in the teaching profession.

Code of Federal Regulations (CFR) A publication of the U.S. government that contains the regulations of the executive agencies of the government (e.g., U.S. Department of Education) that have been instated to implement laws (statutes) passed by Congress (e.g., *PL 94–142*).

codependency A condition in which an individual with a *disability* appears to exhibit more of an inappropriate behavior when he/she is living with another individual. An example would be a person with an alcohol problem who appears to drink more when family members or a spouse is around and may attribute part of his/her reason for drinking to the other person(s). Codependent relationships often do not benefit either partner.

cognition (kahg-nih'-shun) 1. Gaining knowledge through personal experience; the *perception* of knowledge that extends beyond a mere awareness. 2. One of J. P. Guilford's thinking *operations* in the *structure of the intellect* (i.e., to know, recognize, become aware of, understand, become acquainted with).

cognitive Refers to the mental processes of *memory*, reasoning, *comprehension*, and judgment.

cognitive behavior modification Refers to the manipulation of *covert* behavior through a combination of *behavior modification* techniques and self-treatment methods such as self-*monitoring, self-instructional training,* and self-*evaluation*.

cognitive blindness A term to describe *language* competence of *deaf* persons, in which absence of spoken language or words interferes with the development of *concepts*.

cognitive deficit Below-average functioning on *intellectual* or perceptual skills. A student displaying a cognitive *deficit* generally is slow in learning academic subject matter.

cognitive dissonance A state in which two objects, thoughts, or *perceptions* have equal emphasis in one's mind but are conflicting in nature.

cognitive language behavior Arthur Miller's approach to working with children with *autism*. The emphasis is on developing *cognitive* structures through experiential activities. The approach employs a *fading* technique that alters ritualistic behavior by systematically interrupting selected rituals introduced by the *therapist*.

cognitive map 1. A means of *memory* storage in which bits of information are stored in a nonlinear fashion that resembles the way places are coded into a map. Each bit of information in such a system is subject to direct access. 2. A *concept* employed to help *blind* students *visualize* the environment and assist with *mobility*.

cognitive modeling A *self-instructional training* procedure in which a child uses his/her own *verbalizations* to control *overt* behavior. Based upon the work of Donald Meichenbaum, the process involves, first, an adult *modeling* the behavior, and then the child *modeling* the behavior while speaking aloud. Gradually, the *overt* verbal control is *faded* out. (See also *cognitive behavior modification*.)

cognitive style The approach an individual uses consistently in problem-solving and thinking tasks. Some individuals tend to see parts, and others tend toward *gestalt*—seeing things as wholes rather than being aware of components.

cognitive training See *cognitive behavior modification*.

COHI See *crippled and other health impaired*.

coincidental teaching A procedure in which a teacher helps parents identify and use naturally occurring situations in the home and community to teach their child social skills and their *generalization*.

coin-click test A rough *screening* test for *hearing acuity*. The tester clicks two coins together near the pupil's ear and then at various distances as he/she moves away from the pupil. The tester asks the pupil to indicate when he/she ceases to hear the clicks. The tester should know the approximate distance at which a person with normal hearing would cease to hear the clicks in order to recognize *hearing losses* in the population being tested.

collaboration The practice of direct interaction between at least two coequal parties voluntarily engaged in working with students with *disabilities*. Implies that a *special education* teacher and a general education teacher are working together for the education and training of a student with *disabilities*.

collaborative consulting model One of the administrative models used in *inclusion*. It emphasizes *consulting teachers* working with general education teachers who have students who are *disabled* in their classes. Sometimes these *consulting teachers* do not actually directly teach students with disabilities.

collegial teaming A term that means the same as teaming or *co-teaching*. It indicates that a *special education* teacher's instructional group is commingled with that of a general education teacher and that both teachers are sharing equally in the instruction. (See *collaboration*.)

coloboma (kuh-low-boe'-mah) A *congenital* disease of the eyes in which areas of the *retina* are not completely developed, resulting in impaired *visual acuity*. Condition may worsen over time.

colony system A type of *institutional* organization in which the number of individuals in each cottage or unit is kept small and the services that are offered are directed toward specific goals, such as social living, vocational training, and *self-help skills*.

colorblind(ness) A *hereditary* defect in vision characterized by a lack of color *perception* or an inability to *discriminate* between certain colors.

color coding A method of using color to identify various elements of teaching material prepared for students. It is based on the idea that such use of color aids students in the identification of parts and functions and thus facilitates learning. For example, each of the parts of speech in a paragraph could be identified by a separate color (e.g., nouns—red, verbs—blue).

colostomy (koe-lahs'-toe-mee) A surgical operation to create an opening between the colon and the body surface, usually in the side of the abdomen, to compensate for a bowel obstruction and enable the elimination of solid bodily wastes.

coma Complete, prolonged unconsciousness often brought on by a disease condition (as in *diabetic coma*). A person in this condition is said to be **comatose**.

combined method A means of instructing *hard of hearing* or *deaf* persons in which procedures from both the *manual* and *oral methods* are used. (See also *total communication*.)

common reality The reality base from which most people function; constitutes those objects, people, and events experienced in common and accepted as real. Contrasts with idiosyncratic experiences such as *hallucinations*.

communicable disease A condition that can be transmitted readily from one person to another without direct physical contact (e.g., chicken pox, flu).

communication aide A person who works under the supervision of a *speech and language pathologist* to provide *therapy* to students. The *aide* must be offered 50 hours minimum training and cannot serve children without parent approval.

communication board Pictorial or symbol representations used in *nonoral communication* systems such as the *Bliss method*. In such systems, symbols denote thought components, and individuals with little or no speech are taught to communicate by pointing to symbols on the communication board.

communication disorder Any condition that inhibits communication, such as speech or *language* problems.

communication skills Refers to the many ways of transferring thought from one person to another through the commonly used media of speech, written words, and bodily gestures.

communitization The process of providing homes and developmental training environments for persons who are returning to the community from *institutional* living.

community center A site or facility developed to provide services for people in the area who need them. The services are offered by *interdisciplinary* agencies and personnel from the community and are contained in various units such as *day schools*, *diagnostic* and consultation units, *sheltered workshops*, and *alternative living* units. (See also *alternative living*; *group home*.)

community mental health center A facility that provides comprehensive services and continuity of care for individuals with *mental illness* and *emotional disturbance*. This type of center provides in-patient treatment, out-patient treatment, partial hospitalization (day and/or night service), emergency services, and community consultation and education. It functions as one administrative entity but may contract for hospital beds or other services.

community-based instruction A method of instruction in which a student is taught to perform skills in the actual environment rather than being taught skills at school with an expectation for *generalization* and application on the job.

compensation A psychological adjustment technique whereby an individual reacts to conscious or unconscious feelings of inadequacy, inferiority, or incompetence by concentrating on and/or excelling in another area of activity; e.g., individuals with *learning disabilities* may develop certain skill areas to **compensate** for deficiencies in other areas.

compensatory activities 1. Programs substituted for those in which disabling conditions would interfere with satisfactory achievement. 2. The educational means necessary to repair harm done to an individual previously denied the right to an education, regardless of present age.

compensatory education Refers to instructional restitution for situations in which a student has been denied an education or appropriate educational instruction has been lacking due to improper placement or ineffective instruction. Recent court rulings on compensatory education have included the class of students who were not placed within 30 days of the date of their *IEP* team meetings. The *remediation* may include instruction beyond the usual termination date, intensive instruction, or a program during summer vacation time.

competency Mastering the material in a subject area or reaching the specific level of performance for success that has been set in that subject area.

competency-based instruction (CBI) Teaching derived from specific *criteria* that were set prior to the instructional period. The goal of the instruction is to achieve the competencies spelled out in the criteria.

competing equities A term describing a situation in which two or more people or groups of people have rights or privileges that cannot be fully satisfied without infringing on the rights or privileges of one another. For example, children with *disabilities* have some rights to be integrated with nondisabled children, but nondisabled children also have rights to an education that is not disrupted by children with disabilities. In such a case, the competing equities of both groups of children must be weighted against each other and a decision made by a court or other policymakers as to which claims prevail. Another way of thinking about competing equities is to ask: Whose rights or privileges are to be reduced for the benefit of other people?

complex health care A treatment program in which a variety of *disciplines* take part; used for individuals with extensive *disabilities*.

compound fracture A bone break in which an external wound is associated with the break.

comprehension Understanding the meaning of spoken or printed *language* (as contrasted with perceiving or pronouncing words without understanding their meaning).

comprehension monitoring The act of *evaluating* one's own *comprehension* processes. Actions to regulate comprehension and resolve comprehension failure, considered by some to be part of comprehension monitoring, might more suitably be termed comprehension fostering activities. The combination of *monitoring* and regulatory functions constitutes metacomprehension.

comprehensive plan A document produced by a *local education agency* or a state that describes how it intends to meet the needs of all *exceptional children* within its jurisdiction, as *mandated* by federal or state law.

compulsion (adj., **compulsive**) An irresistible impulse to perform an irrational act.

compulsive behavior A *neurotic* form of behavior in which an individual has an irresistible impulse to perform a controversial behavior that might be against his/her better judgment or will.

compulsory school age range The ages required by law for children to attend school. This *range* varies according to the state code; in many states it is from ages 6 to 16.

computer-assisted instruction (CAI) The use of computers for instruction. Microprocessors/microcomputers have come into increasing use in the teaching of children and adults who have *disabilities*.

concave lens A manufactured lens (as in eyeglasses) that has one flat side and one side curved slightly inward toward the middle, producing a "hollow" effect. A concave lens expands the light rays entering the lens, thus lengthening the distance of *focus*. Concave lenses are used to correct *myopia (nearsightedness)*. For comparison, see *convex lens*.

concave-convex lens A manufactured lens that is concave on one side and convex on the other. (See *concave lens*; *convex lens*.)

concentration 1. The act of giving close *attention* to a specific learning situation. 2. The combination of all forces, mental and physical, exerted in an effort to solve a problem or participate in an activity.

concept 1. The accumulation of all that is conveyed to one's mind by a situation, symbol, or object. Sometimes used to refer to a thought, opinion, or general idea of what something should be. 2. The set of characteristics common to a class of objects; e.g., triangularity includes all three-sided figures.

conceptual (n., **conceptualization**) Describes the integration of two or more sets of characteristics that are isolated by a process of abstraction and united by a specific definition.

conceptual disorders Difficulties in generalizing, abstracting, and reasoning, as well as storing and retaining past experiences. Conceptual disorders may become apparent by an individual's lack of ability to remember ideas, *concepts*, rules, or regulations that appear reasonable for the individual's *intellectual* level.

concrete Describes an idea or image of a situation, symbol, or object that can be perceived by the senses and derives from an experience that makes it familiar.

concrete mode A learning or *cognitive style* characterized as learning most efficiently by use of objects and tangible items.

concrete operations A level of individual functioning proposed by Jean Piaget. At this level, the individual structures reality as completely as possible by remaining close to reality in its raw form and without the isolation of variables. This level of functioning is lower or simpler than the more complex abstract level.

concussion 1. The shock produced by bodies or objects crashing together. 2. An injury, with a lowering of *functional* activity, resulting from a fall, a blow, or a similar injury (as in a brain concussion).

conditional aversive stimulus An agent that is not in itself unpleasant to a person but becomes so when repeatedly paired with an agent that does disturb the person.

conditioned reflex (response) (CR) A learned response to an external *stimulus*. The response is developed through training geared toward teaching that response.

conditioned reinforcer A *stimulus* that typically has no *reinforcing* qualities but acquires them as a result of being repeatedly paired with strong reinforcers.

conditioning (adj., **conditioned**) The process of building up the association of a *stimulus* with a response so that in the future the stimulus can produce the response.

conduct disorder One of the classifications of *behavior disorder* in Herbert Quay's *dimensional classification* system. It describes individuals who have *aggressive* and other behaviors that are all negative (e.g., boisterous or bullying behaviors).

conduct problem A term proposed as being applicable to students who do not show signs of *emotional disturbance* but instead represent behaviors of "normal" students who choose to break socially defined rules. Educators who support this *concept* would not have *special education* serve "conduct-disordered" students.

conductive hearing loss A form of *hearing loss* characterized by obstruction along the sound conduction pathway leading to the inner ear. The obstruction reduces the sound transmission through the outer and middle ear, causing a flat *audiogram* and generally a hearing loss of less than 70 *db*. This form of hearing loss is the most preventable and treatable.

confidentiality One of the requirements under federal laws; protects the privacy of student and parent information, including the protection of student files. Stipulates that teachers and other professionals not use the student's name in open discussions.

configuration clue In reading, a hint toward the identity of a word that can be gained from examining its physical characteristics or general outline, rather than its detailed and specific parts.

conformity Adjustment to a social environment by acting within the dictates of the behavior standards of that environment. Teachers sometimes seek conformity of students through classroom control and management.

confrontation A direct verbal or physical response to inappropriate behavior. On the teacher's part, confrontation involves a willingness to enforce rules that have been established.

congenital (kun-jen'-ih-tal) Describes the presence of a condition or characteristic in an individual at birth. The causes of the condition are not, however, limited to *hereditary* factors. Examples of congenital conditions are congenital *deafness* and congenital *heart defects*.

congenital amputee See *amputee*.

congenital anophthalmos (ann-ahf-thal'-mos) Lack of development of the eyes and associated parts of the brain necessary for vision; usually associated with *mental retardation*.

conjunctiva (kon-junk-tie'-vah) A thin, transparent membrane that lines the eyelids and covers the front of the eye. In diseases such as pinkeye, the conjunctiva is *inflamed*.

conjunctivitis (kon-junk-tih-vie'-tis) *Inflammation* of the mucous membrane that lines the inner surface of the eyelid and covers the forepart of the eyeball.

consent agreement 1. An out-of-court agreement, formally approved by the court, that is reached by the parties to a lawsuit. In *Pennsylvania Association for Retarded Children (PARC) v. Commonwealth of Pennsylvania*, a court entered an order that it adopted pursuant to a consent agreement between the *plaintiffs* and *defendants*. 2. A legal term denoting an agreed-upon stipulation regarding an individual's treatment, involvement in research, or other action, based on that person's capacity to make decisions, having adequate information, and in the absence of force or coercion. *Informed consent* means that the individual is apprised of all rights and the consequences of consent.

consent judgment A *contract* acknowledging in open court a mutual agreement that is binding on both parties as fully as other judgments.

consonant An alphabet letter representing a speech sound articulated by narrowing the breath channel enough to cause a brief stoppage of the breath stream or an audible friction (e.g., f, g, l).

constitution The basic makeup of an individual including the factors of physical well-being, health, and vitality.

constitutional disorder Any illness or condition an individual has as a result of his/her unique mental or physical structure. May be inherited or *chronic*, but does not include conditions acquired after birth as a result of accident, disease, or environmental situation. Constitutional disorders can affect the way individuals view themselves, to the extent that they can be considered *disabled* in some instances.

construct A *concept* invented for purposes of theory. Constructs generally are not directly observable.

constructivism (constructivistic philosophy) A philosophical approach to teaching and learning that views students as active, self-regulating learners who construct knowledge in developmentally appropriate ways. It does not endorse *direct instruction* in skills, but rather, more of a total approach. *Whole language* has been given as an example of constructivism because the child is taught reading, writing, spelling, and *language* as a combined approach rather than as individual subject areas.

consultant (consulting teacher) (CT) A resource person in *special education* who offers *diagnostic* and other help and support to teachers, rather than direct services to students. See *collaborative consulting model*.

content validity A measure of the appropriateness of a test to determine how well the material represents the goals the developer had in constructing it. Usually used with *achievement tests* to determine if the subject content really represents the *curriculum*.

contents One of the elements of thinking in J. P. Guilford's model (see *structure of the intellect*); includes *figural*, *conceptual*, symbolic, and behavioral thought.

context 1. The written or spoken material in which a specific word, phrase, or statement is found that helps explain its meaning. 2. The environment or circumstances in which something is found or occurs.

contextual clue 1. A hint toward the meaning or identity of a word that can be gained from adjacent words in the passage or sentence. 2. A hint toward the causes of social behavior that can be gained from the environment or particular circumstances in which that social behavior might be observed.

contingency (kuhn-tin'-jen-see) A structured relationship between behaviors and the delivery of subsequent events.

contingency contract A *contract* in which the parties involved (e.g., teacher-student, parent-child) develop an agreement (usually written) specifying the positive or negative consequences of specific behaviors. The contract is signed by all parties to verify their commitment to meeting its terms.

contingency management The manipulation of consequences in an individual's environment to achieve *target behaviors.*

contingent reinforcement A planned consequence that is forthcoming when a specific response is anticipated from a behavior.

continuing education Learning opportunities offered to youth and adults through special programs, schools, centers, institutes, or colleges, emphasizing specific areas of knowledge and skills rather than traditional course sequences. The programs often are provided to individuals who have completed or have withdrawn from full-time educational programs.

continuous reinforcement A schedule whereby every response is rewarded, or reinforced.

continuum of alternative placements See *service delivery system.*

continuum of services See *service delivery system.*

contract An agreement between two parties stating the conditions under which a consequence will occur. For example, "If Mary stays in her seat for 15 minutes, then she will receive 15 minutes of 'free time.'"

contract plan An educational program especially suited to *accommodate* individual differences in children. The course content is divided into a number of assignments given one at a time, in sequence, to the pupil. Upon completion of a *contract,* the student is allowed to proceed to the next contract, thus allowing time to proceed at the most suitable rate for each individual. Same as *Dalton plan.*

contracture Shrinking or shortening of a muscle, tendon, or other tissue, which may result in distortion or disfiguration of the area of the body involved. If not treated by *physical therapy,* surgery, or other means, the contracture becomes increasingly severe and eventually irreversible.

control braces Devices designed to regulate and direct the movement of students with *physical disabilities* (rather than designed for support). May be used to eliminate purposeless movement or to allow movement in only one or two directions.

control group A unit of individuals used in research who do not receive the experimental treatment but may be exposed to another treatment or no treatment at all. Use of control groups provides a reference or index against which the *experimental group(s)* can be compared.

controlled competition A classroom technique that structures activities in such a way that rivalry among individual pupils or groups is kept to a minimum or at the level the teacher allows.

convergence The *ocular* mechanism that allows the two eyes to look at an object and to see only one object. (See also *fusion.*)

convergent thinking 1. Reaching conclusions that appear to be optimum by drawing from the available information (as contrasted with *divergent thinking*). 2. One of J. P. Guilford's thinking *operations*. (See *structure of the intellect*.)

convex lens A manufactured lens (as in eyeglasses) that has one flat side and the other side curved outward on the exterior surface, producing a bulging effect. Convex lenses compress light rays entering the lens, thus shortening the distance of *focus*. Convex lenses are used to correct *hyperopia* (*farsightedness*). For comparison, see *concave lens*.

convulsion A violent, involuntary contraction or series of contractions of the bodily muscles; often present in the more severe *seizures* of *epilepsy*, causing the body to thrash about in an uncontrolled manner.

convulsive disorder A *clinical syndrome* characterized by frequent *seizures* and loss of consciousness.

cooperative learning A grouping and instructional technique emphasizing cooperative goals that can be reached only if all members of the group work together. Students may contribute and work at different levels, which makes this technique popular with *inclusion* proponents.

cooperative plan A *service delivery system* approach in which students are enrolled in *special classes* and attend general education classes for a portion of the day. This term has been largely replaced by the term *inclusion*.

cooperative work study program A school arrangement, functioning under an established formal agreement between the local school and the state *rehabilitation* services, that provides work training in community business.

coping behavior The actions or strategies that individuals use in dealing with their environments. If an individual is able to deal effectively with the environ-

ment, he/she may be said to have "good coping behavior."

cornea (kor'-nee-uh) The clear, transparent, outer coat of the eyeball forming the covering of the aqueous chamber.

coronary thrombosis A condition in which a blood clot forms or lodges in one of the arteries that nourish the heart's muscles.

correctional counselor See *probation officer*.

corrective braces Physical support structures used for straightening bones (generally leg bones) and allowing joints to move by supporting a part of the body weight. Referred to loosely as *orthopedic* braces.

corrective physical education Programs that involve specific activities or exercises selected to change or improve the function or structure of the body. Often a segment of *rehabilitative* programs in *rehabilitation* hospitals.

correlation A statistic showing the relationship between two scores or characteristics. If the tested relationship occurs frequently, it may be referred to as having a "high correlation"; if it occurs infrequently, it may be referred to as having a "low correlation."

cortex The outer layer of gray matter cells of the *cerebrum* and *cerebellum* (brain parts).

co-teaching See *collegial teaming*.

counselor-centered therapy *Intervention* wherein a counselor gathers information before a session with a client and takes charge during the session in describing what the information means in terms of client action. Also referred to as the *directive approach*.

counter-conditioning A process in which the aversive quality of certain *stimuli* is reduced or eliminated by associating the negative events with positive experiences; e.g., a fear of animals might be reduced by *conditioning* pleasant experiences with fuzzy or furry items.

courtesy stigma The stigma that a family member or other person takes on by his/her relationship with a person with a *disability*. The term is used when describing one's coping mechanisms and the fact that a closely related person with disabilities may be devalued by the community, thus affecting one's status.

covert Refers to an action that cannot be observed. Opposite of *overt*.

CP See *cerebral palsy*.

CPR See *cardiopulmonary resuscitation*.

CR See *conditioned reflex (response)*.

crack A slang term for a derivative of cocaine. Its use has physical, behavioral, and emotional manifestations.

craft-centered curriculum An approach formerly used in a limited number of classes for those with *mental retardation* to prepare those individuals for specific trades. Craft-centered activities alone, however, were found to not meet the needs of students with retardation because they taught isolated skills that became ends in themselves rather than preparing the students to understand life experiences and solve persistent life problems.

cranial (n., **cranium**) Pertaining to the head or skull.

cranial anomaly (kray'-nee-ahl ah-nah'-mah-lee) A *malformation* of the *cranium* (i.e., abnormal shape of the head), usually resulting from an inherited condition.

craniostenosis (kray-nee-oh-steh-no'-sis) Premature closure of the *cranial* sutures during development of the skull, which results in a shortening or narrowing of the *cranium*.

cranium bifidum (biff'-ih-dum) A *hernial* protrusion of spinal—or, more appropriately, *cranial* (brain)—tissue through the skull because of improper closure of the skull cavity; usually results in *retardation, paralysis, hydrocephaly*, and complicated educational and health care problems. (See also *spina bifida*.)

Cranmar abacus An adaptation of the Japanese *abacus* used by individuals who are *blind* to conduct math calculations.

creativity (adj., **creative**) The ability to produce a large number of original and unusual ideas, to have a high degree of flexibility in responses, and to develop ideas and activities in detail. Possessed by most children to some extent; particularly considered as a characteristic of *gifted* children.

creeper A device, usually a flat, rectangular board with wheels at each corner, that may enable an individual with *physical disabilities* lying *prone* on it to push himself/herself about by use of the arms.

cretinism (kree'-tih-nizm) A *clinical type* of *mental retardation* resulting from a *thyroid* deficiency; becomes evident early in life and is characterized by thick, dry skin, roundness of face, *hoarseness* of voice, listlessness, and dullness. If treated early enough, a person having this condition can be helped to develop normally, and mental retardation and associated conditions may be prevented.

cri-du-chat syndrome French for "cry of the cat," this growth disorder involves the fifth *chromosome*. The resulting condition often manifests in *severe mental retardation* and *microcephaly*.

crippled and other health impaired (COHI) A term used for years to refer to *orthopedic disabilities* and such medical conditions as heart abnormalities and *muscular dystrophy*. The term has been replaced largely by *physical disability*.

crisis intervention An immediately available service to meet crucial needs of individuals who present themselves for help in emergency situations.

crisis teacher A *resource teacher* or *itinerant teacher* of children with *emotional/ behavior disorders*. This term came about because the teacher was to respond to behaviors that might be a real threat to the general education classroom but, if dealt with properly, might allow a student to be *mainstreamed*.

criteria of ultimate functioning A term coined by Lou Brown to describe those factors that would be necessary for an individual with *severe disabilities* to function productively and independently in a socially, vocationally, and domestically integrated community environment.

criterion (pl., **criteria**) The goal set in a learning situation or a test to which the student must perform before he/she is considered to have learned the required material or met the minimum requirements of the test.

criterion-referenced testing (CRT) Testing designed to measure the specific knowledge or content a student has learned, in contrast to *norm-referenced testing*, which compares an individual's performance to that of a *norm* group.

cross-age tutoring See *peer tutoring*.

CRT See *criterion-referenced testing*.

CT See *consultant (consulting teacher)*.

cued speech A method of communication developed by Orin Cornett that is used with *deaf* persons. With this method, a combination of hand signals near the chin supplements and clarifies *lip reading* and speech variations. Cannot be used as a *total communication* system.

cueing *Signaling* used to aid a student in remembering a correct behavior. The teacher *signals* the correct behavior just before an action is expected so there is less chance of incorrect performance.

cuisenaire (kwih-zen-air') **rods** An instructional device utilizing various-sized colored wooden rods to teach *arithmetic processes*.

cultural deprivation The cumulative effect on a child of living in an environment of low socioeconomic status, disorganized family life, isolation, crowded conditions, or lack of stimulation; tends to contribute to the child's inability to function adequately.

cultural diversity Describes any situation in which the clients come from nonstandard environments. Their differences in learning and behavior patterns are sufficient to justify accommodating teaching and treatment methods.

cultural-familial Describes a condition in which an individual is *diagnosed* as having *mental retardation* without evidence of cerebral *pathology*, but having a family history of *intellectual* subnormality and *cultural deprivation*.

culture-fair or **culture-free tests** Instruments designed or constructed in such a way as to minimize or eliminate the effects of one's culture on performance. The preferred term is now *nondiscriminatory testing*.

cumulative record A continuous written account of a child's educational experiences, kept by the school. These experiences may include subjects studied, achievement, health, information about the home, attitudes, and other data.

curriculum (adj., **curricular**) A systematic grouping of activities, content, and materials of instruction offered under school supervision for the purpose of preparing students to learn and live effectively.

curriculum consultant A professional who has special training in a specific *curricular* field and who devotes an allotted amount of time to consult with and aid school faculty in that area.

curriculum development The cooperative study of goals and procedures for modifying and improving learning activities and the *curricular* content of a school program.

curriculum-based assessment (CBA) See *curriculum-based measurement*; the terms are used interchangeably, but some professionals distinguish between the two.

curriculum-based measurement (CBM) A system of instruction and repeated measurements of achievement with a prescriptive orientation toward *remediation*. The measurements involve small samples of reading and other subject matter that have previously been taught. The combination of instruction and measurement has been effective in improving the academic functioning of children with and without *disabilities*.

cursive writing A method of handwriting characterized by connected letters and flowing lines. In *special education*, cursive writing may be the preferred and only method of handwriting taught to some children with *perceptual disorders*, to the exclusion of manuscript printing.

custodial A term formerly applied to persons with *profound mental retardation* who required constant care and supervision. This term, which implied nursing care, fell into disuse before 1970.

cutaneous (kyew-tane'-ee-us) Pertaining to the skin or to the skin as a sense organ (cutaneous sense).

CWPT See *classwide peer tutoring*.

cyanosis (sy-ah-no'-sis) A condition characterized by blueness of the skin resulting from a lack of oxygen in the blood; often observed in children with severe *cardiovascular* disorders.

cycloplegia (sy-kloe-plee'-juh) *Paralysis* of the ciliary muscle of the eye; results in an inability to constrict the *pupil*.

cystic fibrosis (sis'-tik fibe-roe'-sis) **(CF)** The most common, and usually fatal, *hereditary* disease of childhood. Involves a *dysfunction* of the *exocrine glands* and affects most body organs, particularly the lungs and *pancreas*. Abnormal mucous secretions obstruct bodily functions, especially the body's ability to clear the lungs, which results in excessive coughing.

cytogenetics (sy-toe-jeh-net'-iks) (adj., **cytogenic**) The study of *chromosomes* and their relationship to *heredity*. Often concerned with the relationship between *chromosomal aberrations* and *pathological* conditions.

cytomegalovirus (CMV) An infectious *virus* that if present during pregnancy may result in children with *hearing loss*, *mental retardation*, and delayed development.

D

dactylology (dak-til-ol'-oh-jee) See *fingerspelling*.

daily living skills See *activities of daily living*.

Dalton plan See *contract plan*.

dance therapy The use of dancing for *habilitation* purposes in treating mental and *emotional disorders*, based on the premise that improved coordination, posture, and rhythm in bodily movements create inner feelings of confidence and greater security.

DAPs See *developmentally appropriate practices*.

day school A facility attended by children during part of the daylight hours but who spend the remainder of their time elsewhere.

db See *decibel.*

DD See *developmental disability.*

de facto A Latin term that means, literally, "by reason of the fact." The following is an example of its use: *Integration* by race and *disability* now is required by law (*de jure* integration), but may not actually occur in some schools or among some students (de facto *segregation*).

de jure A Latin term that means, literally, "by law." In the past, *segregation* of the schools by race or *disability* was required by the laws of some states; thus, de jure segregation was enforced. Present law requires de jure *integration.*

deaf (n., **deafness**) A condition in which the *auditory* sense is not the primary means by which speech and *language* are learned and the sense of hearing is so lacking or drastically reduced as to prohibit normal function as a hearing person.

deaf-blind Describes a person whose vision and hearing are so deficient as to require specialized methods of communication that are different from those used in the fields *deafness* and *blindness.* Such individuals may not have equal *disabilities* in each *modality* and in fact might not meet the legal definition of either deafness or blindness. In teaching them, *residual vision* and *residual hearing* are used in conjunction with the sense of touch.

decibel (db) A unit of measurement expressing the *intensity* of sound; a unit of hearing or *audition.* The extent of hearing is expressed as the number of *decibels* necessary for the person to hear pure tones above the *baseline* used to measure normal hearing.

deciduous (deh-sid'-you-us) **teeth** The first set of teeth, 20 in number, commonly called "baby teeth"; these are shed between ages 5 and 14 and are replaced by "permanent" teeth.

decoding 1. Receptive habits in the *language* process that allow meaningful use of what is received either auditorily or *visually.* 2. Breaking down a complex structure into the simplest understandable units, or translating something that is not understood into something that is comprehended.

decubitus (deh-kue'-bih-tus) **ulcer** Any breakdown of tissue and skin in which the sense of feeling is absent; caused by prolonged pressure. Also called bedsores or pressure sores, these ulcers are common among *quadriplegics* and *paraplegics.*

deductive thinking A term used by learning theorists to describe the process of reasoning from the general to the specific, in which a conclusion is reached by following logical inferences from the beginning. Opposite of *inductive thinking.*

defective syntax A condition in which an individual can use words or short phrases for self-expression but is not able to organize complete sentences for adequate communication.

defendant The party in a lawsuit against whom legal action is taken. For example, when a parent sues a school system, the school system is the defendent.

defense mechanism A behavior used to reduce tension and *anxiety.* The behavior may be *aggressive*, retiring, *diversional*, destructive, or of any other form that achieves the purpose. Often an individual's defense mechanism against admitting failure is to place the blame elsewhere.

deficit A term denoting that an individual is behind age peers in certain basic developmental processes. A deficit in *memory* skills, for example, means that the individual is lacking in that area and indicates redirection of *curricular* efforts to focus on reducing that deficit.

deformity Any distortion of the body or a specific part of the body that is considered disfiguring or repulsive; sometimes accompanied by loss of function.

degeneration (adj., **degenerative**; v., **degenerate** A breaking down or deterioration, usually of a progressive nature. Degeneration of body tissues is accompanied by a steady loss of vitality.

deinstitutionalization A practice arising from the principles of *normalization* and *least restrictive environment* in which individuals with *mental retardation* and *emotional disturbance* are moved out of *institutions* into community *alternative living* arrangements.

delayed recall The ability to remember learned material after a lapse of time.

delayed speech Any condition in which the development of speech is slower than normal; can occur in any of the various stages of speech development.

delinquency (adj., **delinquent**) Offenses against the legal and social standards of society; refers to unacceptable behavior in youth. (See *juvenile delinquency*.)

delirium A mental disturbance of short duration marked by illusions, *hallucinations*, *delusions*, incoherence, and physical restlessness. This condition often accompanies infection and high fever.

delivery model (system) An administrative arrangement to provide services. *Special education* models include *resource room*, *special class*, *itinerant teacher/therapist* program, and others. (See *service delivery system*.) The preferred term in the 1990s is *service options*.

delusion A mental image that an individual accepts and defends as true or real but that in reality is false or unreal.

delusions of grandeur A characteristic of some *psychotic* conditions, in which the individual has an exaggerated misconception of importance, position, abilities, wealth, or accomplishments.

delusions of persecution A characteristic of some *psychotic* conditions, in which the individual believes that another individual(s) is trying to belittle, injure, or harm him/her in some way.

dementia (dih-men'-chuh) British usage: Any acquired *mental deficiency* or disorder, as opposed to *congenital* mental deficiencies or disorders. U.S. usage: One of the lower *functional* levels in *mental retardation*. The term is not currently used.

dementia praecox (dih-men'-chuh pree'-cocks) A mental disorder that results in deterioration of the mind, loss of interest in people, and incoherence of thought and action; culminates in loss of touch with reality. Preferred terminology today includes senility and *Alzheimer's*.

demographic Descriptive term applied to statistical studies of populations, including physical conditions and vital statistics (births, marriages, health, etc.).

denasal speech A condition resulting from obstruction of the nose, characterized by the absence of *resonance* in the voice, as sometimes accompanies the common cold.

denial reaction Behavior of a person with a *disability* who refuses to admit any limiting effects associated with the disability.

deoxyribonucleic (dee'-ox-ee-ri-bo-nu-klay-ik) **acid (DNA)** The principal constituent of *chromosomes* and the prime *carrier* of *hereditary* factors.

dependence A situation in which one is unable to function independently and make decisions without the assistance of another. **Dependency** is a common problem for persons with *disabilities*.

depopulation A procedure for reducing the number of persons in an *institution*, under the *deinstitutionalization concept.* Theoretically, the *concept* means reduction of the residential population to zero.

depression (adj., **depressed**) A psychological/psychiatric term referring to a dejected mood, despondency, *psychomotor retardation*, reduced vitality and vigor, and despair. Mild depression may come and go with no long-term effects, but severe depression is considered a serious *mental health* problem.

depth perception Accurate recognition of distances to or between objects in the environment; enhances the ability to orient one's self in relation to objects.

deregulation The process of removing restrictions or regulations. The term has taken on more meaning in the past few years as the government has reduced the restrictiveness of many regulations governing the implementation of laws. **Deregulatory** actions, for example, were attempted against *PL 94–142*.

dermal Pertaining to the skin.

dermatitis (der-mah-tie'-tiss) *Inflammation* of the skin.

dermatologist A medical doctor who specializes in the *diagnosis* and treatment of skin conditions and disorders.

desensitization A *behavior therapy* technique in which the individual is exposed gradually and systematically to objects, events, and situations that evoke fear, the purpose of which is to reduce fear.

desired learner outcomes (DLOs) Terminal *instructional objectives* as defined

in the Education Sciences Program developed by Jack Cawley. Includes *objectives* written in behavioral terms; e.g., the student will be able to make change correctly for any combinations up to $1.00. (See also *behavioral objective.*)

detachment (of retina) A condition in which the inner layers of the *retina* of the eye become separated from the pigment epithelium, where they are normally attached, resulting in *visual impairment* or *blindness.*

detoxification A treatment process for alcoholism involving the controlled withdrawal of alcohol from the person being detoxified. Sometimes shortened in the vernacular to "detox."

developmental approach A *concept* holding that all individuals learn in the same way and in the same general sequences but that they vary in the rate of learning. Proponents of this theory hold that children with *mental retardation* learn the same way as average children, but at a slower rate. The developmental approach emphasizes *Piagetian, cognitive*, and sensorimotor stages of *intelligence* and the normal sequence of *acquisition* of *language* skills. For comparison, see *nondevelopmental approach.*

developmental curriculum Any instructional approach that emphasizes what students should be able to accomplish at certain *chronological ages* and/or *mental ages.*

developmental disability (DD) A term that came into usage with the Nixon administration; pertains to *disorders* occurring between 18 and 20 years of age, such as *mental retardation, epilepsy*, and *cerebral palsy*. The definition was broadened with *PL 94–103* to *autism* and severe *learning disabilities* if the cause originates from mental retardation. In 1979 PL 95–602 expanded the *concept* to include *physical disabilities* and severe childhood *emotional disorders.*

developmental disorder See *developmental disability.*

developmental dyslexia A type of severe reading disorder that is different from acquired *dyslexia* because it is not caused by *brain injury* or any known agent; often seen in children of above-average *intelligence.*

developmental lag Functioning at a level lower than that expected for one's *chronological age* when compared to *age norms.*

developmental language disorder, expressive type A classification in the *DSM*-IV System; denotes a difficulty in expressing, or an inability to express, one's wishes. Also called *expressive aphasia.*

developmental language disorder, receptive type A classification in the *DSM*-IV System denoting difficulty in understanding the spoken word. Also called *receptive aphasia.*

developmental maximization unit A small *residential* facility located near a state *institution(s)* and used for intensive treatment and training of institutionalized individuals being prepared to return to the community.

developmental period The time between conception and 18 years of age, during which physical and mental growth occurs. This is the period in which *developmental disabilities* originate.

developmental retardation A term that has been suggested as a replacement for *mental retardation.* Proponents believe it emphasizes the correct elements of mental retardation and its use would remove some of the confusion with *mental health* and *mental illness.*

developmental therapy A *psychoeducational* curriculum approach to the treatment of students with *emotional disorders* that emphasizes developmental milestones. This approach, developed by Mary Wood, emphasizes four basic *curricular* areas: behavior, socialization, communication, and academics.

developmental training home (DTH) A group residence for adults with *disabilities* who require a moderate amount of supervision and support in *self-help skills*, training development, and so on. (See also *group home.*)

developmentally appropriate practices (DAPs) Guidelines used to plan and *assess* programs in the field of *early childhood education.* Their development was necessitated by the variability in types of educational and instructional programs in the field.

deviance Achieving, behaving, or adapting in ways that vary noticeably from societal norms in their personal characteristics—mental, emotional, moral, or physical.

deviancy model An approach in educational, *mental health*, and social programs in which a child who does not achieve, behave, or adapt as expected receives certain *interventions* set up to correct the variance the individual expresses.

deviate To turn aside, stray, or differ from a standard, principle, or *norm.* **Deviant** describes a person who varies noticeably from societal norms in some personal characteristic—mental, emotional, moral, or physical.

diabetes (die-uh-bee'-tess) (adj., **diabetic**) A *metabolic disorder* in which the body is unable to properly utilize carbohydrates in the diet because of failure of the *pancreas* to secrete an adequate supply of *insulin* or because of failure of the insulin secreted to function properly in the digestive process; results in an abnormal concentration of sugar in the blood and urine. *Symptoms* are excessive thirst, excessive urination, weight loss, slow healing of cuts and bruises, pain in joints, and drowsiness.

diabetic coma (or **reaction**) Uncontrollable drowsiness and muscular pain, possibly resulting in unconsciousness, caused by too little *insulin* in the system. This condition can become serious if the individual is not administered insulin soon after the onset of *symptoms*.

diabetic retinopathy A condition associated with *diabetes* in which the blood supply to the *retina* of the eye is faulty; results in *blindness*.

diagnosis (adj., **diagnostic**; v., **diagnose**) 1. The act of recognizing a disease or condition by *symptom* identification and/or testing. 2. Judgment that follows critical scrutiny. In *special education*, diagnosis usually is made by an *interdisciplinary* team that analyzes the cause or nature of a condition, situation, or problem.

diagnosogenic (die-ag-no-so-jen'-ik) **theory** A premise that attributes *stuttering* in individuals to influences in their early environment, specifically to the influence of significant persons in that environment who called attention to normal *dysfluencies* and *labeled* them as stuttering.

Diagnostic and Statistical Manual of Mental Disorders (DSM) Classification system of the American Psychiatric Association. This system is widely used, primarily by medical and *mental health clinics*.

diagnostic test A measure designed to analyze or locate an individual's specific areas of weakness or strength, so that they can receive *attention* in future instruction. A **diagnostician** may conduct this testing.

diagnostic-prescriptive center A setting emphasizing short-term *assessment* and teaching with the expressed purpose of determining a student's strengths and weaknesses and developing a specific teaching plan.

diagnostic-prescriptive education See *diagnostic-prescriptive teaching.*

diagnostic-prescriptive teaching (DPT) An approach to instruction that involves the *evaluation* of students on an individual basis, with emphasis on their strengths and weaknesses, followed by the development of teaching prescriptions designed to remedy the weaknesses and develop the strengths.

dialect A noticeable variation of any *language*. The variation differs from the standard or traditional form in such characteristics as pronunciation, voice *inflection*, choice of words and terms, or phraseology. May be the customary speech of a social class, a geographic region, a nationality, or an ethnic or cultural group.

Diana v. State Board of Education A landmark court case in California that set the *precedent* for students to receive testing, placement, and similar considerations based not only on the English *language*, but also on the primary language of the home.

diaphragm (die'-ah-fram) The muscular partition that separates the thoracic, or chest, cavity from the abdominal region of the body; has an important function in breathing.

dichotic (die-kot'-ik) Simultaneous *auditory* stimulation of both ears by different *stimuli*, usually through the use of earphones and two channels of a tape recorder.

dicta A Latin term describing *language* in a judicial opinion that is not essential to the disposition of the case or to the court's reasoning and that is regarded as gratuitous. Dicta are persuasive but not binding on other courts, whereas the court's holding and reasoning are.

diction One's *enunciation* and choice of words to express oneself *orally* with clarity and effectiveness.

Dictionary of Occupational Titles (DOT) A publication that gives an extensive listing and classification of jobs in the United States. Published by the Superintendent of Documents, Washington, DC 20202.

didactic (die-dack'-tik) **method** Any approach to teaching that uses materials that are practical or instructive in and of themselves. The *Montessori method* is especially noted for its emphasis on practical self-instruction.

differential diagnosis An *evaluation* that attempts to distinguish between similar disorders or conditions by identifying features that are characteristic of only one of them.

differential education Educational experiences uniquely designed to involve the capacities and needs of *gifted* individuals, which, in general, are beyond the reach of and not appropriate to the capacities or needs of persons not gifted or endowed with unusual potential for productive or *creative* thinking.

differential reinforcement Providing rewards for behavior in the presence of one *stimulus* situation and not *reinforcing* in the presence of other stimulus conditions.

differential threshold The smallest amount of difference between two *stimuli* that can be detected by use of a receptor, or sense organ. Also referred to as the **just noticeable difference**, or **JND**.

digraph (die'-graf) The *phonetic* combination of two letters to spell a single sound, as "sh" in "shoe."

dimensional classification A system of categorizing the *behavior disorders* of school-age individuals; developed by Herbert Quay.

diopter (die'-op-ter) The unit of measurement for the refractive power of a *lens*; used in testing the eyes and prescribing eyeglasses.

diphthong (dif'-thong) The result of combining two *vowel* sounds that, when combined produce a sound unique to the combined vowels, such as "oy" in "boy."

diplegia (die-plee'-juh) *Paralysis* of the body in which both sides are affected; a result of injury to both *hemispheres* of the brain.

diplopia (die-ploe'-pea-ah) Commonly called "double vision"; a *visual* defect in which single objects are seen as two. Also termed *amblyopia*.

direct assessment A *concept* that originated in the 1980s. Deals with non*norm-referenced testing* in which the individual is assisted in task performance to determine how much he/she might be capable of learning or performing rather than *assessment* of what had already been achieved; in terms of measuring achievement vs. academic potential, the measurement would be focused on instruction that the child is known to have received.

direct consent An agreement elicited by a person directly involved in conducting a research project to allow for collection and use of data.

direct instruction A method of teaching academics to students with *learning disabilities* that emphasizes teaching skills rather than the *remediation* of psychological processes.

Direct Instruction System for Teaching Arithmetic and Reading (DISTAR) One of the most systematic instructional methods derived from the *early child-*

hood education movement. Developed as an outgrowth of the work of Carl Bereiter and Sigfried Engelmann.

direct measurement A method of collecting data in which tangible behaviors are observed and counted. (See also *behavioral assessment*.)

direction taking The act of a *blind* person locating a line or course that better facilitates traveling in a straight line toward an *objective*.

directionality One's ability to differentiate the basic directions involved in the environment, such as right from left, up from down, front from back. Young children express a normal deficiency in this capacity, but older children who lack directionality may have learning problems.

directive approach (or **therapy**) See *counselor-centered therapy*.

directive teaching An instructional approach with emphasis on teaching basic skills combined with the systematic measurement and collection of data on a student's academic performance. Directive teaching is an extension of *prescriptive teaching* and *applied behavioral analysis*, emphasizing intentional academic instruction.

dis- Prefix meaning opposite or absent.

disability (adj., **disabled**) A physical, psychological, or *neurological* deviation in an individual's makeup. A disability may or may not be a *handicap* to an individual, depending on one's adjustment to it. The terms disability and handicap often have been considered and used synonymously, but this is not accurate, as a handicap actually refers to the effect produced by a disability. With the passage of *IDEA*, the field has shifted to the use of disability and has usually abandoned the use of handicap. (See also *presumptive disability*.)

discipline 1. Management of youngsters to prevent unnecessary disruptive behaviors and incidents and promote positive experiences. 2. An area of training in professional services (e.g., *psychology*, teaching).

discovery The process by which a party to a civil suit can find out about matters relevant to the case, including information about what evidence the other side has, what witnesses will be called, and so on. Discovery processes for obtaining information include depositions and interrogatories to obtain testimony, requests for documents or other tangibles, and requests for physical or mental examination.

discrepancy formula A means of expressing the difference in test scores between expected and actual achievement to determine if the difference is large enough to warrant special services. For a child suspected of having a *learning disability*, a special formula is applied to determine if he/she is to be *labeled "LD."*

discrimination (v., **discriminate**) The ability to make judgments regarding sameness or differences between at least two *stimuli*. This ability is of great importance in academic work for judging form, shape, right or wrong, large or small, etc.

disguised rejection An apparent attitude of caring or loving that actually is a "cover" for feelings of guilt or other negative emotions. For example, a parent who appears to be excessively concerned about showing love and is oversolicitous of a child with a *disability* may have really rejected the child and, because of guilt feelings, *compensates* by exaggerated expressions of love and concern.

disinhibition The inability to restrain oneself from reacting to distracting *stimuli*; loss of the effects of *conditioned inhibition*. Disinhibition may be exhibited by those with *learning disabilities* as well as those with *closed head injuries* causing them to respond to or be distracted by all stimuli.

disorientation Loss of ability to keep one's bearings in the surrounding environment, with reference to right and left, location, time, recognition of acquaintances, and, in more severe instances, recognition of one's own identity.

displacement A psychological *defense mechanism* in which an individual substitutes another form of behavior or thinking for what is expected, with the intention that the new behavior will be more acceptable.

dissociation A mental condition in which ideas or desires are separated from the main stream of consciousness or from one's personality to a degree that they are no longer accessible to *memory* or consciousness. The individual has difficulty in perceiving, or is unable to perceive, things or situations as a whole, and instead tends to respond to *stimuli* in terms of parts or segments.

distal Far from the point of attachment or origin; often used with reference to *physical disabilities*. Opposite of *proximal*.

DISTAR See *Direct Instruction System for Teaching Arithmetic and Reading*.

distinctive features Describes individual characteristics of a sound—voiced sound, voiceless sound, duration, tenseness, etc.

distortion (in speech) An *articulatory defect* in which speech sounds are altered, as in saying "shled" for "sled."

distractibility (adj., **distractible**) A behavioral characteristic, often present in children with *central nervous system* disorders, in which the individual is unable to refrain from responding to stimuli that

are essentially unnecessary to immediate adjustment. As a result, the individual is unable to direct *attention* to *stimuli* that are important to adjustment or learning.

distress *Stress* resulting in negative events in one's life, such as disappointments. (See also *eustress* and *stress*.)

diuretic (die-you-ret'-ik) Having the properties of reducing the amount of water retained in the body and increasing the flow of urine; any drug with those properties.

divergent thinking 1. Reaching conclusions in a manner not entirely determined by available information. In divergent thinking, one's thoughts may go in different directions, sometimes searching and seeking variety, so that a number of different responses are produced. Also, a reorganizing of known facts into new relationships. 2. One of J. P. Guilford's thinking *operations* in the *structure of the intellect*. (See also *convergent thinking*, in contrast.)

diversion The act of turning a person or things aside from the course currently being followed. Often used with *exceptional children* in reference to changing a negative or nonprofitable activity or goal into a positive or profitable activity or goal.

diversity Differences within or across groups.

divestiture in special education A term coined in the early 1980s indicating that *special education* should get out of the business of serving students with mild *disabilities*. In the late 1980s proponents of the *concept* spoke instead of the *regular education initiative (REI)*, which recommended total *mainstreaming* with support from special education *consulting teachers*. In the 1990s, the preferred term has changed to *inclusion* because of growing negative reactions toward REI.

dizygotic (die-zie-got'-ik) Describes twins resulting from the simultaneous fertilization of two separate eggs rather than the division of one (*monozygotic*) egg. These twins are referred to as fraternal rather than identical.

DLOs See *desired learner outcomes.*

DNA See *deoxyribonucleic acid.*

DNR See *do not resuscitate.*

D'Nealian manuscript A system for teaching manuscript writing that involves the use of slanted letters. This system is preferred by some professionals because of perceived greater ease in transferring to cursive writing. Little research exists to support its advantages for students with *disabilities*, but its intuitive face validity for such use is appealing to some.

do not resuscitate (DNR) A *concept* to which educators have had to respond as parents and doctors have made requests for some individuals with *severe disabilities* not to be administered life-sustaining techniques, such as being given oxygen, in situations in which it appears that death is imminent. Unfortunately, educators often cannot tell the difference between normal *seizures* or other medical conditions and those that are life threatening.

Doman-Delacato method A neurophysiological approach to the treatment and education of children with *cerebral palsy* and other *disabilities* that was developed at the Center for the Development of Human Potential. This method is best known for *patterning*, in which children are physically aided through developmental activities such as creeping and crawling.

dominant genes Those parts of the *chromosomes* that result in the expression of characteristics, as contrasted to *recessive genes.*

Doppler effect Describes the changes in *pitch* of an object as it gets closer. This phenomenon aids *blind* persons in judging distance and navigating the physical environment, because pitch and *frequency* increase as the object gets closer.

DOT See *Dictionary of Occupational Titles.*

double interlocking reinforcement A *contingency* arrangement whereby a member of a group is rewarded for specified social responses, and the group in turn is reinforced for social responses directed toward the specific individual.

Down syndrome A *clinical type* of *mental retardation* resulting from a specific abnormal *chromosomal* arrangement. Individuals with Down syndrome usually have *intelligence* in the moderate-mild *range* of *retardation.*

DPT See *diagnostic-prescriptive teaching.*

drug addiction A condition in which the body becomes physically dependent on a substance; as tolerance increases, larger amounts may be needed to produce the desired results.

drug therapy 1. Any prescriptive use of medication to modify behavior, to aid in education, or to help improve social acceptability. 2. In medicine, the use of substances in the traditional sense to treat illness or disease.

DSM See *Diagnostic and Statistical Manual of Mental Disorders.*

DTH See *developmental training home.*

dual diagnosis A term indicating that a person has more than one *disability*. The term has been used especially to describe individuals who have both *mental retardation* and *mental illness*, a combination that occurs frequently and poses unique educational and treatment needs.

Duchenne (due-shane') **disease** A childhood form of *muscular dystrophy*, which usually appears between ages 2 and 6 and is characterized in the early stages by waddling, walking on toes, or difficulty in running. (See also *pseudohypertrophy*.)

due process of law A right to have any applicable federal or state law applied reasonably and with sufficient safeguards, such as hearings and notice, to ensure that an individual is dealt with fairly; protects the rights of individuals in identification, *evaluation*, and placement; provides for prior notice, parental consent, impartial hearing, appeals, written decision, and *surrogate parents*. Due process of law is guaranteed under the Fifth and Fourteenth Amendments to the federal Constitution. (See also *procedural due process*.)

dull normal Used in some classification systems to designate students who function just below average or normal in general *intelligence*. A more common and desirable term is *slow learner*.

dullard Commonly used during the 19th century in reference to an individual who was unable to function socially or academically as well as his/her peers; an individual who has moderately subnormal *intelligence*. (This term is not currently acceptable and is relegated to slang usage.)

dwarf (dwarfism) An individual of unusually small stature in whom bodily proportion varies from the *norm*.

dynamic assessment A term that emerged in the 1980s to describe a new type of *intellectual* testing—the American approach to the measurement of *intelligence*, which is similar to R. Feuerstein's (developed in Israel). Its essence is the measurement of ability by finding out the maximum that children can do with help. In this approach children are given

clues or *prompts* to help them understand what the task requires. For example, a child may be asked, "In what ways are an apple and a peach alike?" The tester may prompt, "For example, both are round," thus prompting the understanding of sameness required for future examples.

dynamometer (die-nah-mah'-meh-tur) An instrument used to measure the power in a muscular contraction.

dys- Prefix meaning bad, difficult, or abnormal.

dysacusis (dis-ah-kyew'-sis) A sensorineural condition in which an individual has difficulty understanding speech; can be equated to the reading disorder *dyslexia*, which produces difficulty in deriving meaning from the printed word. Classified under the general category of *aphasia*.

dysarthria (dis-are'-three-uh) A defect in the *central nervous system* that results in faulty *articulation* of speech sounds; usually observed in *cerebral palsy*.

dyscalculia (dis-kal-kyew'-lee-uh) Impaired ability to calculate or manipulate number symbols; often associated with *learning disabilities*.

dysfluency More commonly called *stuttering*; hesitations in or interferences with smooth speech, which may or may not constitute classification as a *disability*. Some dysfluency is normal in all persons. (See also *fluency disorder*.)

dysfunction Partial disturbance, *impairment*, or abnormality in a particular bodily activity.

dysgraphia (dis-graf-ee-ah) A *learning disability* characterized by difficulty in writing; often associated with *neurological dysfunction*.

dyskinesia (dis-kih-nee'-zee-ah) A physical condition caused by partial *impair-*

ment of the coordination of voluntary muscles, which results in clumsy movements and poor physical control.

dyslalia (dis-lay'-lee-ah) A *speech disorder* characterized by problems in *articulation* caused by the abnormal use of external speech organs rather than damage to the *central nervous system.*

dyslexia (dis-leck'-see-ah) An *impairment* in reading ability or a partial inability to read; often associated with *cerebral dysfunction* or *minimal brain dysfunction.* An individual with this condition does not understand clearly what he/she reads. A more *generic* term for learning problems including dyslexia is *learning disability.*

dyslogia (dis-loe'-zhuh) A *linguistic* disturbance characterized by the faulty formulation or *expression* of ideas in the spoken form. Dyslogia may accompany *mental retardation* or *emotional disturbances.* (See also *aphasia.*)

dysmetria (dis-meh'-tree-ah) A *"soft" sign* of *minimal brain dysfunction* in which the individual being tested has difficulty directing a finger to his/her nose with eyes closed.

dysnomia (dis-noe'-mee-ah) The partial loss of ability to comprehend, organize, or express ideas or names in speech, writing, or gestures.

dysphagia (dis-faj'-zhuh) Difficulty with *oral* feeding due to a *severe disability.*

dysphasia (dis-fay'-zhuh) See *aphasia.*

dysphemia (dis-fee'-mee-ah) A *speech disorder*, such as *stuttering*, related to *psychoneurosis*,

dysphonia (dis-fone'-ee-ah) A *voice disorder* characterized by faulty *phonation* or *resonance* and *pitch* deviations.

dysplasia (dis-play'-zee-ah) Abnormal development of the body or cells.

dyspraxia (dis-prak'-see-ah) An *inhibition* of the ability to coordinate body movements, especially speech. (See *apraxia.*)

dysrhythmia (dis-rith'-mee-ah) A malfunction of the neuromotor system that causes poor rhythm or a loss of ability to move with rhythm.

dystonia (dis-toe'-nee-ah) A rare disease of the *central nervous system* that causes a loss of muscle tone and use in young children.

dystrophy See *muscular dystrophy.*

E

ear defenders Protective devices or objects used to cover and protect the ears from loud noises and dangers.

eardrum See *tympanic membrane.*

early childhood education A practice of teaching or intervening with children before traditional schooling begins, to aid subsequent learning in youngsters thought to be *at-risk* or identified as having some problem. It can be applied from birth and emphasizes preventive *intervention.* (See also *preschool education.*)

early infantile autism A term first used by Leo Kanner in 1943 to describe what is now called *autism.*

Eastern Nebraska Community Office of Retardation (ENCOR) State office that developed a comprehensive system of services and model program. Professionals sometimes refer to the "ENCOR standards."

E/BD See *emotional/behavior disorder.*

eccentric gazing A behavioral characteristic of some *partially sighted* students who see more clearly by using *peripheral vision* and thus not looking directly at instructional material or teachers. This behavior should not be viewed as daydreaming and should not be discouraged.

echocardiograph Examination of the function of the heart by means of *ultrasound* equipment.

echoencephalography (ek-oh-en-sef-ah-log'-ruh-fee) Examination or measurement of the internal structure of the *cranial* cavity by means of *ultrasound* equipment.

echolalia (ek-oh-lay'-lee-uh) A speech condition characterized by the involuntary repetition of words, syllables, or sounds spoken by others, as if echoing them. A common characteristic of persons with *severe mental retardation*.

echolocation A technique used by *blind* persons of producing a sound with an *echolocation device* and interpreting the qualities of the reflected echo to aid in *mobility* and *obstacle perception*.

echolocation device An aid to *blind* persons that emits high-*frequency* sound waves that bounce off objects. The loudness of the returning signals indicates the size of an object, and the *pitch* indicates distance.

eclectic (ek-lek'-tik) **method** A teaching and counseling approach in which the teacher uses those methods from various systems and philosophies that are most appropriate to the situation, the child, and the classroom.

eco-behavioral conditions Environmental conditions, such as crowding, lighting, and furniture mismatched to student size, that contribute to the potential for disruptive behaviors.

ecological approach One of the treatment *concepts* used with individuals who have *behavior disorders*. It emphasizes that the individual is not sick but, rather, that an interaction of the individual and his/her environment causes the individual's behavior. With this approach, a change in the environment is one method of bringing about a change in the individual.

ecological inventory A listing of activities and skills that an individual with a *severe disability* is required to perform in a living, working, and school environment.

ecological model See *ecological approach*; *ecosystem*.

ecosystem (or **ecological system**) The combination of all forces existing in the environment or in a certain realm, as in the "family ecosystem." In the *ecological approach*, it is believed that the ecosystem determines the behavior of individuals within it; thus, the focus on a disturbed child would be away from internal factors and toward external, environmental factors.

ectomorphic (ek-toe-more'-fik) One of the body types (*somatotypes*) characterized by slender stature and slight muscular development.

eczema (ek'-zeh-mah or ek-zee'-mah) An *inflammatory dermatitis* (skin condition) characterized by redness, itching, tiny pustules, oozing, crusting, and later scaling.

ED Refers to the U.S. Department of Education.

EDA See *electrodermal audiometry*.

edema (eh-dee'-mah) Swelling caused by localized fluid in the tissues.

edible reinforcer Any food enjoyed by pupils that can be used to reward appropriate behavior contingent on performance of the behavior.

educability The capacity of an individual to learn by experience and to use learning to adjust to the environment.

educable Having the ability to learn more than routine training tasks with a degree of academics up to the sixth-grade level. The term was originally part of the educational classification systems and was the equivalent of the term *mild mental retardation*. It is now seldom used except as a general term.

educable mentally retarded (EMR)/educable mentally handicapped (EMH) The term ascribed to the highest level of *mental retardation*, including individuals capable of becoming self-sufficient and learning academic skills through the upper elementary grades. EMR is the equivalent of *mildly retarded* in the American Association on Mental Retardation classification system. The most accepted *IQ range* is 2 to 3 *standard deviations* below the *mean* on an individually administered *intelligence* test, or an *IQ* of approximately 55–70. In recent years, because of the change from *handicap* to *disability*, the preferred term has become mildly *disabled* or *mild intellectual disability*.

educateur A professional employed in France and parts of the United States to provide an educational and treatment program for children with *behavior disorders*.

Education for All Handicapped Children Act of 1975 (EHA or PL 94–142) A federal law, described as a "Bill of Rights for the Handicapped," that includes many provisions and special features designed to protect the rights of children with *disabilities*. Includes provisions for *free appropriate public education*, definitions of the various *handicaps*, priorities for *special education* services, protective safeguards, and procedures for developing mandatory *individualized education programs*.

educational diagnosis Determination of the academic level of students and how they learn through the use of tests and *evaluative* instruments. Information collected through educational *diagnosis* is used in selecting services for the students and in planning educational activities for them.

educational potential The theoretical maximum academic performance an individual will reach at maturity.

educational retardation Failure to develop in *academic achievement* as rapidly or as far as expected for one's *chronological age* even though one may not have *mental retardation*.

educational therapist A term often used in *clinical* teaching programs when referring to an educator who does educational *assessment* and prescribes educational activities for students with *disabilities*.

educationally blind Describes students for whom vision is reduced to such a degree that education must occur through braille, listening, and other nonstandard means. This term has not gained wide usage. (See also *functionally blind*, which is an equivalent term.) Those who are educationally blind make up only a small percent of those *labeled legally blind*.

educationally handicapped (EH) A term used in some state educational codes to refer to children who have difficulties at school that result from either *learning* or *behavior disorders* or a combination of the two. This term has been replaced in some states by *learning handicapped*, which includes *mild mental retardation*, *behavior disorders*, and *learning disabilities*.

educationally subnormal A term of British origin referring to a level of *intellectual* functioning comparable to the educational classification of *educable mentally retarded* or *mild mental retardation*.

EEG See *electroencephalogram*.

effective instruction Those practices that research has shown to be of unusual significance in yielding increased learning and behavior among general education and *special education* students; provides a rationale for fast-paced instruction, time on task, allotted time for instruction, and summary of instruction.

efferent (ef'-er-ent) **nerves** The nerves of the body that convey impulses outward from the nerve centers or the *central nervous system.*

efficacy (ef'-ih-kah-see) The producing of a desired outcome, or the power to produce desired outcomes. Often used in *special education* to refer to studies that seek to *evaluate* the effectiveness of educational programs or methodology.

efficiency The ability to produce an effective operation in achieving desired results, as measured by a comparison of the cost in time, energy, and money against the amount of work accomplished.

egalitarianism (ee-gal-ih-tare'-ee-an-izm) A legal principle under which persons with unequal physical and mental abilities are granted equal opportunities. The outcomes of their education may require greater expenditure, but it is not necessary that they reach the same goals.

ego First discussed in Sigmund Freud's writings on *psychoanalytic* theory in the 1890s, the term refers to the aspect of one's being that serves as an arbitrator between one's inner needs and wishes and the external demands of the environment, thus helping one better to perceive reality; the conscious subject of one's experiences that provides awareness of personal identity.

egocentric Self-centered. An individual who regards everything as it relates to himself/herself and does not heed the needs or rights of others.

EH See *educationally handicapped.*

EHA See *Education for All Handicapped Children Act of 1975.*

EHLR An abbreviation for *Education for the Handicapped Law Reporter*; used in the works of a commercial publisher that report the opinions and judgments of many of the *special education* cases decided by state and federal courts.

EKG See *electrocardiogram.*

elaboration One of J. P. Guilford's *products of thinking*, which provides for constructing more complex objects or organizations from available information. (See *structure of the intellect.*)

elective mutism One of the classifications of the *DSM*-IV System in which the individual refuses to speak. The person may appear to be incapable of hearing or speaking but may not be *hearing impaired.*

electrocardiogram (eh-lek-troe-kar'-dee-oh-gram) **(EKG)** A mechanical tracing made by an **electrocardiograph** that depicts the electric charges caused by contraction of the heart muscles.

electrocautery (ee-lek-troe-caw'-ter-ee) Cauterizing by use of electricity. See *cauterize.*

electrodermal audiometry (EDA) A form of *audiometry* used to test the hearing of hard-to-test children and adults. The test is based on measuring skin resistance when responding to sounds. This form of testing is nearly obsolete.

electroencephalogram (eh-lek-troe-en-sef'-ah-loe-gram) **(EEG)** A mechanical tracing made by an **electroencephalograph** that depicts the electrical output of brain waves. An EEG is useful in studying *seizures* accompanying brain injuries, *epilepsy*, etc.

electrolarynx A mechanical device used by individuals who have had laryngectomies; simulates the actions of the *lar-*

ynx that has been removed, allowing the person to produce speech.

electromyographic Describes an *intervention* strategy employing *biofeedback* that is used to control *hyperactivity.*

electroretinograph (ee-lek-troe-reh-tin'-oh-graf) An instrument used to measure the electrical response of the *retina* when stimulated by light.

electroshock therapy Treatment of *mental illness* through the administration of electrical current, which induces *neurological* reactions.

Elementary and Secondary Education Act (ESEA) The first general support of *special education* by the federal government. This act, passed during the Johnson administration, included support for Titles I through V, and Title VI was added to cover persons with *disabilities.*

eligibility The process of an *assessment* team deciding if an individual meets the *criteria*, according to state rules and regulations, to be classified by one type of *disability* or another. Also the determination process for deciding if a client meets the requirements for *rehabilitation* services.

ELP See *estimated learning potential.*

embolism (em'-boe-lizm) The sudden clogging of an artery by a clot or foreign object.

embryonic The second stage of *fetal* development, which lasts from about the end of the second week to the eighth week after conception.

EMH See *educable mentally retarded.*

emmetropia (em-eh-troe'-pea-ah) The refractive condition of the eye when it is perfectly *focused* for distance, so that the image of an object *focuses* directly on the *retina* without *accommodation.* Condition of the normal eye.

emotional disorder (disturbance) A term applied to individuals who are not able to control their emotions well enough to maintain their behavior within an acceptable *range.* Mildly disturbed students may be served through continued placement in general education classes with supporting service from an *itinerant* or *crisis teacher.* A comparable term used in many states is *behavior disordered.*

emotional lability A condition in which an individual displays unstable moods often characterized by rapid shifts from one extreme to another.

emotional/behavior disorder (E/BD) A *disability* characterized by behavioral or emotional responses in school so different from appropriate age, cultural, or ethnic norms that they adversely affect educational performance. Educational performance includes the development and demonstration of academic, social, vocational and personal skills. The term *emotional/behavior disorder* came into use in the 1990s to replace *emotional disturbance* and *behavior disorders.*

empathy A mental reaction in which one identifies himself/herself in a positive manner with another individual or group. This trait often is cited as being important in relating to or teaching individuals with *disabilities.*

empirical Describes the use of observation or experience, sometimes without the establishment of a research design, to gather data to support a conclusion.

employee assistance programs Counseling and *therapy* services offered within agencies and private companies to help employees deal with drug and/or emotional problems and thus have a chance of retaining their jobs.

EMR See *educable mentally retarded.*

en banc A French term meaning, literally, "on the bench." Refers to a situation in which a court consisting of more than one member (such as the federal appeals courts) hears a case with all of its members present at the hearing and participating in the decision. Usually, federal courts of appeals are divided into panels (or groups) of judges, and only one panel hears a case and makes the judgment of the court, without the participation of the other members of the court. Sometimes, however, a case is so difficult or important that all members of the court hear the case and decide the outcome. The court then sits en banc—all together on the bench.

encephalitis (en-sef-ah-lie'-tis) 1. Any condition that causes *inflammation* of the brain. The condition may result in residual *neurological* or physiological *disabilities* that inhibit a child's *educational potential*. 2. A disease of the brain caused by a *virus* infection that is contagious; commonly referred to as "sleeping sickness."

encephalography (en-sef-ah-log'-rah-fee) *X-ray* examination of the head following removal of the *cerebrospinal fluid* and replacement of that fluid with air. This *diagnostic* technique allows *X rays* of the air spaces of the brain that otherwise would not be possible. Also called *pneumoencephalography*.

encephalopathy (en-sef-ah-lop'-ah-thee) Any *degenerative* disease of the brain.

enclave Refers to a group of three to four individuals with *severe disabilities* who are placed as a group in a supportive employment situation with a *job coach*.

encoding A *psycholinguistic* process that involves expressing ideas in symbols. An individual may encode by speech or writing. A simpler, synonymous term is *expression*.

encopresis (en-koe-pree'-sis) Inability to control one's bowels; *incontinence* of *feces* that is not attributable to *organic* defect or illness.

ENCOR See *Eastern Nebraska Community Office of Retardation*.

endocarditis (en-doe-kar-die'-tis) *Inflammation* of the endocardium, the membrane lining of the heart. This condition especially involves the heart valves.

endocrine (en'-doe-krin) **gland** One of the ductless glands that produce chemical substances, such as *hormones*, that pass directly into body fluids. These substances help regulate body functions. Examples are the *thyroid* and the *pituitary gland*.

endogenous (en-dodge'-eh-nus) Describes conditions resulting from internal rather than external factors; includes *hereditary* conditions. In the field of *mental retardation*, usually refers to inherited *mental retardation*. Opposite of *exogenous*.

endomorphic A body type (*somatotype*) characterized by a fat, stout body and large abdomen, squatness and general roundness of form, and little or no muscle definition.

endorphins (en'-dore-fins) A class of brain peptides that plays a role in neurochemical aspects of learning, *memory*, pain, and behavior.

engaged time A term used in *effective instruction* to indicate the minutes a child is actually paying *attention* and working.

engineered classroom A program developed by Frank Hewett and others for students with educational or learning problems. Pupils are assigned specific work based on prior achievement. As new work is completed, a *checkmark system* and *reinforcement* are employed. Cards filled with checkmarks can be exchanged for tangible items or special privileges. The program derives its name from the structure and systematic reinforcement system. Extraneous *visual stimuli* in the room are carefully restricted.

enrichment The most common approach to teaching *gifted* pupils; *curricular* activities or experiences are expanded to provide greater depth of understanding and application than activities for other students. Enrichment may include resource reading, *creative* projects, community application, special assignments, small-group work, and other adaptations of instruction.

entry behavior A student's behavior before receiving instruction. Instruction or *therapy* should start with reference to such behaviors.

enucleation (ee-noo-klee-ay'-shun) Removal of an eye, usually necessary when a disease does not respond to treatment and results in *blindness* or when the eye is severely injured by an accident. Treatment may include the fitting of an artificial eye to improve appearance and prevent deterioration of the eye socket.

enunciation (eh-nun-see-ay'-shun) The pronunciation of words with a distinctness of *articulation* that makes them clearly intelligible to the listener.

enuresis (en-yuh-ree'-sis) A condition in which an individual involuntarily discharges urine.

environmental deprivation The *concept* that lack of stimulation in certain environments can reduce a person's learning capacity.

environmental engineering The use of circumstances and space around a person or group to provide a better learning environment or to effect better control of individual or group behavior. The term *ecological system*, or *ecosystem*, refers to the systematic study of the effect of environment on individuals and groups; this field of investigation has demonstrated that factors affecting learning may relate to more than the student and teacher; other noninstructional factors can have a strong influence as well.

environmentalism A school of thought that minimizes *heredity's* effect on one's development and life and emphasizes the influence of one's cultural, physical, and psychological surroundings.

enzyme (en'-zime) An *organic*, protein compound that serves as a catalyst in producing change in substances. Bodily enzymes are important in the digestive process of converting food to energy as well as in cellular processes.

epicanthus (ep-ih-kan'-thus) (or **epicanthal fold**) A vertical fold of skin on either side of the nose, which covers the innermost portion of the eye. The presence of this fold gives individuals with *Down syndrome* the appearance of having slanted eyes.

epidemiology (ep-ih-de-mee-ahl'-oh-jee) The branch of medicine that deals with the origin and treatment of epidemic diseases. In *mental retardation* or any other field, an **epidemiological** study deals with the search for causes.

epiglottis (ep-i-glah'-tis) A lid-like *cartilaginous* structure in the back of the throat that overhangs the *larynx* and prevents food from entering the *trachea*.

epilepsy (adj., **epileptic**) A *chronic* condition of the *central nervous system* characterized by periodic *seizures* accompanied by *convulsions* of the muscles and, with the more severe attacks, loss of consciousness. (See also *grand mal, petit mal, akinetic seizure,* and *myoclonic seizure.*)

epiphysis (eh-pih'-fih-sis) The ends of long bones, where growth takes place. Injury to this area may slow or stop growth in a leg or arm.

equal protection The principle set forth in the Fourteenth Amendment that guarantees the same legal rights and benefits to all citizens, unless the withholding of rights and benefits has a justifiable reason—e.g., to protect others, an uncontrolled person with *seizures* may not be allowed a driver's license and certain other rights.

equivalent form Describes a test or measure that closely parallels another measure with respect to content and number and difficulty of items; an individual can be expected to obtain similar scores on both measures.

ergonomic (air'-go-nah-mik) **principle** The science of the natural laws of work and the design of tools and machines to facilitate human interaction. This principle is increasingly employed in developing environments that are supportive of those with *disabilities*, aiding them in accomplishing certain goals or allowing them easier access to more normal lives.

errorless prompt An exaggerated, external, and basically irrelevant cue temporarily used to draw a student's *attention* to a correct response; promotes correct responding for students with *severe disabilities*.

erythroblastosis (uh-rith-roe-blas-toh'-sis) A condition originating before birth as a result of incompatibility of the mother's and baby's blood; characterized in the infant by *anemia*, *jaundice*, and possibly *kernicterus*. (See also *Rh factor*.)

erythrocytes (uh-rith'-roe-sites) The red blood cells that perform the important function of carrying oxygen to body cells.

ESEA See *Elementary and Secondary Education Act*.

esophageal (eh-sahf-ah-jee'-ul) **speech** A form of speech developed by persons who have had laryngectomies. This form of speaking has limited volume and *pitch*, but is adequate for communication.

esophagus The tube in the alimentary canal that connects the *pharynx* and stomach. Its primary function is to carry food to the stomach.

esophoria (es-oh-for'-ee-ah); **esotropia** (es-oh-troe'-pea-ah) A muscular defect causing one or both eyes to turn inward, toward the nose. (See *strabismus*.) Esophoria refers to the tendency to turn inward. Esotropia refers to the eyes remaining inward, requiring surgery to correct. Failure to correct the condition causes *deficits* in *depth perception*.

estimated learning potential (ELP) A term employed in the *System of Multicultural Pluralistic Assessment*, developed by Jane Mercer, to indicate the expected learning capacity of children when compared to others of similar sociocultural levels. Basically, it is a way to measure *intelligence* while removing some of the effects of culture.

ESY See *extended school year*.

et seq. A Latin abbreviation for "and following" (et means "and"; seq. is an abbreviation for sequens, which means "following"). It is used in citations, where it always follows a noun (e.g., Vol. 20, *United States Code*, Sections 1401 et seq.—hence, "and following sections").

etiology (et-ee-ahl'-oh-jee) The study or assignment of causes, reasons, or origins, especially of diseases or conditions such as behavior and *learning disorders*.

eugenics (you-jen'-iks) The study of influences for improving the inborn or *hereditary* qualities of a race or breed;

application of the knowledge of *heredity* to improve the human race.

eustachian (you-stay'-shun) **tube** A passageway connecting the middle ear with the *posterior* part of the *nasal* cavity *(nasopharynx)*; serves to equalize air pressure on both sides of the *eardrum*.

eustress (you'-stres) *Stress* resulting from positive events in one's life, such as taking a vacation or getting a raise. (See also *stress* and *distress*.)

euthanasia (you-thuh-nay'-zhuh) The practice of painlessly putting someone to death, particularly an individual suffering from a fatal, unbearable disease or condition. (See also *infanticide*.) In some cultures, children with *severe disabilities* are euthanized.

euthenics (you-then'-iks) The science dealing with the improvement of living conditions, especially physical aspects such as food, clothing, light, ventilation, and shelter, for the purpose of producing more efficient human beings.

evaluation (v., **evaluate**; adj., **evaluative**) 1. An appraisal or estimation of certain specific characteristics, such as *intelligence*, personality, or physical aspects of an individual. 2. In J. P. Guilford's model (see *structure of the intellect*), judgment of the suitability of information that has been cognized, memorized, or generated.

event recorder A mechanical device for counting the frequency of specific occurrences of an event in a given time period.

event recording A system of collecting observational data in which the number of times a behavior occurs is noted. If rocking were the behavior, for example, the teacher would count the number of times the rocking occurred.

evoked-response audiometry A form of *audiometry* based on the changes in brain wave activity when the brain's response

to sounds is measured by an *electroencephalograph*.

ex rel. A Latin abbreviation for ex relationale that indicates a lawsuit is brought on behalf of one person by another (e.g., the attorney general of a state may sue on behalf of an individual; thus, the case is captioned "State of Kansas, ex rel. Jane Doe, an incompetent, v. Superintendent, State Hospital"). The lawsuit normally is one in which the state attorney general seeks to vindicate a legal position that is favorable to the state and its citizens on behalf of a person not able to bring a lawsuit directly.

exacerbation (egg-zas-er-bay'-shun) Increased severity, as in a disease or *symptoms*.

exceptional child(ren) (exceptionality) A child who *deviates* markedly, either above or below the group *norm*, from other children in mental, emotional, physical, social, or *sensory* traits, to a degree that special services are required to help the child benefit from educational experiences.

excess costs That portion of the annual expenditure for the education of an *exceptional child* that exceeds the average expenditure for a nonexceptional child. Some states fund services under this system.

exocrine glands Glands that release a secretion through a duct, as contrasted with ductless, or *endocrine,* glands.

exogenous (egg-zah'-jen-us) Describes a condition resulting from external factors, such as a physical, nonhereditary condition. Opposite of *endogenous*.

exophoria (ek-so-for'-ee-ah); **exotropia** (ek-so-troe'-pea-ah) A deviation in the alignment of the *visual* axis so that one or both eyes turn outward, away from the nose. Opposite of *esophoria* and *esotropia*. (See also *strabismus*, a broader term.) Exophoria refers to the tendency to turn outward. Exotropia refers to the eyes remaining outward, requiring surgery to correct. Failure to correct the condition causes *deficits* in *depth perception*.

exophthalmos (ek-sof-thal'-moss) Abnormal bulging or protrusion of the eyeballs from their sockets.

expectancy table A design measure used to predict how persons with a specific set of scores will perform. In planning and setting goals for students, ability often is compared to expectancy in achievement.

experience chart A summary of the important knowledge, facts, or principles involved in a topic of classroom discussion or a learning *unit*; the chart is developed cooperatively by the class, is usually written on large sheets of newsprint, is often illustrated with pictures, and is held on an easel for display.

experimental group Unit of individuals used for experimental treatment in research. Outcomes are referenced against outcomes of the *control group*.

expert witness A person called to testify in a case because he/she has a recognized competence in an area. For example, experts in the right-to-education cases had doctoral degrees in the field of *special education*, were authors of numerous professional publications pertaining to *exceptional children*, and were *consultants* to advisory committees on education.

expression See *encoding*.

expressive aphasia Defect in, or loss of the power of, *expression* through speech, writing, or gestures resulting from injury to or disease of the brain centers.

expressive language The aspect of communication whereby messages are conveyed verbally, symbolically, or in writing. In contrast, see *receptive language*.

expressive therapy A form of *psychotherapy* used in treating *behavior disorders* in which the emphasis is on the individual's talking out or through his/her problems.

expulsion The forced removal of a student from a school program for more than 10 days because he/she committed behaviors that were highly disruptive or dangerous. Expulsion necessitates a revision of the student's *IEP* and must be used with caution with students with *disabilities*.

expunction of records The legally protected review of a child's school records for error and the elimination of any error found.

expungement (egg-sponge'-ment) A process whereby parents and their children with *disabilities* can have inappropriate school, court, and other records destroyed.

extended care The provision of prolonged or continuous supervision, care, protection, or custody of an individual.

extended family A term of sociological origin referring to the implications of a home or living environment that includes not only the primary family unit, but grandparents, aunts, uncles, cousins, etc. This larger family unit was common among some ethnic groups in the past but does not usually characterize the modern family.

extended program A *special education* program that goes beyond high school graduation or past the traditional school age, many times having *vocational education* or *sheltered workshop* elements. Also may be used to refer to day programs that exceed the normal school day in length.

extended school year (ESY) Refers to school programs for students with *disabilities* that extend beyond 180 days. The term came into wide use in the 1980s with litigation to extend the school year for some youngsters with disabilities for whom being out of school for the summer caused significant *regression* in skills.

extensive mental retardation A term in the 1992 American Association on Mental Retardation definition scheme that is for all purposes equivalent to the term *severe mental retardation*. It implies the extensive need for support from family and social agencies.

extensor A muscle that functions to straighten or extend a joint.

extensor thrust reflex A reaction by some individuals with *cerebral palsy* who are overly sensitive to being supported by the back part of the head during feeding or dressing; the *reflex* causes them to stiffen the body and possibly slide out of the chair.

external locus of control A hypothetical *construct* that holds that some individuals believe their life, destiny, success, and failure are controlled by outside forces. Opposite of *internal locus of control*. (See also *locus of control*.)

external otitis (oh-tite'-iss) Often called "swimmer's ear"; an infection of the skin of the external *auditory* canal.

extinction The dying out or extinguishing of a specific behavior; may occur as a result of a planned adjustment of goals or needs or the removal of *reinforcement* for a response.

extracurricular activities Programs organized and sponsored by a school to allow the exercise of pupil abilities and interests that are not a part of the regular, required curriculum. At the secondary level, particularly, students receiving *special education* services should have the opportunity to be involved in extracurricular activities in which they are interested and for which they are suited.

extralinguistic Describes nonlanguage activities, such as the failure to *discriminate visual* tasks, *distractibility*, and *stereotypic* or self-destructive behaviors that are noncommunicative.

extrapunitive Describes the behavior of blaming others or expressing one's own anger against others.

extremities Limbs of the body; the arms and legs.

extrinsic motivation The use of *incentives* external to the activity in which a student is involved but valued by the learner, with the intent of improving or facilitating the student's performance of the activity; often involves offering prizes or material rewards for outstanding work.

extrovert (extravert) A person who is predominantly interested in the external world and social life, as contrasted with an *introvert*, who is predominantly concerned with mental processes involving deep understandings such as reflections or *introspections*.

eye coordination The ability of an individual's eyes to work together to *focus* on a single *visual* image.

eye-hand coordination The ability of an individual to combine and coordinate functions of the eyes and the hands in carrying out manipulative activities involving the hands.

F

F. Supp. An abbreviation for *Federal Supplement*; used in citations to a lawsuit's reported judgment and order. Indicates that the case was decided by a federal trial court (a "district" court) and is reported in a certain volume of the reports of the federal trial courts. The volume of the reports precedes the F. Supp. designation; and the identity of the court and the date of the judgment are set out in parentheses after the page. Thus, in *PARC v. Commonwealth of Pennsylvania*, 343 F. Supp. 279 (E.D. Pa. 1972), the case is reported in volume 343 of the *Federal Supplement*, beginning at page 279, and was the decision of the federal district court for the Eastern District (section) of Pennsylvania in 1972.

F.2d An abbreviation for *Federal Report, 2d Series*; used in citations to a lawsuit's reported judgment and order. Indicates that the case was decided by a federal court of appeals and is reported in a certain volume of the reports of the federal courts of appeals. The volume of the reports precedes the F.2d designation; the page at which the report begins follows the F.2d designation; and the identity of the court and the date of the judgment are set out in parentheses after the page number. Thus, *Smuck v. Hobson*, 408 F.2d 175 (D.C. Cir. 1969), shows that the appellate judgment (in the case involving school classification practices of the District of Columbia Board of Education) is reported in volume 408 of the *Federal Report, 2d Series*, beginning at page 175, and was a decision of the federal court of appeals (D.C. Circuit Court of Appeals) for the District of Columbia in 1969.

FAC See *facilitative communication*.

facial vision A term used to express the ability of *blind* people to "feel" objects or to perceive their presence with the face. This ability may be more related to the sense of hearing than any special facial senses.

facilitative (facilitated) communication (FAC) A controversial technique that allows a student with *severe disabilities* to communicate in an augmentative system. The teacher or other "facilitator" assists the student, perhaps by holding or pushing against the student's arm, physically moving his/her hand or pointing on the *communication board* without actually imposing the teacher's wishes.

facio-scapulo-humeral dystrophy A type of *muscular dystrophy* that usually begins in the muscles of the face, shoulders, and upper arms. The *symptoms* may vary in *intensity*, but weakness of the facial muscles is usually the most noticeable.

fading (v., **fade**) Gradually changing or reducing a *stimulus* or *reinforcement* as an individual acquires the desired skills.

Fair Labor Standards Act Commonly known as the Federal Wage and Hour Law; establishes minimum wage, child labor control, overtime, and equal pay standards for employment. This law applies to those with and without *disabilities* who are employed.

false imprisonment In education, usually refers to teachers' exceeding their authority in confining a student with no reasonable exit. False imprisonment may involve the misuse of *time-out* procedures.

familial Occurring in members of the same family and across generations.

familial mental retardation *Retardation* that is not *diagnosed* as a *clinical type* and is not caused by *organic brain injury*, but rather has arisen from such causes as cultural inheritance, common exposure to agents associated with social customs, transmission of deleterious *genes*, economic poverty, and factors related to social structure (even when unrelated to economic level).

family care service A term sometimes used in place of *foster home*; includes an expanded role for the *contract* care of persons with *disabilities* so that they can live in the community.

Family Education Rights and Privacy Act (FERA or Buckley Amendment) A law that gives parents of students under 18 years of age and students over 18 the right of access to the students' school records on a "need to know" basis only. The *local education agency* must maintain confidential students' records and make them available within 45 days of a request.

family involvement program An educational innovation developed by Merle Karnes and others that emphasizes parents, family, and home as instructional *units*.

family neurosis A mental disorder that affects all members of a family group to some degree. Members show tension, *anxiety*, *hysteria*, *phobias*, obsessions, and, in general, unusual mannerisms.

family support A program of state cash support for parents to assist them in keeping their children with *mental retardation* or *severe disabilities* in their home. The payments are available in all but three states for *respite care* and other types of family support.

family systems theory Theorizes that the essence and strength of families lies within the interactions of its components.

family therapy A counseling or *therapeutic* method in which problems are viewed as being those of the entire family and therefore are treated in the *context* of the family unit.

fantasy A product of a vivid imagination usually dealing with fictitious images. Fantasy can be a means of adjusting to strong desires or emotions. In moderation, it may be satisfying, but when allowed to replace constructive thoughts, it can become an educational interference.

FAPE See *free appropriate public education*.

farsighted(ness) See *hyperopia*.

FAS See *fetal alcohol syndrome*.

febrile (feb'-ril) Accompanied or marked by fever.

feces (fee'-seez) (adj., **fecal**) Waste matter discharged from the body during bowel movements; stools.

Fed. Reg. An abbreviation for *Federal Register*, a daily publication of Congress that contains the text of new laws and regulations and comments by members of Congress on matters of public policy.

feeblemindedness A term of British origin that refers to a level of *intelligence* comparable to the educational classification of *educable mentally retarded* or the American Association on Mental Retardation's classification of *mild mental retardation*. The *intellectual* level when *assessed* with an individual intelligence test involves *IQ* scores ranging from 50 to 70. (This term is no longer used in current literature.)

feedback Transmittal of information that allows improvement of *motor* or *cognitive* responses based on previous information or response.

femur The large bone located between the hip and the knee.

fenestration (fen-eh-stray'-shun) **operation** Surgery in which an opening is cut in the bone between the *eardrum* and the inner ear to replace an obstructed natural opening that was causing *hearing impairment*.

feral (fer'-uhl) **child** A child who has been reared in isolation or by animals in the wild and is, therefore, uncivilized. Some 23 cases have been recorded, of which the most noted was Victor, with whom Jean Itard worked.

Fernald method A *multisensory* approach to learning reading words. The words to be learned are written in large letters on newsprint or in sand. The child then traces the letters with his/her index finger while saying them aloud. The combined *visual*, *tactile*, and *auditory* stimulation increases the potential for learning the words. (See also *VAKT*.)

FERPA See *Family Education Rights and Privacy Act*.

fetal alcohol syndrome (FAS) A condition found in some infants of alcoholic mothers, marked by low birth weight, *mental retardation*, and *cardiac* and physical defects.

fetal stage The *developmental period* of the *fetus* from about the eighth week of pregnancy until birth.

fetoscopy (fee'-toe-skop-ee) A *diagnostic* technique used during the *prenatal* period to examine *visually* the *uterine* environment. A needlelike device with a light and lens is inserted through the mother's abdomen to allow examination of *fetal* disorders not picked up by *amniocentesis* and *alpha-fetoprotein screening* or *ultrasound.*

fetus (adj., **fetal**) The developing organism during the period of pregnancy from the eighth week after conception until birth; the term is often applied to all *pre*-birth existence.

fibrosis (fie-broe'-sis) The formation of fibrous tissue, as in *cystic fibrosis.*

fibula (fib'-yew-luh) The smaller of the two bones of the lower leg, situated to the outer side of the larger bone, the *tibia*.

field defect A *blind* area in the *field of vision*; the individual does not see in that portion of the eye.

field of vision The entire area one can see without shifting one's gaze. In *partially sighted* individuals, a reduction in the field of vision can be considered as a *disability.*

figural One of J. P. Guilford's *contents* of thought (see *structure of the intellect*), which includes *visual* objects with their properties of shape, size, color, etc.; *auditory* elements in the form of rhythms, melodies, and speech sounds; and *tactual* and *kinesthetic* materials.

figure-background disturbance The tendency to confuse immediately important components of the environment, which are referred to as "figure," with less important aspects of the environment, which are referred to as "background" or "ground." May cause individuals to show poor judgment in selecting figures, or completely reverse the background and figure, which interferes with problem-solving activities.

filial therapy Nondirective, or client-centered, *therapy* conducted by parents under the direction of a professional *therapist.*

fine motor Refers to skills involving the small muscle groups, primarily of the hands. Fine *motor skills* are involved, for example, in drawing. In contrast, see *gross motor*.

fingerspelling A method of communication used by *deaf* persons; involves using different combinations of the hands and fingers to indicate letters in spelling words. Also termed *dactylology* . Used to facilitate *manual method* by spelling out letter-by-letter proper names and other words that lack manual signs.

First Chance Programs established by Congress in 1968 that give opportunities for educational training to young children with *disabilities* and their families, encourage further training in the model procedures used, and stimulate the development of new programs for these young children.

first priority children Defined by *PL 94–142* as school-age students with *disabilities* who are not receiving any education and must be served first educationally.

fissure Any opening or failure to close, as in *cleft palate.*

Fitzgerald key A system of teaching *language* structure by classifying the parts of sentences according to function. The Fitzgerald key was developed for use with *deaf* children, but its application has broadened to programs for students with other *disabilities* as well.

fixed interval reinforcement A system of rewards in which the *reinforcement* is given following the lapse of a specified amount of time (e.g., *reinforcement* is given every 5 minutes if the desired behavior is apparent).

fixed rate reinforcement A schedule of rewards in which the *reinforcement* is given after a behavior has been successfully performed a specified number of times (e.g., reinforcement is given after three math problems have been answered correctly).

flaccid (flas'-sid) (n., **flaccidity**) Describes poor muscle tone in which the muscle is flabby, soft, weak, and considered unhealthy. In contrast, see *tonus.*

Flanders interaction analysis system A procedure for observing a classroom in which the interactions between the teacher and pupils are recorded and analyzed to determine how well the teacher is interacting with the pupils.

flat affect A behavioral/emotional characteristic sometimes found in individuals with *emotional/behavior disorders* and those with head injuries in which joy, anger, or other excitable emotional responses are missing. This characteristic may be masked by socially correct facial expressions like smiles, frowns, etc., but it still limits the development of close relationships.

flex (v.) To bend, as in flexing a joint or muscle in a continuous *reciprocal* motion.

flexibility of thinking One of J. P. Guilford's factors in *creative* thinking; represents the variety of ideas produced by a person. (See *structure of the intellect.*)

flow-through funds Monies available under *IDEA* that are passed through the *state education agency* to the *local education agency.*

fluency 1. Uninterrupted smoothness and rapidity, as in reading or speaking. 2. In J. P. Guilford's *structure of the intellect*, the factors in *creative* thinking that represent the quality and the number of ideas produced.

fluency disorder A type of communication or speech problem characterized by an interrupted flow or rhythm of speech. The best example is *stuttering.* (See also *dysfluency.*)

focal length The distance from the eye to the object in the line of sight.

focal seizure A malfunction, beginning with a twitching in a specific part of the body (e.g., a finger), that is associated with a *lesion* in the corresponding *motor* area of the brain and that may generalize to *grand mal seizures*. (See also *Jacksonian seizure.*)

focus (n.) The point at which light rays converge to project a clear image (as on the *retina*). (v.) To adjust a lens system to produce a sharp, clear picture.

follow up (v.) To provide *diagnosis* and treatment after the initial diagnosis and treatment of a condition. Also, to continue supervisory and training services after an individual leaves a vocational work-study or *rehabilitation* program.

Also used as a noun and an adjective to denote any contact or service subsequent to the first one.

following technique The act of a *blind* person lightly holding onto a sighted person's elbow while walking. Also called *sighted guide technique.*

fonator (foe'-nay-ter) An electronic device that converts spoken words into vibrations or vibrator speech patterns. Can be used by *hearing impaired* children as an aid to their "hearing" and learning of speech; adds *tactual* information to the *visual* signals already received.

fontanel (fon-tah-nel') The soft-spot area in the skull, or *cranium*, of a newborn that has not yet become *ossified* and hardened. Sometimes called the "birth spot."

footedness A preference for using one foot (either the right or left) over the other, especially for performing tasks that require the use of only one foot. (See *laterality.*)

form constancy The ability to recognize letters or other basic shapes regardless of their color, size, or other variations. This ability is extremely important in reading when different typefaces and typestyles are used.

formal assessment (testing) A procedure in which normed or *norm-referenced tests* are used to measure specified characteristics. These tests, usually produced and sold commercially, are often referred to as *standardized tests.* The individual's score is compared to the *norm*, or to how other children typically perform.

forward chaining Teaching behaviors for completing an act (such as putting on a jacket) by beginning with the first behavioral segment and adding each behavioral segment in natural order. *Reinforcement* is provided for larger and larger component sequences until the entire behavior pattern is maintained by the final *reinforcing* event. In contrast, see *backward (reverse) chaining.*

Foster Grandparents A program initiated in 1965 that uses older Americans in volunteer programs for children, particularly children who have *mental retardation* and are in *institutions.*

foster home A living environment, other than with the parents, in which a child may be placed for rearing; the placement is usually made by a family or welfare agency. (See also *family care service* and *developmental training home.*)

foster parent An individual who assumes legal responsibility for rearing a child and takes the place of the child's parents for a period of time but does not necessarily adopt the child. (See also *advocacy/ advocate.*)

fovea (foe'-vee-ah) A small area of the *retina* in which vision is the most distinct or clear.

fracture A break of a bone. Can be any of the following types: (a) *compound*— a fracture with external wounds; (b) comminuted—the bone is crushed or splintered; (c) compression—the joint is jammed together; (d) greenstick—a fracture on one side of the bone with the other side bent; (e) impacted—one fragment is driven into another.

fragile X syndrome A subgroup of the X-linked *genetic* abnormalities most often associated with *mental retardation* and postpubertal physical anomalies in males. Affects males, and females are *carriers* of the condition.

fragmented perception Having only partial or incomplete understanding of information received, as occurs in conjunction with a *learning disorder.*

free appropriate public education (FAPE) One of the key stipulations of

PL 94–142 and IDEA, which requires an educational program for all children without cost to parents. This stipulation does not require the best possible education, but when combined with the legal requirement for the *least restrictive environment*, it implies that the individual is to receive the education and *related services* that will bring about an adequate program.

free association A technique used to encourage *creative* thought or to appraise thought processes; requires the individual to report thoughts as they come to mind.

Freedom for All A series of acts that incorporate the principle of restoring rights to those who have *physical*, mental, and *sensory disabilities* by repealing all other acts or portions of acts that restrict their rights. Such acts have reinstated the rights of persons with *epilepsy*, for example, to marry, to vote, etc.

freedom from peonage A principle based on the Thirteenth Amendment that guarantees all persons freedom from having to work without pay. As applied to persons with *disabilities*, the principle guarantees that such individuals do not have to work unless they so choose and that, if they do work, they are assured fair labor standards and a decent wage.

frenum (free'-num) A fold of skin under the tongue, which, if attached too near the end, results in a condition that has been referred to as "tongue-tied." The condition can be corrected early in life through simple surgery.

frequency In hearing, the physical parameter of sound that refers to the number of vibrations of a sound in one second. Expressed in *hertz (Hz)*.

frequency distribution When counting behaviors, the record of the number of times that a behavior occurs in a given time interval or intervals.

fricative (frick'-uh-tiv) A *consonant* sound produced by forcing voiced or unvoiced breath through a limited opening (such as "f" in "fat," "sh" in "shut").

Friedreich's ataxia A *hereditary* disease that causes hardening of the spinal cord and results in *paralysis* of the lower limbs and *impairment* of speech. The condition affects males and females equally and usually appears in the 7 to 10 years after birth. The disorder is progressive, usually resulting in death by 30 years of age.

Fröalich's syndrome A combination of conditions including *mental retardation*, obesity, small stature, and failure of sexual development that results from *pituitary gland hypothalmic dysfunction*.

frustration-aggression hypothesis A theory holding that frustration leads to *aggression* as a natural consequence.

FTE See *full-time equivalent*.

full inclusion A term introduced in the 1990s to refer to the practice of expecting all students with *disabilities*, regardless of severity, to be enrolled in general education full time. All *special education* services are delivered in the general education classroom through teachers, *aides*, or special *motivations* provided in a supportive role. (See *inclusion* and *total inclusion*.) Some authors differentiate between full inclusion and total inclusion. Such differentiations believe that full inclusion is when not all students with disabilities are assigned to general education settings, but those who are participate fully.

full-time equivalent (FTE) A *concept* incorporated into some state financial formulas in which teacher loads for six periods are used to figure teacher allotment.

functional Denotes nonorganic or without apparent structural cause. In *mental* *retardation*, it signifies the lack of *brain injury*.

functional analysis A procedure used to identify environmental conditions that serve as *antecedents* or consequences to problematic behaviors.

functional curriculum An educational program for persons with *mild mental retardation* that emphasizes preparing them to cope with and solve persistent life problems so that they will be able to live successfully in the community. (See also *community-based instruction*.)

functional hearing loss An inability to hear stemming from psychological problems rather than from *impairment* of the ear or *auditory* mechanism.

functional language A communication system that is usable and allows an individual to make known his/her needs. The term is used primarily with reference to individuals with *severe disabilities* to connote a *language* goal or function the teacher is seeking to develop.

functional literacy The level of communication ability that is necessary for living adequately in society. An individual usually has to be able to read above the fourth-grade level to have much chance for success in independent living.

functionally blind A condition of *visual impairment* in which the individual is not able to use print as a reading medium. (See also *educationally blind*.)

functionally illiterate Implies that the individual at adulthood has not reached the level of communication or reading needed to operate independently in society.

Functional illiteracy can result from a lack of education or from certain types of *disabilities*.

fundamentals The basic knowledge or skills of an area of study or activity, such as the fundamentals of arithmetic.

fusion In vision, the process of combining the images seen by both eyes into one image.

G

galactosemia (gah-lak-toe-see'-mee-ah) A *hereditary* disease identified by the body's inability to convert the galactose part of the lactose molecule in milk to glucose in a normal way for proper body use. If not identified and treated by a controlled diet, results in *mental retardation* and, sometimes, *cataracts* and liver damage.

Gallaudet (gal-uh-det') **College** A federally supported *institution* of higher learning for *deaf* students; located in Washington, DC.

gamma globulin (gam'-ah glob'-you-lin) The part of the blood *plasma* that contains *antibodies* to fight infection and diseases.

gargoyle, gargoylism (gar'-goil-izm) See *Hurler's Syndrome*.

gastric Pertaining to, originating in, or affecting the stomach.

gene Specific part of any *chromosome* that carries *hereditary* characteristics.

geneology (jee-nee-ahl'-oh-jee) The study and recording of the descent of an individual or a family from its ancestors.

general learning disability (GLD) A proposed term for *educable mental retardation*; implies *generalized* learning problems as opposed to a *specific learning disability*. This term has not received wide usage.

generalization 1. v., **generalize** The ability of a child who has learned a behavior to respond appropriately with that behavior in new settings. Generalization is one of the main *objectives* in the instruction of individuals with *mental retardation*. The goal is to have a child who has learned, for example, to make a bed in one situation be able to *transfer* or generalize bed making to other situations. 2. **generalization (of learning)** A statement of, or a process of forming, a conclusion based on or inferred from a number of specific facts or instances. A lack of ability to generalize learning to situations other than that in which the learning occurred is characteristic of children with reduced *intelligence*.

generalization training Instruction designed to help pupils *transfer* knowledge or skills learned in one situation to other situations.

generic (jeh-nare'-ik) (adv., **generically**) Having to do with a group of similar things and inclusive of all things in the group or class. Usually used in reference to a set of materials or teaching techniques applied with children of differing *diagnoses*.

genetic (jeh-net'-ik) Pertaining to *heredity*, or features transmitted by *chromosomes* from parents to their offspring. Certain physical characteristics, such as skin, hair, and eye coloring, and conditions such as *Down syndrome* are **genetically** determined.

genetics (and **genetic counseling**) The systematic study of biological inheritance. Genetics has become an integral part of counseling for family planning when there is concern that offspring might inherit a disabling condition; genetic counseling reveals the likelihood of conditions based on probability statistics, *chromosome* studies, *amniocentesis*, and other factors.

genius An individual who demonstrates exceptionally high mental ability. No specific *IQ* score has been universally accepted as indicating such a level; however, an IQ of 150 or more would in most cases be considered as genius level.

Many professionals prefer reserving this term for those individuals with exceptional production, such as Edison and Einstein.

genotype (jee'-noe-tipe) The total inherited characteristics of an individual. This *genetic* endowment establishes a *range* within which behavior can develop in relation to the individual's environment.

geriatrics (jare-ee-at'-trix); **gerontology** (jare-un-tol'-oh-jee) The study of problems accompanying old age and the treatment of diseases during this period of life.

German measles (rubella) A *communicable disease* caused by a *viral* infection that is characterized by pink eruptions on the skin. Although milder than typical *measles*, when contracted by a woman during early stages of pregnancy, results in a high *incidence* of *severe disabilities* in the offspring including *mental retardation*, *cardiac* abnormalities, *cerebral palsy*, and *sensory disabilities* (in hearing and vision). Vaccinations to prevent *rubella* are now routinely given to children.

gestalt (geh-stawlt' or geh-shtalt') A theory based on the viewpoint that events or behaviors do not occur through the summation of separate parts but that the whole becomes more than the sum of the parts.

gestation (jeh-stay'-shun) The time period in which a developing baby is carried in the *uterus*; the period of pregnancy.

gifted(ness) A designation for an individual who possesses unusually high ability. No specific *IQ* has been universally set to indicate the *intellectual* level of giftedness; however, an IQ of 130 or more, in conjunction with other traits such as *creativity*, sometimes has been used as a standard.

gifted and talented A more encompassing term than *gifted*; includes high ability in the *creative* and performing arts.

Gillingham method A highly structured *phonic* system of teaching reading; begins by teaching the sounds of letters and builds these letter sounds systematically into words. This system is used by the Orton Society in its programs, most often with individuals who have *specific learning disabilities*.

glaucoma (glaw-koe'-muh) A condition of the eye in which internal pressure causes hardening of the eyeballs; if not treated, results in *impairment* of vision or *blindness*.

GLD See *general learning disability*.

global intelligence Refers to the combined effect of all the traits in one's *intellect*.

glottis (glot'-iss) One's vocal apparatus, consisting of the vocal cords and the space between them.

glycemia (gly-see'-mee-ah) The presence of glucose in the blood. (See also *hyperglycemia*.)

Goals 2000 A national effort to enumerate specific accomplishments expected of public education by the year 2000.

gonococcus (gon-oh-kok'-us) The microorganism that causes *gonorrhea*.

gonorrhea (gon-oh-ree'-ah) A *venereal disease* occurring in both sexes that may lead to *cutaneous lesions*, *arthritis*, and sterility. A *fetus* may contract gonorrhea from an infected mother at birth.

Gower's sign A *symptom* of *Duchenne disease*, a type of *muscular dystrophy*, in which a weakness of the back and stomach muscles causes a child to "walk up" his/her legs using the hands to facilitate reaching an upright standing position.

grade equivalent A *raw score* expressed in terms of average school achievement. For example, if a *raw score* of 24 is interpreted as the score achieved by average children in the fifth month of the fourth grade, it might be expressed as 4.5. (See also *age equivalent*.)

grade level An indication of educational maturity designated by the school grade corresponding to an individual's achievement record. Usually, grade level can be established by subtracting 5 from an individual's *chronological age*.

grade norm See *grade equivalent*.

Grade I braille The first, or introductory, level of *braille*, in which every word is spelled out.

Grade II braille The advanced level of *braille*, in which students are taught to use and read contractions of words and phrases. Its use improves the speed of reading and transcription because it is a shortened form.

grand mal A severe form of *epileptic seizure* involving loss of consciousness and extreme *convulsions*.

grapheme (graf'-eem) A written symbol that represents a spoken *language* sound. The printed representation of a *phoneme*.

graphesthesia (graf-es-thee'-zee-ah) The ability to recognize letters traced on the skin. Lack of this ability may be considered a *"soft" sign* of *minimal brain dysfunction*.

gross motor Refers to skills involving large muscles. Gross *motor skills* are involved, for example, in such activities as rolling, crawling, walking, running, throwing, and jumping. In contrast, see *fine motor*.

group home A form of *alternative living* arrangement in which individuals with *severe disabilities* live in a community setting rather than in an *institution*. (See also *developmental training home*.)

group intelligence test Any instrument designed to measure *intelligence* that can be administered to several persons at a time as opposed to being administered individually.

group therapy An approach to *psychotherapy* in which small units of individuals are treated by the same *therapist(s)* at the same time. Positive factors of this approach are that it is financially economical, uses professional personnel more efficiently than the one-to-one approach, and allows individuals in the group to help each other.

guardianship A legally sanctioned relationship between a competent adult and a minor or individual with a *disability*. The guardian has the authority and duty to make and effect decisions concerning the minor or individual with disabilities within the limits set by the court.

guide dog A trained dog used by *blind* persons in *mobility*. Also called *lead dog* or *seeing eye dog* (the latter is the least preferred).

gurney A stretcher on wheels such as is commonly used in hospitals to move patients to and from surgery. The increasing survival rate of students with *severe disabilities* (especially those who are *medically fragile*) has brought the term into special educators' vocabularies.

guttural speech A speech and *voice disorder* in which the *pitch* is likely to be lower than normal and the voice gives the impression of falling back into the throat; sometimes referred to as "raspy" speech.

gynecology (guy-neh-kahl'-oh-jee) A branch of medicine that deals with treating females and their unique diseases.

H

habilitation The process of training and providing services for the improvement of an individual's total *range* of function. Habilitation implies the development of skills for successful living or employment, in most cases, whereas *rehabilitation* implies that the person once had normal functioning or employment and is being retrained or rehabilitated.

habilitation plan A program for an individual receiving *developmental disabilities* funds; includes a written *assessment* and treatment plan.

halfway house A temporary *residential* unit usually operated by an *institution* for the purpose of training the residents to live with a greater degree of independence than is provided within the institutional setting. The training may be directed at preparing the individuals to live independently within the community.

hallucination An abnormal mental condition in which a person has the impression that imaginary things are real. The person also may see or hear nonexisting objects or sounds.

hallucinogen (adj., **hallucinogenic**) Any drug that causes *hallucinations*.

halo effect Any impression given by an individual or group (as in research studies) that causes a rater's estimate of specific abilities or traits of that individual or group to be consistently too high if behavior is positive, or too low if behavior is negative.

handedness A preference for predominantly using either the right or the left hand in performing tasks, particularly tasks requiring the use of only one hand.

handicap (adj., **handicapped**) The result of any condition (*disability*) or deviation, physical, mental, or emotional, that inhibits or prevents achievement or acceptance. The term was largely replaced by disability in the early 1990s. (See also disability, which is the preferred term.)

handicapism A term referring to prejudice, stereotyping, and *discrimination* against those with *disabilities*.

haptic A term first used by Victor Lowenfeld to refer to the *kinesthetic* and *tactile feedback* that a child receives through movement and touch. Includes all the sensations derived from the skin receptors for contact, pressure, pain, warmth, and cold. If the haptic sense is impaired, individuals may have difficulty making the correct *motor* responses. Some children with *learning disabilities* appear to have haptic deficiencies.

hard of hearing A condition in which *auditory acuity* is reduced to the degree that special services, such as *auditory training*, speech (or *lip*) *reading*, *speech therapy*, or a *hearing aid* may be required. With proper adaptations, many hard of hearing individuals can be educated as effectively as hearing children.

hard palate See *palate*.

hardware Pieces of electronic equipment used in providing a service (e.g., teaching machines, microcomputers, amplification equipment). Such equipment utilizes software.

harelip See *cleft lip*, the preferred term.

Head Start A nationwide program instituted in 1965 to provide preschool experiences for economically disadvantaged children.

health impairment Any condition or disease that interferes with an individual's state of optimal physical, mental, or social well-being. Often used in reference to diseases that result in low vitality or progressive deterioration. In children,

may result in the need for *special education*.

health service system Term for all health, medical, and *related services* coordinated by one agency or plan.

hearing acuity How well one can hear. Commonly measured by audiometric testing, or *audiometry*.

hearing aid Any of a number of devices used for collecting, conducting, and amplifying sound waves to help an individual utilize his/her hearing capacity to the maximum.

hearing loss (impairment) A deficiency in one's ability to hear. May *range* from a mild loss to a total lack of hearing ability. At the level of severe loss (*deafness*), defined as 70–90 *db*, measured on an *audiometer*, **hearing impaired** individuals require extensive training in communication methods.

hearing officer A person trained by the state to conduct *due process* hearings and render decisions. Many hearing officers are lawyers, but the primary requirement is that they are not employed by the school system.

hearing threshold The level at which an individual with average hearing can detect sound 50% of the time. The hearing level is measured in *decibels* on an *audiometer*.

heart defect Any of a number of *cardiac* conditions resulting from *malformations*, mechanical imperfections, or injuries to the heart, its muscles, or the vessels leading to and from it. Heart defects most often are classified as *congenital* or acquired. Congenital conditions are usually malformations or mechanical defects; acquired conditions may result from injuries or may be the residual effects of diseases such as *rheumatic fever*.

Hebb's theory A viewpoint of *conceptual* and perceptual neural organization that advocates that the stimulation of a sense organ activates a chain of upper *central nervous system* cells called a "cell assembly" and that such activation, upon repetition, produces a stable *perception*. The production of a series of cell assemblies by related *stimuli* forms a "phase sequence," which allows sequential perceptions, while the relating of the stimuli to previously learned perceptions is handled by another neural organization called "phase cycles." Hebb's theory often has been applied in *mental retardation* as a basis for instructional technology and research.

Heller's disease (dementia infantilis) A *degenerative metabolic disorder* involving *atrophy* of the brain and nerve cells. This condition usually occurs at about 3 or 4 years of age, at which time the child becomes irritable, negativistic, and disobedient.

hematology (hee-muh-tahl'-oh-jee) The study and science of the composition and function of the blood.

hematoma (hee-mah-toe'-mah) A tumor filled with blood.

hemi- A prefix meaning half.

hemiatrophy (hem-ee-at'-roe-fee) The *degeneration* or wasting away of an organ or muscular portion of the body on one side only. The word stems from *hemi* (half) and *atrophy* (wasting away).

hemiplegia (heh-mih-plee'-juh); **hemiparesis** *Paralysis* of the arm and leg on one side of the body. The latter term implies lesser severity.

hemisphere One half of any spherical body structure or organ. One can refer, for example, to the right and left *hemispheres* of the brain.

hemoglobin The red pigment in the red blood cells that performs the function of carrying oxygen.

hemophilia (hee-moe-fee'-lee-ah) A condition, usually *hereditary*, characterized by failure of the blood to clot following an injury. Profuse bleeding, internal as well as external, occurs from even slight injuries. Found primarily in males, because of *hereditary* determination factors. An individual with this affliction is called a **hemophiliac**.

hemorrhage An abnormal discharge of blood from a blood vessel. Hemorrhages are usually caused by an injury, but may also be caused by a rupture, or break, of a vessel under excessive pressure changes.

hepatitis (hep-ah-tie'-tiss) Any of the disease conditions in which the primary characteristic is *inflammation* of the liver. (See also *infectious hepatitis*.)

hepatolenticular (hep-ah-toe-len-tih'-cue-lar) **degeneration** See *Wilson's disease*.

heredity (adj., **hereditary**) The biological *genetic* process by which an organism produces offspring of similar or comparable structure. Significant in *special education* because of the number of traits or types of deficiencies transferred to offspring by *genes*

hernia (adj., **hernial**) The protrusion of a part of an organ or a tissue through an abnormal opening of the body; results from the breaking down of specific muscles.

herpes (her'-peez) 1. One of several types of organisms that cause infection on the lips and genitals. Pregnant mothers with the genital type of infection can give birth to children who have *mental retardation*. 2. **herpes simplex** Any of several *viral* diseases of the skin, the most common type of which results in cold sores or fever blisters. Another type causes ulcers on the adult genitalia, which may infect an infant progressing down the birth canal. Herpes in infants attacks the brain and in many newborns is rapidly fatal. If the baby lives, *brain damage* usually is profound. Herpes in the newborn may be prevented by good *prenatal* care and delivery of the baby by *caesarean section*.

hertz (Hz) A unit of measurement of *frequency*, or vibrations per second, of sound waves; formerly, cycles per second (cps).

heterogeneous (het-er-oh-jee'-nee-us); **heterogenous** (het-er-ah'-jen-us) Consisting of dissimilar parts that may come from a wide *range* of sources and not have uniform quality throughout (e.g., a group of students with a wide range of abilities). Opposite of *homogeneous*, or *homogenous*.

heterophoria (het-er-oh-fore'-ee-uh) A general term for a defect in the muscle balance of the eyes, in which the deviation is latent and not as apparent as in *strabismus*. When the eyes pull toward the nose, it is called *esophoria*; when the eyes pull away from the nose, it is called *exophoria*; when the eyes tend to pull up, it is called *hyperphoria*; and when they pull down, it is *hypophoria*.

"high grade" mental retardate An archaic term of *institutional* origin classifying individuals with less *severe retardation* (in contrast to those with more severe retardation, who were classified as "*low grade*"). Comparable to the preferred term *mild mental retardation*.

high risk Describes children who come from families with a record of *disabilities* or potential for disabilities. The risk may have *genetic* origins or result from a lack of activities that stimulate development. (See also *at-risk*.)

higher functioning autistic disorder Students with this condition are *diagnosed* as "autistic-like" or having "autistic tendencies." While these students have the same types of problems as children with *autism*, the severity of their *language*, communication, social, and *cognitive* disorders is more mild. (See also *autoid*.)

hirsutism (her'-suit-izm) Abnormal hairiness, often an *adverse reaction* to certain kinds of *drug therapy*. Also known as *hypertrichosis*. In contrast, see *hypotrichosis*.

histidinemia (hiss-tih-deh-nee'-mee-ah) A *metabolic disorder* caused by an abnormal level of **histidose**. Many people with this disorder have *mental retardation*, *retarded* growth, and speech *impairments*.

HIV See *human immunodeficiency virus*.

hives An eruptive skin condition usually caused by a reaction of the body to a specific substance; sometimes considered to be of emotional origin.

hoarseness A *voice disorder* characterized by harshness and a grating, *breathy* quality comparable to that otherwise accompanying a cold or other irritation of the *larynx*.

Hodgkin's disease A *malignant* condition involving a painless, progressive enlargement of the lymph nodes and spleen. Related *symptoms* may be loss of appetite, weight loss, fever, night sweating, and *anemia*.

holophrastic (hoe-loe-fras'-tik) **speech** Use of a single word to express an underlying complex intention or situation. For example, a child may say "bottle" and mean, "I want my bottle." Also called *kernel sentence*.

home school The school to which a student would have been assigned had he/she no *disability*. Also referred to as *neighborhood school*.

home schooling A practice by parents, especially in the 1990s, to keep their children out of the public schools; parents educate them at home, free from the influence of society. At times this practice has been employed by parents of those with *disabilities*.

home-based instruction Teaching at a student's home, provided for students who are unable to attend school. Home-based instruction represents one of the options in the *service delivery system* of *special education*; also called homebound.

homeostasis (hoe-mee-oh-stay'-sis) A condition of stability in body functions. Homeostasis is achieved by a system of control mechanisms that are activated when body functions become unbalanced.

homogeneous (hoe-moe-jee'-nee-us); **homogenous** (hoe-mah'-jeh-nus) Consisting of similar parts and having a uniform quality throughout. For example, a *self-contained class* would be more homogeneous than a general education classroom. Opposite of *heterogeneous*, or *heterogenous*.

homophones (adj., **homophonous**) (hoe-mah'-fuh-nus) 1. Different sounds that are produced by the same external lip movement (e.g., p*a*n, p*e*n, p*i*n). Homophones cannot be distinguished by *hearing impaired* speech readers. 2. Words pronounced alike but different in meaning (e.g., hear, here).

honeymoon period The time period following the start of a program when students may not express the behaviors for which they were referred. Research and data collection during such early stages may yield inappropriate or misleading results.

Honig v. Doe A landmark case in which the Supreme Court set forth limitations on *suspensions* and *expulsions* of students with *disabilities*. With this decision, suspensions beyond 10 days cumulative are considered as changes of placement. Under more recent federal legislations, longer suspensions are not a change in placement if the inappropriate behavior for which the student was suspended was not a manifestation of his or her disability and qualifies under the Gun Free Schools Act.

honor society (or **honors program**) A selective system of membership recognizing individuals with a high level of *academic achievement*. Often a part of a school's provision for *gifted* students. A student who achieves at or above a specific high level, as stipulated by school policy, may receive the designation of **honor student**.

Hoover cane A long, thin cane designed by Richard Hoover to assist *blind* persons in safe and effective *mobility*, or movement from one place to another. Also called *long cane*.

hormone A chemical substance produced by the ductless glands of the body. Hormones are secreted directly into the bloodstream and are involved in helping to regulate body functions.

hortitherapy A term coined by Karl Menninger in the 1930s to describe the *therapeutic* treatment of individuals with *disabilities* growing and working with plants. The therapeutic benefits led to the establishment of the National Council for Therapy and Rehabilitation through Horticulture (NCTRH).

hospital-based instruction The teaching of students in the hospital who are confined there because of illness, accident, recuperation following surgery, or any disabling condition that does not allow them to attend school; also called hospital bound.

houseparent A person employed as a *surrogate parent* in a *residential* setting such as an *institution*, a *group home*, or a *halfway house* to provide supervision and guidance to children, adolescents, or adults.

human immunodeficiency virus (HIV) The agent that causes *AIDS*.

human service system Term used to refer to the coordination of educational, *rehabilitative*, medical, welfare, and other needs in a unified program to reduce confusion in services.

human services counselor A term used in Canada since the late 1980s to refer to *caseworkers* and others who were previously called welfare workers or *social workers*.

humanistic education An approach to teaching or instructing people that emphasizes the dignity and worth of each individual and holds that a person has within himself/herself the ability to correct the imbalance between an individual and his/her environment. Incorporates the thinking of Carl Rogers and others.

Huntington's chorea (koe-ree'-uh) A *hereditary* condition that results in a wide variety of rapid, jerky, involuntary movements.

Hurler's syndrome A *hereditary metabolic disorder* characterized by such physical abnormalities as thickened lips and broad bridge of nose as well as possible *mental retardation* and general progressive physical deterioration; if not treated, death occurs. Sometimes called *gargoylism*.

huskiness A voice quality characterized by roughness in tone and a relatively low *pitch*. Could be a *symptom* of a *voice disorder*.

hyaline membrane disease (hi'-e-len) A condition that affects the lungs of newborn infants; caused by the formation of a membrane between the lung capillaries and the tiny air sacs (alveoli) of the lungs. The membrane interferes with the passage of oxygen into the blood and of carbon dioxide out of the blood after it returns as waste from the lungs. Sometimes results in death.

hydrocephalus (hie-dro-sef'-uh-lus); **hydrocephaly** (-lee) A condition of excess *cerebrospinal fluid* accumulation in the *cranial* cavity, causing undue pressure on the brain and resulting in an enlarged head. Sometimes referred to formerly as "waterhead." Now, surgical procedures such as *shunting* are used to reduce fluid pressure and head enlargement. If unchecked, the condition usually causes *mental retardation*.

hydrotherapy A method of treating *disabilities* or disease using water, as in creating pressure by a forced flow of water.

hyper- A prefix designating an excess, more than desirable.

hyperactive (adj.) (n., **hyperactivity**) Describes behavior characterized by abnormal, excessive activity or movement. This activity may interfere with a child's learning and cause considerable problems in managing behavior.

hyperglycemia (hie-purr-glie-see'-mee-ah) A condition of excessive sugar in the blood, resulting in excessive thirst, frequent urination, weakness, rapid breathing, and sometimes *coma*. In contrast, see *hypoglycemia*.

hyperhemolytic (hie-purr-hee-moe-lit'-ik) **crisis** An abnormal destruction of red blood cells resulting in loss of *hemoglobin* and interfering with the nourishment of cells, as in *sickle cell anemia*.

hyperkinetic (adj.) (n., **hyperkinesis**) (hie-purr-kin-ee'-sis) Characterized by excessive *motor* activity, inattention, and *impulsivity*. This terminology is used in the medical field with reference to children who have *hyperactivity* and *distractibility*.

hyperlexia A *learning disorder* in which an individual pronounces words by sight with little or no *comprehension* of their meanings.

hypermetropia See *hyperopia*.

hypernasal (hypernasality) Describes excessive sound emission through *nasal* passages during speech, as in *cleft palate* speech.

hyperopia (hie-purr-oh'-pea-ah) **(far-sightedness)** Poor vision at close *range*, due to the eyeball being shortened from back to front so that light rays tend to *focus* behind the *retina*. Hyperopia most often is corrected by using *convex lenses*, which bend the rays so they will focus on the retina. In contrast, see *myopia*.

hyperoxia (hie-purr-ock'-see-ah) An excess of oxygen in the body.

hyperphoria A muscle defect of the eyes that causes the eyes to pull up. (See also *heterophoria*.)

hyperplasia (hie-purr-play'-zee-ah) An abnormal multiplication of elements constituting a part of the body, such as cells of an organ or a tissue.

hypertelorism (hy-per-teel'-oe-ris-um) A condition characterized by an abnormally great distance between the eyes and a broadening of the base of the nose. In itself, hypertelorism is not a disease, but it is associated with several forms of *mental retardation*.

hypertension A condition characterized by abnormally high arterial blood pressure. An individual with hypertension may have no *symptoms* or may have *symptoms* such as headaches, dizziness, or nervousness. Hypertension may lead to a *stroke*.

hyperthyroidism A condition characterized by excessive activity of the *thyroid* gland, which may result in weight changes, *hyperactivity*, nervousness, and similar behaviors.

hypertonia Excessive muscular tension.

hypertrichosis (hie-purr-trik-oh'-sis) A biological condition characterized by excessive body hair. (See also *hirsutism*.)

hypertrophy (hy-per'-troe-fee) Abnormal enlargement of a body organ or part. Hypertrophy of the gums is a possible side effect from use of the drug Dilantin.

hyperventilation Excessive respiration characterized by short, rapid breath and possibly a loss of consciousness. The condition causes (usually temporarily) an abnormal loss of carbon dioxide from the blood.

hypnosis (adj., **hypnotic**) An induced state of passivity in which the subject shows increased responsiveness to suggestions and commands provided that they do not conflict with his/her conscious wishes.

hypnotherapy (hip-no-ther'-a-pee) The use of *hypnosis* to change behavior or treat a disease.

hypo- A prefix designating lower, or less than desirable.

hypoactive Showing an obvious loss or absence of physical activity. Opposite of *hyperactive*.

hypochondria (hie-poe-kahn'-dree-ah) A state of being unusually anxious about one's health, often accompanied by *delusions* of physical illnesses.

hypodermic Describes the administration of medicine under the skin, as with an injection.

hypogenitalism (hie-poe-jeh'-nih-tah-lizm) Decreased growth of sexual organs and development of secondary sexual characteristics.

hypoglycemia (hie-poe-glie-see'-mee-ah) Low glucose content in the blood caused by an increase in *metabolism* resulting from too much exercise, too much *insulin* (*insulin* reaction), not enough food, or nervous tension. In contrast, see *hyperglycemia.*

hypokinesia (hie-poe-kih-nee'-zee-ah) Abnormally reduced *motor* activity with the possible appearance of laziness.

hypolexia (hy-poe-lex'-ee-ah) Low reading level or ability in a person of high *intelligence.*

hypometabolism Abnormally low *metabolic* rate and utilization of material by the body.

hyponasality See *denasal speech.*

hypophoria (hy-poe-for'-ee-ah) A defect in the eye muscles that causes the eyes to pull down. (See also *heterophoria.*)

hypoplasia (hie-poe-play'-zee-ah) The decreased or arrested growth of an organ or tissue. In some forms of *mental retardation*, the genitals do not develop normally and the person is said to have hypoplasia.

hypotension Below-normal blood pressure. Often a result of shock but may derive from other causes.

hypothalamus (hie-poe-thal'-ah-mus) (adj., **hypothalmic**) A nerve center of the brain that lies beneath the thalamus on each side. It encompasses the regulatory centers of *autonomic nervous system* (involuntary) body functions.

hypothyroidism A condition caused by abnormally low secretion of the *thyroid* gland. If this condition occurs to a severe degree during early childhood and is not treated, *cretinism* may result.

hypotonia A neuromuscular disorder characterized by weak, *flaccid* muscles.

hypotrichosis (hy-po-trih-ko'-sis) A condition characterized by less than the usual amount of body hair. In contrast, see *hirsutism.*

hypoxemia (hie-pok-see'-mee-ah) Reduced oxygen supply in the blood.

hypoxia (hie-pok'-see-ah) A condition characterized by a low content of oxygen in the air being inhaled, which results in a deficiency of oxygen carried by the blood.

hysteria (adj., **hysterical**) An outbreak of wild emotionalism, which can become *chronic*. If hysteria persists as a *psychoneurotic* condition, it may become a *functional* nervous disorder with varying manifestations of an emotional, mental, and physical nature including *blindness, deafness,* or *paralysis.*

Hz See *hertz.*

I

-ia Suffix denoting *pathology*, as in *kleptomania.*

iatrogenic (aye-at-troe-jen'-ik) Describes any adverse condition in a patient that occurs as a result of the medication or treatment.

ichthyosis (ik-thee-oh'-sis) A *congenital hereditary* skin disease that produces dryness and scaling.

id A term first discussed in Sigmund Freud's writings on *psychoanalytic* theory in the 1890s; represents or contains components of one's instinctual life. The two basic instinctual drives are, first, the fixed quantity of sexual energy available to an individual from birth, called libido, and, second, *aggression.*

IDEA See *Individuals with Disabilities Education Act.*

identification 1. A *defense mechanism* in which an individual associates himself/herself with other persons, groups, or organizations in an attempt to feel more secure and to relieve frustrations. 2. A method for effecting behavior change and learning in which the pupil is led to think, feel, and behave as though the characteristics of another person or group belong to him/her. Identification with the model of the other person or group may be done consciously or unconsciously. 3. Pinpointing the need of an individual for further treatment, *assessment*, or training.

idiolalia (id-ee-oh-lay'-lee-ah) A form of spoken communication that consists of invented *language*. It occurs most often between twins, who can understand their own language while no one else can. It may delay normal communication to the extent that some **idiolalic** children have been misidentified as *mentally retarded*.

idiopathic (id-ee-oh-path'-ik) Describes a condition of unknown causes, as in certain *epileptic seizures*.

idiot (old usage) A term of British and *clinical* origins that refers to a level of *intellectual* functioning comparable to the educational classification of *severe mental retardation* or the American Association on Mental Retardation's classification of *profound mental retardation*. The intellectual level, *assessed* with an individual *intelligence* test, would be *IQ* scores ranging from approximately 0 to 20. The term has negative connotations in the United States.

idiot savant See *savant syndrome*.

IEP See *individualized education program*.

IEP manager The person agreed upon at the IEP conference to oversee implementation of the child's *individualized education program*.

IFSP See *individual family service plan*.

IHSS See *in-home support services*.

IIP See *individual implementation plan*.

ileostomy (ill-ee-ahs'-toe-mee) A surgical procedure for diverting the urine, via an *ilioconduit*, through a *stoma* exiting on the abdomen.

ilioconduit (ilial loop) Refers to the means of diverting liquid feces or waste out through a *stoma* on the abdomen. With *paraplegics* and *incontinent* individuals, this procedure helps prevent kidney damage. (See also *ileostomy* and *clean intermittent catheterization*.)

illiteracy The inability to read and write at a *functional* reading level, usually considered to be below fourth-grade level.

ILS See *independent living skills*.

imagery A *learning strategy*, used especially with children who have *learning disabilities* or *retardation*; individual is encouraged to make a *visual* picture of the *stimulus* item. The interaction between the stimulus item and *visualization* is what improves learning.

imbecile (old usage) A term of British and *clinical* origins that refers to a level of *intellectual* functioning comparable to the educational classification of *trainable mentally retarded* or the American Association on Mental Retardation's classification of *moderate mental retardation*. The intellectual level, *assessed* with an individual *intelligence* test, would involve *IQ* scores ranging from 20 to 50. The term has negative connotations in the United States.

IMC See *instructional materials center*.

immitance (im-mit'-ans) **testing** A measurement made by *audiologists* to determine the flexibility of the *eardrum* and the amount of pressure in the middle ear. This type of test does not determine *hearing acuity* but rather is used to determine the possible cause of a *conductive hearing loss*.

immunity The body's ability to resist a particular disease or infection, as in immunity to chicken pox.

impaction A state in which a material becomes firmly wedged or lodged, as in wax impaction in the ear or *fecal* impaction in the rectum.

impairment A general term indicating injury, deficiency, or lessening of function. For example, *visual impairment* indicates that vision is less than normal.

impedance (imm-peed'-ans) **audiometry** An approach to measuring middle ear function by determining the reaction in the middle ear to changes of pressure in the *auditory canal*. The preferred term is now *immitance testing*.

imperception Lack of ability to understand or interpret *sensory* information accurately; involves *impairment* of *cognitive* functions rather than *sensory* impairments.

impulsivity Responding abruptly without consideration of consequences or alternatives.

in loco parentis (in low'-koe pair-en'-tiss) A legal term referring to situations in which teachers are allowed or expected to act in place of parents. This authority varies according to state law, but in most states may be exercised only when the situation requires *intervention* to maintain order in the school or safety of student(s), and the teacher is acting without excess emotion.

in re A Latin term in the title of a law case that indicates "in the matter of." It is always followed by the name of a party to the lawsuit (e.g., In Re: John Doe, a minor; here, the title to the lawsuit means, "In the matter of John Doe, a minor/child").

inborn error of metabolism Any one of the inherited disorders caused by the absence of certain *enzymes* in the body, which results in a *metabolic* block or incomplete *metabolism*.

incentive (in-sen'-tiv) Anything that incites action toward achieving an *objective*; can be tangible or intangible.

incidence The number of cases of a given condition identified and reported for a population (e.g., the number of children born with *Down syndrome*), usually reported as a numerical ratio (say, one child with Down syndrome per 1,000 live births) or expressed as the number or percentage to have a given condition at some time in their life. (See also *prevalence*.)

incidental learning *Acquisition* of knowledge that takes place not as a primary goal but as a part of the peripheral effects of the experience.

inclusion A term connoting the expectation that for the majority of students with *disabilities* the *least restrictive environment* is in general education with support. Inclusion does not mean full-time enrollment in general education but connotes that it is the preferred placement for all students and that the majority of the services will be delivered there. See also *full* inclusion and *total inclusion*.

inclusion (alternative definition) According to James M. Kauffman, John Wills Lloyd, John Baker, and Teresa M. Riedel, a more humane definition of inclusion is "one that allows for a variety of placements that offer the conditions under which every individual feels safe, accepted, and valued and is helped to develop his or her *affective* and *intellectual* capacities."

inclusion philosophy The theoretical basis for *inclusion*, which considers that all students with *disabilities* should be educated with nondisabled students whenever appropriate. Courts have used *reasonable expectation of benefit* as a *criterion* by which to judge appropriateness of placement.

inclusion transition plan A document or a portion of the individualized education plan that addresses those steps and actions necessary for a student with *disabilities* to move through the *continuum of services* to a more inclusive environment. These documents are written to assist in the *transition* of students to the new environment.

inclusive education A general term implying that students with *disabilities* have a right to be educated with nondisabled students as much as is possible.

inclusive schools Schools in which the philosophy is to include all students with *disabilities* in general education classes.

incontinence (adj., **incontinent**) The inability to control one's bladder or bowel functions. Opposite of continence.

incorrigible Describes behavior that is rebellious and unmanageable. The term is more likely to be used as slang to characterize some students with *behavior disorders* or those who are *socially maladjusted.*

incus (ing'-kus) The second of the three small bones of the middle ear that conduct vibrations from the *tympanic membrane (eardrum)* to the inner ear. This bone is sometimes referred to as the anvil. The other two bones are the *malleus* and the *stapes.* Together, these three bones are called the *ossicles.*

independent living rehabilitation services Programs to help train individuals who have *severe disabilities* to live and work in the community with or without supervision.

independent living skills (ILS) Practical learning imparted to persons with *mental retardation* so that they can function in home or community environ-

ments. (See also *activities of daily living.*)

individual family service plan (IFSP) A feature of *PL 99–457*; an expanded *individualized education program* that is written for preschool children with *disabilities* and their families. The plan outlines the family's strengths and needs related to enhancing the child's development.

individual implementation plan (IIP) The portion of the *individualized education program* that states the *short-term objectives* for the student and the specific strategies for *intervention.*

individual reading inventory (IRI) A nonstandardized procedure teachers use to establish a student's reading level for independent and assisted instruction; involves having the student read from selected reading passages and computing the number of errors. (See also *informal reading inventory.*)

individual services plan (ISP) A statement of proposed services to guide the service provider and client throughout the duration of service. Similar in meaning to the *individualized progress plan.*

individual test A measure designed to be administered to one person at a time, as contrasted with measures administered to a group in one setting.

individualized education program (IEP) A component of the *Education for All Handicapped Children Act*, which requires a written plan of instruction for each child receiving special services; gives a statement of the child's present levels of educational performance, *annual goals, short-term objectives*, specific services needed by the child, dates when these services will begin and be in effect, and related information. The program is undertaken by a team that includes the parents.

individualized instruction Teaching and study approaches designed specifically for a given pupil's interests, needs, and abilities.

individualized planning conference A meeting for the purpose of developing, reviewing, or revising a child's *individualized education program*.

individualized program plan (IPP) Approximates an *individualized education program* or *habilitation plan*. Specifies the appropriate instruction, *therapies*, etc., needed by an individual child or adult.

individualized progress plan (IPP) A plan of instruction or *habilitation* called for in *PL 94–103* (the Developmental Disabilities Act of 1975). (See also *individually prescribed instruction* and *individualized program plan*.)

individually prescribed instruction (IPI) Teaching based on an *individualized education program* or *habilitation plan*.

Individuals with Disabilities Education Act (IDEA) When *PL 94–142*, the *Education for All Handicapped Children Act*, was updated during the One Hundred and First Congress (PL 101–476), it was renamed the Individuals with Disabilities Education Act. The new act carried forth all the provisions of PL 94–142 but also included additional elements.

inductive learning The *acquisition* of knowledge through guided discovery. In this approach, students are presented with several illustrations of a rule or an occurrence and are then asked to infer the principle involved.

inductive thinking A term used by learning theorists to describe the process of reasoning from parts to the whole, often resulting in a general principle inferred from particulars in the environment. Opposite of *deductive thinking*.

infant education A shift in emphasis, which occurred following the passage of *PL 99–457*, to include many more children with *disabilities* in education programs from birth to age 3.

infanticide (in-fan'-ti-side) A term similar to *euthanasia* except that it is exclusive to young children; refers to the act of letting babies whose *prognosis* is clearly terminal die by withholding treatment, withdrawing treatment, and/or withholding sustenance.

infantile Describes behavior characteristic of an infant.

infantile amaurotic family idiocy See *amaurotic family idiocy* and *Tay-Sachs disease*.

infantile (progressive spinal muscular) atrophy A severe and rapidly advancing neuromuscular disorder of infants. See also *marasmus*.

infantile autism See *autism*.

infectious hepatitis An *inflammation* of the liver caused by a specific *virus*. Early *symptoms* are nausea, vomiting, and pain in the upper abdomen; *jaundice* may or may not be present. This disease may infect anyone but usually occurs in children between ages 5 and 15.

infectious mononucleosis (mah-noe-new-klee-oh'-sis) A condition, thought to be caused by a *virus*, characterized by fever, sore throat, chills, headache, stomach pain, body rash, initial enlargement of the lymph nodes, possible *central nervous system* involvement, and low vitality. Treatment involves bed rest and restriction of activity.

inferiority complex A psychological term indicating a severe lack of self-confidence that sometimes results in introvertive tendencies. Usually stems from experiencing failure, but may result from frustrating self-love experiences as a child.

inflammation (adj., **inflammatory**; v., **inflamed**) A condition of body tissues characterized by pain, redness, and swelling, and resulting from infection, injury, or overexertion.

inflection (adj., **inflectional**) The changing degree of loudness and the rise and fall of *pitch* during speech that give different shades of meaning to words and phrases.

influenza (flu) An epidemic disease caused by any number of *viral* infections that is often characterized by *acute inflammation* of the throat and bronchi and is usually accompanied by aching muscles and fever. If a woman contracts influenza during early pregnancy, the chances of having a baby with *disabilities* are increased.

informal assessment (testing) A procedure in which instructional materials that have not been normed are used to measure specified characteristics. An *informal reading inventory* is an example.

informal reading inventory A procedure in which graded reading materials are used to *assess* a student's reading level. The *inventory* is not a normed or *norm-referenced test*, but is designed to provide a basis for beginning instruction.

information theory A broad view of communication that emphasizes a computer-like approach to the treatment of knowledge; *concepts* of input and output variables and mathematical probabilities are applied to human *processing* of information.

information-processing system A framework for understanding how learning occurs.

informed consent See *consent agreement*.

informed decision See *due process*.

infra A Latin word in a discussion of a case indicating that the same case is referred to in a later part of the same article, chapter, book, judicial opinion, or other writing (e.g., the court may refer to the *Rowley* case, infra, meaning that it is discussed later in its opinion or, literally, within its opinion). Opposite of *supra*.

inhibition The process whereby an individual restrains an impulse or activity by utilizing an opposing internal force. Inhibition is not always the result of a conscious effort but may be the result of some force or experience of which the individual is not aware.

in-home support services (IHSS) Those services that individuals with *disabilities* require to live "independently" in a community. They include the provision of personal *aides*, nursing and *medical services*, and any other services that would prevent the individual from having to live in a more restrictive environment.

initial teaching alphabet (ITA) A system of representing speech sounds in which each sound is represented by a single written character. (See also *phonetic alphabet*.)

injunctive relief A remedy granted by a court forbidding or requiring some action by the *defendant*. Injunctive relief includes temporary restraining orders and preliminary and final injunctions. These types of *relief* differ in the lengths of time, stages of the litigative process, and bases of degrees of proof.

innate response system The unlearned *motor* instincts with which a child is endowed at birth. The *startle response* in infants is an example.

inner speech Term originated by Leo Vygotsky referring to mental images of words produced by *visual*, *auditory*, and *kinesthetic* sensations. Children with *disabilities* are often instructed in producing such images.

in-school suspension (ISS) A practice in which disruptive students are removed from the regular classroom and receive individually oriented instruction in skills and knowledge areas in which their low *achievement levels* are contributing to their adjustment problems. Since the 1980s, ISS has been a response of school systems toward keeping students with behavioral problems in school rather than suspending or expelling them.

in-school work experience A method prescribed in the student's *IEP*; elicits information about student's *incentives* and attitudes toward productive labor to prepare them for ultimate placement in a job in the competitive market by assigning them supervised duties within the school. An in-school work program is most valuable when it emphasizes factors that may be *generalized* to any type of employment (e.g., punctuality, socialization, completion of tasks, respect for authority).

inservice training In the *context* of *special education* and *rehabilitation*, refers to special instruction in these areas conducted by a school district for its teachers. Inservice training has been heavily emphasized to improve teaching competencies. Current vocabulary favors the term *staff development*.

insight The ability to grasp, apprehend, or understand a situation quickly. This quality often is evident in *gifted* children but usually lacking in individuals with *mental retardation*.

institution (adj., **institutional**) A public or private facility or building(s) providing specified services to persons on a 24-hour *residential* basis.

institutionalization Placement and residence within a specialized structure, particularly with reference to persons who have *mental retardation* or *behavior disorders*. Such placement may have an inhibiting effect on development because of the generally limited *sensory* stimulation and personal experiences within an *institution*, and has been shown in some instances to result in a decrease in *intellectual* functioning.

instructional materials center (IMC) 1. Any of the regional offices forming a national network designed to gather, *evaluate*, store, and make available materials for use by individuals involved in teaching. 2. *Generically*, a name applied to settings in which the above function is performed; also termed *resource centers* or *learning resource centers*—now part of the national Area Learning Resource Centers (ALRCs).

instructional objective The outcome toward which teaching effort is directed.

instructional plan The part of the *individualized education program* that states *short-term objectives* and specific strategies for *intervention*.

instrumental enrichment The term used by R. Feuerstein in his training of persons with *mental retardation* to indicate the nature of the *curriculum* used. The goal of this curriculum is to change the overall *cognitive* structure of the students by transforming passive and dependent *cognitive styles* into independent and autonomous thinking. It is a paper and pencil curriculum administered three to five times a week over a 2- or 3-year period, with each lesson lasting about an hour.

insulin A *hormone* produced by the *pancreas*. The insulin used to treat *diabetes* is extracted from the pancreatic glands of animals or produced synthetically.

insulin shock A reaction brought on in *diabetics* as a result of receiving too much *insulin*, not eating enough food, or participating in too much exercise; the reaction is characterized by feelings of hunger, trembling, perspiring, and muscular contractions. When in insulin shock, the body needs sugar, so eating candy, pure sugar, or an orange usually relieves the condition.

integrated life experience curriculum An approach used in instructing students with *mental retardation* in which *units*, *experience charts*, dramatizations, and other means of pupil participation provide firsthand experiences that help the students better understand their environment and solve persistent life problems.

integrated plan An administrative approach to assigning *exceptional children* for educational experiences whereby the pupil is carried on the roll of a general education classroom but a specially trained teacher is available to assist in a *special class* or *resource room*. This terminology largely has been replaced by *resource room*, *mainstreaming*, and *inclusion*.

integrated skills method An approach to teaching reading, developed out of the work with talking typewriters, in which reading is independent of any specific traditional program or approach. The method integrates pupil needs with teacher knowledge, skills, and teaching styles, and emphasizes three major components—a beginning skills *unit*, integrated skills lessons, and applied reading.

integration The placement of children with *disabilities* in educational programs for nondisabled students. Similar terms are *mainstreaming* and *inclusion*.

intellect (adj., **intellectual**) The substance of a person's thinking or *intelli-gence*, represented by such abilities as observing, reasoning, comprehending, judging, and understanding.

intellectual disability A term used worldwide to refer to individuals with *mental retardation*. Does not have the negative connotations associated with the term mental retardation.

intelligence The ability to understand, comprehend, and adapt rapidly to new situations and learn from experiences. Also, an individual's degree of ability, as displayed by performance on tests constructed for the purpose of measuring mental development level.

intelligence quotient (IQ) The numerical figure commonly used to express an individual's level of mental development. IQ is computed by dividing the individual's *mental age* (as measured by performance on an *intelligence* test) by his/her *chronological age* and multiplying by 100. The resulting score (frequently referred to as measured IQ) represents an estimate of that person's mental development, which may vary over time or in future *assessments*. In most modern IQ tests, statistical methods are used to express a student's level of performance in relation to others in the population.

intensity 1. The magnitude or degree of tension, activity, or energy. 2. The physical parameter of sound expressed in *decibels* (the psychological correlate is loudness).

intensive training residence (ITR) A community *residential alternative* that emphasizes training in skill *acquisition* and the elimination of unsocialized behavior; an extension of the *group home concept*. ITRs were started to provide the expertise necessary for working with "hard core" *deinstitutionalization* cases.

interdisciplinary Involving members of two or more professions who share a common function or goal (e.g., a *diagnostic* team consisting of a physician, a *psychologist*, a *social worker*, and a special educator). Similar to *multidisciplinary*.

interindividual differences A *concept* based on the idea that each person is unique. The term is used in describing differences among children in weight, height, reading ability, learning capacity, etc. Compare with *intraindividual differences* (differences within a person).

interjacent child A term coined by Edgar Doll in the 1950s to refer to students now called *learning disabled*.

intermediate district See *shared services*.

intermediate level 1. A school grade placement equivalent to the fourth, fifth, and sixth grades. 2. A grouping for *special education* classes involving pupils approximately 9 through 12 years of age.

intermittent mental retardation A term that replaced the older term *mild mental retardation* in the 1992 American Association on Mental Retardation's definition of *mental retardation*. Intermittent mental retardation is not exactly the same as mild mental retardation, but according to the definition, the term can be used in a similar manner to imply a mild condition with intermittent support required. This classification system has not been embraced by the field.

intermittent reinforcement A procedure whereby only selected, not all, responses are rewarded during training. This strategy builds more resistance to *extinction* than does *continuous reinforcement*.

internal locus of control A hypothetical *construct* that holds that some individuals believe they are largely in control of their own destinies. Opposite of

external locus of control. (See also *locus of control*.)

international phonetic alphabet (IPA) A system of representing speech sounds in which each sound is represented by a single written character. (See also *phonetic alphabet*.)

internship A period of continuous, full-time participation in the profession for which one is being trained, during which time the **intern** receives direction and supervision. In the case of teaching or administration, the direction and supervision come from a local supervising teacher or administrator as well as from a supervisor from the college or university granting credit for the experience.

interpersonal relations The linkage between a person and others with whom he/she interacts, such as a *peer group*, family, and authority figures. One's effectiveness in this regard seems to be related closely to one's ability to recognize and respond to the needs of others in the surrounding environment.

interpreter (for deaf persons) A person who uses *sign language* and/or *fingerspelling* to translate spoken communication so *deaf* individuals can understand it.

interrelated A term used in some states as the equivalent to mild *disability*. Includes students with *mild mental retardation*, mild *learning disabilities*, and mild *behavior disorders*. Interrelated is similar to *noncategorical*.

intersensory integration An interdependent and facilitating relationship involving several *sensory* modalities; can result in *sensory processing* that is superior to that of one sense alone.

interservice transition plan (ITP) A *transition* on employment plan written for a student by a team of school, community, and agency personnel before he/

she leaves school. Those writing the plan are not necessarily obligated to implement it. In recent years, it has been largely replaced by the term transition plan or transition planning.

interval recording Keeping an account, at regular, equally spaced times, of the occurrence of a behavior.

intervention The interception of unproductive or undesired behaviors or conditions and the process of changing or directing them in ways that are more advantageous.

intonation (in-toe-nay'-shun) The speaking patterns characteristic of specific *languages* or used to create inferences for various meanings.

intracranial Located within the skull.

intraindividual differences A *concept* applied to the comparison of abilities and *disabilities* within a person, as opposed to *interindividual differences* (differences between persons).

intrauterine growth retardation A condition in a newborn characterized by having a small placenta and low birth weight. Also known as *Warkany's syndrome.*

intrinsic motivation The property causing improved performance in a given task through *incentives* within the task itself; that is, a child's interest in learning or performing the task motivates him/her to perform it.

introjection Making an occurrence or characteristic a part of oneself or turning hostility felt toward another against oneself.

introspection (adj., **introspective**) Examining one's own thoughts and feelings; self-analysis.

introvert (intravert) One who tends to shrink from social relationships and becomes involved with himself/herself, sometimes in *fantasy* and the symbolic;

inner-directed rather than outer-directed; *introspective.* Opposite of *extrovert.*

invalid One who is seriously, usually chronically, *disabled* by ill health. An invalid is often dependent upon others, is often limited in getting around, and may have negative, *depressed* feelings as a result of these limitations. The term has been used most often with reference to elderly people who have *disabilities.*

invasion of privacy A situation in which information (say, concerning an individual) is shared with a third party without a *consent agreement.*

inventory A questionnaire or checklist used to elicit pertinent information. A skills inventory, for example, often is used to determine arithmetic knowledge in a nonstandardized manner; other inventories may be used to measure personality characteristics.

inversion A *reversal* in order, form, relationship, or position (e.g., a change in the normal sentence structure by placing a verb before its subject, as is observed sometimes in those whose primary *language* is different from the one in which the inversions occur).

IPA See *international phonetic alphabet.*

IPI See *individually prescribed instruction.*

IPP See *individualized program/progress plan.*

IQ See *intelligence quotient.*

IRI See *individual reading inventory.*

iris The colored portion of the eye, which contracts or expands involuntarily depending upon the amount of light entering the eye. The iris functions similarly to the shutter of a camera.

iritis (eye-rih'-tis) A condition marked by *inflammation* of the *iris* of the eye and in which one experiences pain and discomfort from light.

Ishihari color plates Specific materials developed to identify and measure *colorblindness*. Certain colors used in the plates are visible to persons who are not *colorblind* but cannot be *discriminated* by those who are *colorblind*.

ISO standard The normal listener's average *threshold* levels to sound pressure from which *hearing acuity* is determined, as set by the International Standards Organization. This standard has been used to determine a slight *hearing loss* to be from 25 to 40 *decibels* (*db*); a mild loss to be 40 to 55 db; a marked loss to be 55 to 70 db; a severe loss, 70 to 90 db; and an extreme loss, +90 db.

ISP See *individual services plan.*

ISS See *in-school suspension.*

ITA See *initial teaching alphabet.*

itinerant teacher/therapist A professional who renders service to students in small groups or individually, traveling to more than one school. Usually applied to *speech and language pathologists* and teachers of *low-incidence* exceptionalities such as those with low vision.

ITP See *interservice transition plan.*

ITR See *intensive training residence.*

J

Jacksonian seizure A form of *epileptic* activity in which muscular contractions begin in one part of the body (e.g., the left hand) and may subside without loss of consciousness or may spread to the entire body and develop into a *grand mal seizure.* (See also *focal seizure.*)

jactitation (jack-tih-tay'-shun) Jerking and twitching of the body.

Jaeger chart Utilizing different sizes of print, serves as an aid to determine *visual* competence and the best print size for *partially sighted* individuals.

jargon 1. Speech characterized by an unintelligible jumble of syllables; may occur in early speech development of infants or in speech efforts of individuals who have *profound mental retardation.* 2. Specialized vocabulary used by professionals in a specific field of study or work.

jaundice A condition in which an abnormal presence of bile pigments in the blood and tissues causes yellowness of the skin and eyes and a deep yellow color of the urine. May occur in young children; if caused by the *Rh factor*, can result in *mental retardation.* (See *erythroblastosis.*)

Jena (hay'-nuh) **method** A procedure for teaching lip (speech) reading to individuals with *hearing impairments* that is based on exposing them to the sensations of movement during the production of speech.

jig A device specially designed to help workers perform tasks faster, more accurately, and with greater ease. Jigs are often used in *sheltered workshops* for persons with *mental retardation* to limit or control their work operations so they can perform their work under conditions of minimum supervision and reduced hazards.

job club An organization in which individuals can share with peers (both *disabled* and nondisabled) stories about their job experiences and suggestions on how to look for and adjust to employment.

job coach A person designated as a work supervisor for a person with *severe disabilities* in competitive employment. The job coach serves in an instructional capacity working and *modeling* alongside the individual with *disabilities.*

job sample A selected sampling of a standard work activity that involves all or part of the total operations required by a given job. Job samples often are taken to *evaluate* or determine if a worker or workshop can accomplish certain things prior to hiring the worker or setting up the complete workshop.

job shadowing The process employed by job teachers or others who serve as models or *mentors* for students with *disabilities* proceeding through job skills.

job-coached employee An individual with *disabilities* who is placed in competitive employment with a supervisor or other supportive person to help him/her cope and be successful on the job.

Jukes family The subject of a study by Richard L. Dugdale, published in 1875, which popularized the position that people living under poor social conditions would *degenerate* from generation to generation. The study emphasized the *familial* aspects of *mental retardation*.

juvenile court A court of law that hears only cases involving minor, or underage, children. Many cases brought before these courts involve *neglected*, dependent, or *delinquent* children.

juvenile delinquency The adjudged behavior on the part of young people, classified by the state as underage, that causes them to be charged as lawbreakers.

juvenile rheumatoid arthritis (JRA) One of the most *chronic* of all diseases and the form of *arthritis* most often contracted by children. In severe cases, the pain and stiffness become so debilitating that periods of *paralysis* occur.

juxtospinal Close to the spinal column.

K

Kallikak family The subject and title of a book written by Henry H. Goddard in 1912, which supported the position that *mental retardation* is *hereditary*. Goddard studied the genealogy of an *institutional*

patient and found that the patient's great-great-grandmother had 480 descendants, of which approximately three fourths were considered *"degenerates"* of some type. The patient's great-great-grandfather, however, later married a woman of average *intelligence* and produced 496 direct descendants, all of whom were considered responsible individuals and of normal intelligence.

Kanner's syndrome See *autism*.

karotype 1. An analysis of the *chromosomal* makeup of an individual. 2. A systematic array of the metaphase *chromosomes* of a single cell arranged in pairs in descending order of size.

keratitis (kare-ih-tie'-tiss) *Inflammation* of the *cornea* of the eye with residual scarring.

kernel sentence See *holophrastic speech*.

kernicterus (kur-nik'-ter-us) A condition in a *fetus* resulting from a blood incompatibility between the mother and the developing fetus. The consequent *allergic* reaction in the fetus causes a breakdown of the red blood cells, which releases large amounts of *bilirubin* (the red pigment in the red blood cells). The residual effects of kernicterus may include *mental retardation*, *cerebral palsy*, and other *impairments*.

ketone (kee'-tone) Any compound containing a carbonyl group. Ketone bodies are usually found in the blood and urine of those with uncontrolled *diabetes*. Any condition in which ketone bodies are found in the urine is called ketonuria.

kinesthesis (kih-nes-thee'-sis) The sensation of movement stimulated by nerves in the muscles or joints or by the *vestibular* mechanism in the inner ear.

kinesthetic See *haptic*.

kinesthetic method An approach to teaching reading and related skills in which students trace symbols in the air, in clay, or on paper. This use of the senses enhances learning in some children who have had difficulty with other forms of instruction. (See *VAKT*.)

kinesthetic sense A general term referring to *tactile* sensations and the sensation of muscle movement in any part of the body. Described as a receptive *feedback* of information to the brain to aid sensorimotor coordination and planning for immediate action. Activities such as reading, writing, and speech depend tremendously on accurate kinesthetic information.

kleptomania (klep-toe-may'-nee-uh) A persistent impulse to steal articles that are often of little or no value; monetary profit is not a motive.

Klinefelter's syndrome A condition *(clinical type)* occurring in males, caused by sex *chromosome aberrations*, in which affected boys at *puberty* develop feminine-like breasts and have sparse beards and scant pubic hair. Individuals with this disorder are usually sterile and frequently have *mental retardation*.

knee jerk reflex Involuntary movement of the quadriceps muscle causing extension of the leg when the tendon below the kneecap is tapped. Absence of this *reflex* is an indicator to physicians of the presence of certain conditions.

kolytic (koe-lit'-ik) Describes a calm, self-controlled temperament with a tendency toward being passive.

Kurzweil (curz'-well) **machine** A device that optically reads print and reproduces it as *synthetic speech*; used by *visually* impaired persons.

kwashiorkor (kwash-ee-or'-core) A condition caused by a severe protein deficiency and characterized by retarded growth, skin and hair pigment changes, *eczema*, *pathological* changes in the liver, and mental *apathy*.

kymograph (kye'-moe-graf) An instrument used to record variations in any physiological or muscle process.

kyphosis (kye-foe'-sis) A condition in which the spine is curved in a stooped position, causing the back to be rounded around the shoulders.

L

labeling (or **labelling/label**) The practice of attaching a generalized descriptor to a person with a *disability*, such as *mentally retarded, cerebral palsied, learning disabled*. Although labels may entitle an individual to special services, they carry the risk of creating stigmas and nowadays are used with caution.

labial (lay'-bee-uhl) 1. Pertaining to the lips. 2. Describes a speech sound produced with the aid of the lips (e.g., *p, b*).

lability (lah-bill'-ih-tee) **of affect** A behavioral/emotional characteristic, often noticed in persons with brain injuries, in which an individual overreacts to minimal stimulation, for example, by bursting into tears upon completing a certain task, giggling when insecure, or showing other indications of unstable control of impulses.

lacrimal (lak'-rih-mal) **gland** Located just above the outer corner of each eye, it has the function of secreting tears.

lahlophobia (lah-loe-foe'-bee-ah) An abnormal fear of speaking.

lallation (lah-lay'-shun) An ear-voice *reflex* occurring in children of about 6 months of age, in which the *stimulus* of hearing a spoken sound is sufficient to set the vocal mechanism into operation to produce the sound again, which again stimulates the ear, which again stimulates the speech mechanism, etc. This reflex explains why a child may say "da-da-da-da-da."

lalopathy (lah-loe'-pah-thee) Any *speech disorder*.

laloplegia (lah-loe-plee'-jah) *Paralysis* of the speech organs.

landmark 1. Any familiar object, sound, odor, temperature, or *tactual* clue that a *blind* person can easily recognize as having a known and exact location in the environment; used for *direction taking*. 2. A store, factory, or other object that individuals with *mental retardation* are taught signifies that their bus or rapid transit stop is approaching. The store or other landmark serves as the *stimulus* that it is time to pull the cord for disembarking. 3. Important or significant event.

language 1. A system of words or symbols and the rules for putting them together to form a method of communication among a group of individuals. (See also *functional language*.) 2. A code used by a programmer for purposes of organizing a computer's circuits so the machine will perform specific tasks on demand.

language bifurcation (bie-fer-kay'-shun) Inadequate learning of both the primary and secondary *language* by *bilingual* or ethnic minority individuals.

language development The growth in an individual's ability to communicate through the use of vocal and written symbols.

language disorder A problem in comprehending, expressing, or otherwise functionally utilizing spoken *language*.

language-experience approach A method of teaching reading and other *language* skills that incorporates the pupils' experiences. This method frequently uses an *experience chart* dictated by the pupils and recorded by the teacher, which provides material for teaching language and reading.

large type A print, usually produced to aid *partially sighted* individuals in reading, that is approximately twice as large as regular print. (See also *clear type*.)

Larry P. v. Riles A landmark court case in which California schools were ordered not to use *IQ* as the primary determinant for placement in classes for students with *mild mental retardation*. The case was brought because the percentage of blacks in *special education* far exceeded their percentage in the general population, and tests to determine IQ were considered culturally biased.

laryngectomy (lair-un-jek'-toe-mee) Surgical removal of the *larynx* (voice box) because of a diseased condition or *trauma* to the vocal folds.

laryngitis (lair-en-jite'-iss) Temporary *inflammation* of the *larynx* (voice box), which results in *hoarseness*, soreness of the throat, and sometimes loss of voice.

laryngologist (lair-en-gahl'-oh-jist) A medical doctor who *diagnoses* and treats disorders of the throat, *pharynx*, *larynx*, and *nasopharynx*.

laryngology (lair-en-gahl'-oh-jee) The branch of medicine dealing with the throat, *pharynx*, *larynx*, and *nasopharynx*.

laryngoscope (lair-in'-go-skope) An instrument designed for the direct *visual* examination of the interior of the *larynx* (voice box) through the process known as **laryngoscopy** (lair-en-gahs'-koe-pee).

larynx (lair'-inks) The organ of voice, located in the upper part of the *trachea* (windpipe), that contains the vocal cords and essential musculature for the production of speech.

laser cane A cane housing an electronic device that emits a sound; used by *blind* persons as a *mobility aid*. As the individual approaches an object, the *pitch* of the emitted sound rises.

latchkey Contemporary term applied to children whose parents work outside the home and who must be at home unsupervised from the end of the school day until their parents get home. Some research has indicated that these children have a much greater chance of becoming *socially maladjusted* than do children who have supervision.

laterality (or **lateral dominance**) One's preference for using either the right or left side of the body; also, correctly interpreting the position and sidedness of the body.

lazy eye See *amblyopia*.

LD See *learning disability/learning disabled*.

LEA See *local education(al) agency*.

lead dog See *guide dog*.

lead poisoning A *toxic* condition resulting from the ingestion of lead. Results in *central nervous system* damage and *mental retardation*. Most often caused by the ingestion of lead paint from old houses or old pipes.

learned helplessness An evolved state in which an individual does not attempt to perform a task or solve a problem even though he/she has the ability to do so. Occurs because the person has come to feel that his/her efforts are useless or unimportant to the outcome.

learning curve A graphic representation of progress or achievement as indicated by plotting the results of periodic *evaluations* during a *curricular* sequence; often used to allow pupils to keep a record of their achievements in a specific area.

learning disability (adj., **learning disabled**) **(LD)** A lack of achievement or ability in a specific learning area(s) within the *range* of achievement of individuals with comparable mental ability. Most definitions emphasize a basic disorder in the psychological processes involved in understanding and using *language*, spoken or written. As used in *special education* in Britain (United Kingdom), the term refers to those individuals the rest of the world would *label* as *mentally retarded*.

learning disorder A generalized physical or *neurological impairment* that interferes with *academic achievement*.

learning handicapped A term that was used in California to indicate a category of the *service delivery system* in which students with mild *disabilities* who were formerly *labeled educable mentally retarded*, behaviorally disordered, and *learning disabled* were served within the same program through a resource-type rather than a *self-contained program*.

learning resource center See *instructional materials center*.

learning strategies Techniques, principles, or methods that help a student in the *acquisition*, manipulation, storage, and retrieval of information. Learning strategies are particularly needed by those who lack thinking, *attention*, or *memory* skills and consequently have difficulty with academic learning.

learning strategies approach An instructional method that advocates teaching students skills that will aid them in their learning. Because students with *learning disabilities* and other mild *disabilities* seem to lack skills that are *prerequisite* to academic skills, the instruction emphasizes thinking, *memory*, and listening skills—"how to learn"—rather than teaching basic content.

learning style Refers to the way a child learns. Two different meanings have been applied: 1. Preferred *sensory* modalities and how a child learns relative to the use of *visual, tactile,* and other sensory modes. 2. Personality characteristics that have implications for behavioral patterns in learning situations.

least prompts A teaching method that advocates use of the fewest possible means of assistance. In teaching a task, the teacher helps only to the extent necessary for the child to get to the next learning stage. Includes *modeling* and physical *prompts.*

least restrictive alternative A legal term that antedates the term *least restrictive environment* but is essentially synonymous with it. The term was first used in 1918 in relation to branch banking but has subsequently been employed in such law cases as *Wyatt v. Stickney* (1971) and *PARC v. Commonwealth of Pennsylvania* (1971).

least restrictive environment (LRE) A *concept* expressed by the courts in the 1970s mandating that each person with a *disability* should be educated or served in the most "normal" setting and atmosphere possible. LRE led to the concept and practice of *mainstreaming.* Under *PL 94–142* and *IDEA,* the concept of LRE includes educational placement as similar to that of nondisabled children as feasible.

legal advocacy Activities by an individual or group to promote desired changes to benefit another individual or group. The activities include convincing one or more of the three legally constituted avenues of government—legislative, administrative, and judicial—to react concretely upon the desired changes. (See also *advocacy.*)

legal blindness (legally blind) A term for the level of *visual impairment* at which one is eligible for special consideration, services, or funding. Defined as 20/200 in the better eye after correction or vision that does not exceed 20 degrees in the *visual field.*

legal commitment A court order requiring specified care, confinement, or treatment for an individual.

Legg-Calve-Perthes (leg-cav-perth'-ez) A disease of the circulatory system that can result in destruction of the head of the *femur.* It occurs most often in boys between 5 and 9 years of age. Its effects can be prevented by immobilization.

leisure life skills (leisure time activities) Tasks taught to persons with *disabilities* to assist them in the wise, pleasant use of the time when they are not working or attending classes. Because many such individuals are restricted in work and other uses of time, effective use of free time is an important area for development. Other terminology is *outdoor education.*

Lekotek (lek'-oh-tek) The name of a worldwide system of play libraries for children with *disabilities.* The centers were first established in Sweden. Their primary role is to provide consultation and to lend toys and instructive materials to families so that young children with *severe mental retardation* can be maintained and their early education accomplished in their homes.

lens (of the eye) The transparent component of the eye between the *posterior* chamber and the *vitreous humor* that functions in *focusing* light rays and images on the *retina.*

lesion (lee'-zhun) Any change in the structure of organs or tissues as a result of injury or disease.

lesson plan An orderly, detailed schedule of the important points of a teaching session; specifies *objectives* to be achieved, order of presentation, materials to be used, teaching methods, and student assignments.

leukemia (lew-kee'-mee-uh) A disease of the blood-forming organs that is marked by an increase in the number of white blood cells and results in progressive deterioration of the body. Great strides have been made in treating this condition, especially in children.

life experience unit A teaching block of related skills and facts based on real-life situations and problems. Life experience units are commonly included in educational programs for students with *mild mental retardation*.

life space Commonly used in reference to the immediate environment in which an individual functions.

lifelong career development A systematic approach for persons with *disabilities* to acquire the skills and resources they need to maintain the maximum degree of independent living throughout their life.

life-space interviewing A form of treatment following a crisis situation, advocated by William Morse and others, in which the teacher or *crisis teacher* serves as a *nonjudgmental* recorder of events and helps children work out the response they should make in similar situations in the future.

limited guardianship A legal arrangement under which the guardian of an individual with developmental or other *disabilities* has prespecified restricted authority and responsibility. The extent of *guardianship* is determined by the court and is dependent upon the extent of *adaptive behavior*, the *intellectual* level, and the *self-care skills* of the *disabled* individual as well as the capabilities and qualifications of the guardian.

limited mental retardation A term in the 1992 American Association on Mental Retardation definition scheme that is for all practical reasons equivalent to *moderate mental retardation*. It implies a limited need for support from family and/or social agencies. This term has not been readily accepted as a substitute for *moderate mental retardation*.

lingual (ling'-gwuhl) A speech sound basically formed by the tongue and in which the tongue is considered to have the major *articulatory* role.

linguistics (adj., **linguistic**) The science or study of *language* and human speech, which includes the origin, structure, and *semantics* of *language*.

lip reading (speech reading) A skill taught to *deaf* and *hard of hearing* persons through which they can understand much of what another person is saying by observing the *context* of the situation and the *visual* cues of speech production, such as movements of the lips and facial muscles.

lisp An *articulatory* defect of speech in which the sounds of *s* and *z* are improperly produced with an accompanying emission of air. A person with a lisp might, for example, say "thaw" for saw or "thebra" for zebra.

listening ear dog An animal trained to assist individuals with limited hearing. This type of dog learns to respond to bells, alarms, sirens, a baby's cry, and other audible signals.

literacy The ability to read and write; usually considered to be *functional* reading above the fourth-grade level.

local education(al) agency (LEA) An administrative arrangement referred to by federal and state legislation to designate the entity responsible for providing public education through 12th grade— usually a school district.

local school system (LSS) Same as *local education(al) agency.*

lock-step education Describes a rigid, structured system of pupil progression from grade to grade, regardless of ability or a need to progress more rapidly or more slowly. (See also *social promotion*.)

locus of control A hypothetical *construct* used to describe an individual's expectations for the occurrence of behaviors. *Gifted* children generally score high on *internal locus of control*. Many individuals with *disabilities* have an *external locus of control*.

logical consequences A treatment procedure in which a *contingency* is logically related to a misbehavior (e.g., losing freedom to move around the classroom after disrupting the work of other students).

logopedics (lahg-oh-peed'-iks) The study and treatment of *speech defects*.

long cane See *Hoover cane*.

longitudinal study Research that follows a case or situation over a considerable time, usually a number of years.

long-range goal An element specified in the *individualized education program* as the ultimate learning aim for the term or school year. It is based on already-specified *short-term objectives*.

long-term goals See *annual goals*.

long-term memory Denotes ideas, impressions, or sensations that the individual can recall over a relatively long period of time, in contrast to *short-term memory*, which is brief in duration. Telephone numbers, for example, usually go into *short-term memory* instead of long-term *memory*.

lordosis (lor-doe'-sis) Irregular curvature in the lumbar and cervical regions of the spine when viewed from the side. Other terms used are "hollowback" and "swayback."

low functioning An outdated term that refers to individuals with *cognitive disabilities* whose *adaptive skills* are minimal.

"low grade" mental retardate An archaic term of *institutional* origin classifying individuals with *severe mental retardation* (in contrast to those with less severe retardation, who were classified as *"high grade"*).

low-incidence disability A classification of *impairments* that are few in number in relation to other *disabilities* of the general population (e.g., those involving vision, hearing, or bone structure). Also known as **low-incidence handicap**; however, low-incidence disability is the preferred term.

low-vision aid Equipment designed to improve an individual's sight, usually through magnification. Used by individuals who may be classed as *blind* but who have enough *residual vision* to be able to see better by using these devices.

LRE See *least restrictive environment*.

LSS See *local school system*.

lupus erythematosis (lew'-pus air-ih-them-ah-toe'-sis) A *degenerative, chronic inflammation* of the skin.

M

MA See *mental age*.

macrocephalic (mack-roe-seh-fal'-ik) A term used to describe an abnormally large head. (See also *hydrocephalus*.)

macula (mack'-yuh-luh) The portion of the *retina* that provides the clearest vision.

macular degeneration Deterioration of the portion of the *retina* responsible for detailed vision. Results in a progressive loss of central vision; however, the individual retains *peripheral vision*.

macular pathology Diseases or *degeneration* of the *macula* of the eye.

Madison Plan A *noncategorical* approach to educating students with mild *disabilities* that employs a specialized *resource room* with three activity centers—Preacademic Area I, emphasizing appropriate behavior; Academic Area II, emphasizing intense academic *remediation* in small groups; and Academic Area III, emphasizing larger group instruction and partial *integration* with nondisabled students. The Madison Plan refers specifically to a school in the Santa Monica, California, school system, at which the program was an extension of an earlier *engineered classroom*. (Same as *Santa Monica Project*.)

mainstreaming (adj., **mainstreamed**) The *concept* of serving students with *disabilities* within the general education program, with the aid of *support services* and personnel, rather than placing the children in *self-contained special classes*. This practice relates to the concept of *least restrictive environment*. It has been most successful when appropriate personnel such as *resource teachers* have been used and when the students have had *mild disabilities*. This term has largely been replaced by the term *inclusion*.

major life activities Areas that are expected to be necessary for learning and surviving in society. Under various definitions and federal laws, an individual with a *disability* is defined as a person expressing substantial limitations in these major life activities. The limitations may involve *impairment* in communication, *mobility, activities of daily living*, and other skills to such an extent that the individual will be entitled to receive those services provided for individuals with sufficient deficiencies.

major work classes A term originating in Cleveland to designate classes for *gifted* students that have operated since the 1920s.

makaton (may'-ka-tahn) A complete communication system for individuals with severe *intellectual disabilities*. It involves a developmentally based core vocabulary taught with signs and/or symbols and is always accompanied by speech. Provides an alternative to *sign language* and other forms of *augmentative communication* for nonoral individuals with a variety of *severe disabilities*.

mal- A prefix meaning abnormal, inadequate, or bad.

maladaptive behavior A person's actions that are considered outside the bounds of the socially accepted standards of the society.

maladjustment A condition of being out of harmony with one's environment and a failure to reach satisfactory compatibility between self-desires and behavior; this condition has a harmful effect on the person, the surrounding society, or both.

malformed (n., **malformation**) Irregular in structure or possessing characteristics of being ill-formed when compared to a standard, acceptable configuration.

malignant Tending or threatening to produce death (often used to denote a cancerous condition). Opposite of *benign*.

malinger (v.) To consciously, willfully, and deliberately feign or exaggerate for personal gain or advantage. **Malingering** is a behavior in which an individual pretends to be ill or unable to do something in order to gain advantages (e.g., he/she pretends to have a *hearing loss* to acquire *disability* payments). An individual who displays such behaviors is called a **malingerer**.

malleus (mal'-ee-us) The largest of the chain of three small bones in the middle ear that conduct vibrations from the *tympanic membrane* to the inner ear. Also called the hammer. The other two bones are the *incus* and the *stapes.*

malocclusion (mal-oh-kloo'-zhun) Faulty *positioning* of the teeth that results in an abnormal overbite or underbite.

mandates (mandatory legislation) Previously referred to state laws requiring school districts to provide services to children with *disabilities.* Since the passage of *PL 94–142,* these laws have become moot, because PL 94–142 and *IDEA* require all states to serve children regardless of the severity of their disability or other considerations.

mania (may'-nee-uh) A mental disorder characterized by extreme *hyperactivity,* disorganized behavior, and restlessness.

manic-depressive psychosis A serious mental disorder characterized by behavior alternating between excessive activity *(mania)* and *depression.* Current preferred term is *bipolar disorder.*

manneristic behaviors A behavior pattern, such as swaying the body back and forth or moving the head from side to side, that is a characteristic motion of *blind* persons. Such behavior patterns are interpreted to be acts of involuntary *self-stimulatory behavior* resulting from a lack of meaningful activity. Formerly called *blindisms,* the terminology is changing to *stereotypic behavior* or manneristic behavior because the *symptoms* are also observed in children with *emotional disturbance, brain injury,* and *retardation.*

manual alphabet (finger alphabet) A communication system used by *deaf* persons in which letters are indicated through a variety of positions of the fingers. One type requires both hands to form the letters, but the single-hand alphabet is most common. (See also *fingerspelling.*)

manual method (manualism) A system of communication for *deaf* persons in which *fingerspelling, sign language,* or both are used in place of speech.

Manually Coded English (MCE) A communication system for *deaf* persons in which signing is done on a syllable-by-syllable basis. It differs from *fingerspelling* because syllables and not individual letters are signed, but both systems are similar in terms of the time required.

marasmus (mah-raz'-muss) A form of malnutrition usually occurring during infancy and early childhood. It results in growth *retardation* and progressive wasting away of fatty tissues and muscles. Also called *infantile atrophy.*

masking (v., **mask**) 1. The transmission of white noise (sounds of average amplitude across all audible *frequencies*) into one ear while the other ear is being tested; used to prevent the stronger ear from receiving sound vibrations from the test sound through *bone conduction* and thereby interfering with the test results. 2. In *amblyopia,* one eye controls the sight, resulting in the other eye, whose sight it masks, being a *lazy eye.*

mastoid bone The portion of the temporal bone of the skull that extends behind the ear. *Bone conduction hearing aids* are shaped to fit behind the ear against the mastoid bone. Removal of this bone is termed a **mastoidectomy.**

mastoiditis (mass-toid-ite'-iss) *Inflammation* of the mastoid process of the temporal bone. This condition is painful and may interfere with hearing.

maturational lag A slowness of development that may affect growth, *intelligence,* or emotional independence.

maximum benefit Although federal law requires only a *reasonable expectation of benefit* from instruction as a test of the *concept* of *least restrictive environment*, some states require that the additional services and supports required to maximize the child's potential to benefit from instruction be afforded. In such states, the higher standard prevails.

MBD See *minimal brain dysfunction.*

MCE See *Manually Coded English.*

MCT See *minimum competency testing.*

MD See *muscular dystrophy.*

mean The arithmetic average; the sum of all the scores divided by the number of scores.

measles See *German measles* or *rubeola.*

mediated learning experience (MLE) A theory from R. Feuerstein that seeks to explain how children learn *cognitively.* In addition to the ordinary direct learning, Feuerstein postulated that mediating agents such as parents, siblings, and teachers frame, filter, or select the material, sequence, and other factors to promote learning. This theory is especially pertinent to individuals with *mental retardation* and *learning disabilities.*

mediation 1. The process through which parents and school districts attempt to agree mutually on solutions to their differences in regard to the identification, *evaluation*, placement, and provision of *free appropriate public education* for *exceptional children.* Usually facilitated by a professional **mediator.** 2. A strategy of attaching a verbal label to information to be learned to facilitate its recall. Even the use of music can serve as a mediator to assist learning and its recall.

medical services Those services provided by a licensed physician for other than *diagnostic* or *evaluative* purposes. Thus, *related services* such as *catheterization*, which can be accomplished by a nurse or other personnel, would not be considered medical services.

medically fragile Describes individuals who have *chronic* or recurrent physical or psychiatric disorders that require closely available or constantly present *medical services.*

megalomania (meg-ah-loe-may'-nee-ah) A *psychotic* or serious emotional condition characterized by *delusions of grandeur.*

megavitamin therapy A term coined by Linus Pauling in 1968 for the treatment of *behavior* and *learning disorders* with large doses of water-soluble vitamins.

melancholia (mel-an-koe'-lee-uh) (adj., **melancholy**) A *mental illness* in which the patient feels *depressed*, sad, and without hope.

melodic intonation therapy (MIT) A technique used with *aphasic* individuals that requires them to produce vocal sounds at different *pitches* organized into simple melodies in an effort to improve their *language* abilities.

memory One of J. P. Guilford's five thinking *operations* (see *structure of the intellect*); has to do with remembering, mastering facts, and acquiring distinct knowledge.

meninges (men-in'-gees) The three membranes (dura mater, arachnoid, and pia mater) that surround the brain and spinal cord.

meningitis (men-in-jite'-iss) *Inflammation* of the membranes that surround the brain and spinal cord.

meningocele (meh-nin'-juh-seel) A sac-like membranous pouch that protrudes through an abnormal opening in the skull or spinal column. The sac contains *cerebrospinal fluid* but no spinal nerves. (See also *spina bifida* and *neural tube defect.*)

meningomyelocele (meh-nin-juh-my'-loe-seel) A *meningocele* pouch, as in craniobifida and *spina bifida*, that contains spinal nerves. (See also *meningocele*.)

mental age (MA) The level of an individual's mental ability expressed in terms of the average *chronological age* of others answering the same number of items correctly on a test of mental ability. As an example, a child who has a mental ability equal to that of the average 10-year-old would have a mental age of 10 years, regardless of his/her actual chronological age.

mental deficiency A term that has been replaced by *mental retardation*. Traditionally, the term was related more to the lower levels of functioning than to the full *range* of functioning the term mental retardation covers today; referred mainly to individuals with demonstrable *organic* involvement.

mental health A state of mind representing wholesomeness or *adequacy* of adjustment.

mental hygiene The fostering of healthy emotional attitudes, habits of thinking, and environmental conditions that help individuals resist personality *maladjustment* or *mental illness*.

mental illness A condition that results in *deviant* thoughts, feelings, and behaviors to a degree that causes difficulty in adjusting to life.

mental retardation (adj., **mentally retarded**) **(MR)** A broadly used term that refers to significantly subaverage general *intellectual* functioning that becomes evident during the *developmental period* and exists concurrently with *impairment* in *adaptive behavior*. Most of the time, the term indicates a person having an *IQ* of 70 or less and showing impairment in adaptation or social ability. The 1992 AAMR definition emphasizes impairment in several life skills and places less emphasis on IQ.

mental retardation (American Association on Mental Retardation [AAMR] 1992 classification) Refers to substantial limitations in present functioning. According to this definition, individuals with mental retardation are characterized by significantly subaverage *intellectual* functioning existing concurrently with related limitations in two or more adaptive skill areas. It is hard to predict the impact of this definition. It requires clinicians to measure *adaptive behavior* in 10 areas; if the individual falls below the sixth *percentile* in at least 2 of the areas, that person can be considered to have *mental retardation*. The 10 areas are similar to the life skills areas of competence, including communications, feeding, and employment. The definition is adult oriented and will not provide good guidance to clinicians classifying young children. The 1992 definition also discontinued the use of mild/moderate/severe/profound, replacing those terms with intermittent/limited/extensive/pervasive.

mental retardation service centers Term that has largely replaced "training centers for the *retarded*" and "developmental training centers."

mentor Refers to an experienced teacher who serves as a model or *consultant* for a beginning teacher or to someone who serves as a professional role model for a *gifted* student.

mentorship An instructional approach that involves assigning a *gifted* student to a community member who serves as a trusted guide, educator, or counselor.

mesomorphic (mess-oh-more'-fik) One of the three classifications of body types (*somatotypes*); refers to a body of medium stature with a predominance of muscle and bone—usually considered an athletic body build.

metabolic (meh-tuh-bah'-lik) **disorder** Any condition or disease related to a *dysfunction* in the chemical processes and activities of the body.

metabolism (meh-tab'-oh-lizm) The sum of all the continuous physical and chemical processes by which living cells and tissues undergo the changes necessary for the maintenance of life.

metacognition (adj., **metacognitive**) Involves understanding and controlling one's thinking and learning process; often considered of great importance in teaching children with *learning disorders*.

metalinguistic skills The ability to reflect on *language* or to use language to talk about language. Thus, metalinguistic skills pertain to the mental ability to understand the use of language and to derive meaning from language.

metamemory Refers to one's knowledge of how he/she remembers things best. The *concept* was first applied in the 1980s to children with *mental retardation* and *learning disabilities*; they were instructed to think about when and how they had been able to remember information like that which they were currently trying to learn.

MI An abbreviation for mild *disabilities* or *mild mental retardation* commonly used in *local school systems*. Another similar term is MIMH for "mildly mentally *handicapped*."

microcephalus (my-crow-sef'-uh-lus); (n., **microcephaly**) (-lee) A condition in which the head and brain size are small because of an inherited defect, which also causes *severe mental retardation*.

micturate (mik'-chew-rate) To urinate.

MID See *mild intellectual disability*.

midline The middle of the body or the center of gravity. Individuals with *neurological* problems or *brain injury* may have difficulty crossing a side of their body over the midline in their activities.

migraine A complex of *symptoms* characterized by periodic attacks of headaches of severe *intensity* often accompanied by irritability, nausea, and vomiting.

migrant children Youngsters in families who move periodically seeking seasonal employment; as a result, the family does not establish a permanent residence, and the children do not remain in school for a complete term. The lack of a consistent school program may inhibit the development of these children to the extent that they function below their ability levels.

mild handicap A term that was applied to individuals with the least severe learning and behavior problems and who typically were educated in general education programs. Usually, those with *learning disabilities*, *behavior disorders*, and/or *mild mental retardation* were included in this category. (See also *learning handicapped*, *interrelated*.) The preferred terminology is now mild *disability* or mildly *disabled*.

mild hearing loss An *impairment* demonstrated by difficulty in hearing faint sounds. Individuals with mild hearing losses need favorable seating arrangements and may benefit from *speech reading* and vocabulary and *language* instruction.

mild intellectual disability (MID) Equivalent to *mild mental retardation*.

mild learning disorder Usually refers to individuals with *intellectual* functioning one to two *standard deviations* below the *mean*. These individuals function above those with *mild mental retardation*. Historically, they were called *slow learners*.

mild mental retardation (adj., **mildly retarded**) A term introduced by the American Association on Mental Retardation that referred to a level of *intellectual* functioning comparable to the educational classification of *educable mental retardation*. The intellectual level of individuals with mild mental retardation, *assessed* with an individual *intelligence* test, involves *IQ* scores ranging from 55 to 70. In the association's 1992 definition, the term was changed to *intermittent mental retardation*.

milieu (meel-you') A social setting or environment, and the effects of this environment on one's behavior. Synonymous with *ecosystem*. **Milieu therapy** is a treatment approach based on consideration of the total environment in which the client functions; has many commonalities with *ecosystem* approaches.

Mills v. Board of Education A *class action* court case brought on behalf of seven students with *multiple disabilities* against the Washington, DC, Board of Education; resulted in a judgment that children cannot be denied a publicly supported education merely because of their *disabilities*.

minimal brain dysfunction (MBD) Refers to the presence of *learning* or *behavior disorders* in individuals of near average, average, or above average *intelligence* that result from *diagnosed* or suspected deviations in functions of the *central nervous system*. The preferred term is *learning disability*.

minimum competency testing (MCT) A movement, which started in the late 1970s and continues in the 1990s, in which school systems set expectancies or test score requirements for the promotion of students to the next grade or for graduation. The testing program itself is often simply called MCT. The intent is to ensure that students attain a certain skill level by the time of their graduation rather than merely being "passed upward." The *concept* has been particularly controversial in its implications for students with *disabilities*.

minority group A subgroup of the population whose characteristics differ considerably from the *norm*. Because minority groups have a smaller number of members than belong to the majority, they lack authority or the power to decree action as a group.

mirror reading An *impairment* in which images of words are thought to be seen in reverse, as in a mirror, and are read from right to left, which may create substantial reading problems.

mirror writing A distorted *perception* that causes one to write from right to left, so that what is written becomes legible when read from the reflection in a mirror. This is not uncommon among young children, who tend to "outgrow" it.

misting A mild form of *aversive stimuli*, in which a hand-held sprayer is used to spray water into the faces of children who are hand biting, head banging, rocking, etc.

MIT See *melodic intonation therapy*.

mixed cerebral palsy A combined form of *cerebral palsy* (e.g., *spastic-athetoid cerebral palsy*). Mixed cerebral palsy represents a large portion of the cases of this *disability*.

mixed dominance A condition in which neither side of the body is consistently used (e.g., a person may favor use of the left hand and of the right foot). This condition is slightly more evident among individuals with *learning disabilities*.

mixed hearing loss A type of *hearing impairment* in which both *conductive* and *sensorineural hearing loss* are present.

mixed laterality Confusion of sidedness of the body.

MLE See *mediated learning experience.*

mnemonic (neh-mahn'-ik) A strategy or technique to aid *memory.* The individual makes up a jingle or the like to facilitate recall. In medical school, for example, students use the mnemonic "*On old Olympus's towering top a Fin...*" to help them remember the twelve *cranial* nerves (which begin with the letters OOOTTAFAJUSH). Mnemonic techniques can help children with learning problems learn material for tests, enabling them to remember larger amounts of information than they normally would.

MO An abbreviation used by many *local school systems* to refer to *moderate mental retardation.* Some teachers use MOMH as an equivalent term.

mobility The process of moving about safely and effectively within the environment. It is an especially important ability for *blind* persons, who must coordinate mental *orientation* and physical locomotion to achieve safe, effective movement. They may use **mobility aids** such as canes, *guide dogs, sighted guides,* or electronic devices to help them move about.

mobility specialist An instructor in the art of *orientation* and *mobility* skills. (See also *peripatology.*)

mobility training Special instruction of *blind* individuals in the ability to move about safely and effectively from one place to another. Mobility training involves a wide variety of specific techniques according to the needs of the students, including *orientation*, foot travel, moving in traffic, crossing streets, accepting human assistance, using a cane,

making use of the senses in getting about, and, in some instances, the use of *guide dogs.*

modality 1. The form or application of a treatment. 2. A channel of learning (e.g., *visual* modality). 3. Specific treatment used in *physical therapy.*

modeling A teaching technique in which the teacher performs a desired behavior and encourages the pupil to try the same behavior, using the teacher's demonstrated behavior as an example.

modem Computer terminology indicating the telephone connection or connection equipment that allows one type of computer to be connected with another or with auxiliary equipment.

moderate hearing loss A deficiency in the ability to hear in which one can understand conversational speech at up to 3–5 feet but probably needs a *hearing aid, auditory training, speech reading* instruction, favorable seating, and/or *speech therapy.* Described generally as a 40–55 *db* loss.

moderate mental retardation (adj., **moderately retarded**) A term introduced by the American Association on Mental Retardation to refer to a level of *intelligence* comparable to the educational classification of *trainable mental retardation.* The *intellectual* level of individuals with moderate mental retardation, *assessed* with an individual intelligence test, involves *IQ* scores ranging from 40 to 55. In the association's 1992 definition, the term was changed to *limited mental retardation.*

moderate training residence Terminology that has emerged to replace the term *group home.* It represents the same *concepts* but removes the negative association attached to the earlier *label.*

mon- or **mono-** Prefix meaning one or single.

monaural amplification Magnification of sound in one ear through the use of a *hearing aid.*

mongolism See *Down syndrome*, the preferred term.

monitoring 1. A requirement of *PL 94–142* and *IDEA* that all school systems receiving federal funds under that act must undergo a thorough external *evaluation*. 2. In general, the function that involves checking a program in process to determine its effectiveness.

mononucleosis (mah-noe-new-klee-oh'-sis) See *infectious mononucleosis.*

monoplegia (mon-oh-plee'-juh) *Paralysis* of one limb only.

monozygotic (mah-noe-zie-gah'-tik) Describes twins resulting from the splitting of a single fertilized egg, and therefore identical in *genetic* composition and appearance. These twins are referred to as identical rather than fraternal.

Montessori (mahnt-eh-soar'-ee) **method** An instructional format developed by Maria Montessori, an Italian *psychiatrist*, which emphasizes individual instruction using extensive *sensory* and *motor* training, early development of reading and writing skills, and much free physical activity. The method originally was intended for preschool and primary levels but in some situations has been used at other levels.

Moro reflex The response of an infant to a loud, sharp noise or to being dropped gently on his/her back; characterized by the infant fanning out his/her arms and crying. The Moro reflex is commonly referred to as the *startle response* because the behavior is characteristic of what happens when a person is startled.

morpheme (more'-feem) Any sound or group of sounds that has *linguistic* meaning and cannot be further reduced and still retain meaning. The smallest unit of meaningful *language.*

morphology (more-fahl'-oh-jee) 1. In *language development*, the structural level at which meaningful units are created from sounds. 2. The study of word formation.

mosaicism (moe-zay'-ih-siz-im) A form of *Down syndrome* named for its unusual *chromosome* pattern, in which not all cells have an abnormal *chromosomal* composition.

motivation The *incentive*, force, or thought that makes one act to satisfy needs or achieve goals.

motokinesthetic (mo-to-kin-es-thet'-ic) **method** A technique used in *speech pathology* in which the *speech clinician* directs the movement of the production of speech sounds by placing his/her hands on the *articulatory* mechanism of the client and also employing the client's sense of feeling on the speech mechanism.

motor Refers to the movement of body muscles. In the education field, the motor function is often differentiated into *fine motor* and *gross motor skills.*

motor aphasia (ah-fay'-zee-ah) Inability to speak because of a lack of physical coordination to form words. In many cases, the individual may know the words and can communicate by pointing and by gestures. (See also *expressive aphasia* and *apraxia.*)

motor disinhibition A form of *distractibility* in which one is unable to resist responding to any *stimulus* that produces a physical activity. Thus, any object that can be pushed, pulled, twisted, poked, traced, bent, folded, or mutilated likely will elicit a response.

motor skills Any acts requiring the ability to control and direct the voluntary muscles of the body. Usually classified as *fine motor* or *gross motor* skills.

mouthstick A device that individuals with severe *physical disabilities* hold in the mouth to activate electric typewriters, microcomputer keyboards, and *autotelic* devices.

movement therapy A technique often applied in *special education* in which children practice body actions within space to improve body knowledge and *orientation*.

movigenics An approach to the learning process and *curriculum* based on theories proposed by Raymond H. Barsch in 1967 and 1968; involves much *perceptual-motor* activity and considers *perception*, movement, and *language* as a dynamic triad for curriculum implementation.

MR See *mental retardation*.

MS See *multiple sclerosis*.

M-team See *multidisciplinary team*.

multi- Prefix meaning many.

multidisciplinary Involving members of several professions who are involved in or contribute to a common *objective*, such as a *screening committee* consisting of a special educator, a medical doctor, a *psychologist*, a *social worker*, and a school administrator. Similar to *interdisciplinary*.

multidisciplinary team (M-team) A group involving members from a variety of *disciplines* who pool their expertise toward making a decision, such as in a *prereferral screening* process.

multifactored testing A term popularized by *PL 94–142* that means *assessment* using a variety of instruments; such testing is conducted to avoid arriving at a *diagnosis* of *mental retardation* or other *disability* based on only one score.

multihandicapped Having a *physical* or *sensory disability* plus one or more additional disabilities that inhibit learning. Special services usually are required. The term *multiple disability* is now preferred over multihandicapped.

multimodal The use of a number of senses at the same time. Similar to *multisensory*.

multiple disability Preferred term for having a *physical* or *sensory disability* plus one or more additional disabilities that inhibit learning, usually requiring special services. The term *multihandicapped* was previously used.

multiple sclerosis (skler-oh'-sis) **(MS)** A disease of progressive deterioration in which the protective *myelin* sheath surrounding the nerves *degenerates* and causes failure in the body's *neurological* system. MS appears most often in individuals between the ages of 20 and 40.

multiply handicapped See *multiple disability*.

multisensory A term generally applied to training procedures that simultaneously utilize more than one sense *modality*. Multisensory learning results from two or more sense modalities being employed as the means for instruction.

muscular dystrophy (MD) A *hereditary* disorder that causes a loss of vitality and progressive deterioration of the body as a result of *atrophy*, or the replacement of muscle tissue with fatty tissue.

music therapy The scientific application of music to accomplish treatment aims; the use of music by a *therapist* to influence changes in behavior.

mutation (mew-tay'-shun) An unexpected difference that occurs in a specific characteristic of certain offspring; results from a modification in the determining *genetic* structure. An offspring that has undergone mutation is called a **mutant**.

mute One who cannot speak. **Mutism** is the inability to speak or, sometimes, the refusal to speak.

myasthenia gravis (my-uhs-thee'-nee-uh grav'-iss) A *syndrome* of fatigue and exhaustion of the muscular system marked by progressive *paralysis* of muscles without *sensory* disturbance or *atrophy*. At times, for no apparent reason, myasthenia gravis goes into *remission*.

myelin A soft, white, fatty-like substance that forms a protective sheath around certain nerve fibers. *Degeneration* of this myelin sheath is associated with *multiple sclerosis*.

myelomeningocele (my-eh-loe-meh-nin'-goe-seel) See *meningomyelocele*.

myoclonic seizure An *epileptic* activity characterized by jerking of the arms and bending of the trunk of the body, which may result in falling.

myopathy (my-op'-ah-thee) Any disease of a muscle characterized by weakness and deterioration without *neurological impairment*.

myopia (my-oh'-pea-ah) **(nearsightedness)** A condition in which one's distance vision is poor, usually due to the eyeball being lengthened in diameter from front to back so that the image comes in *focus* at a point in front of the *retina*. Myopia usually is corrected by using *concave lenses*. In contrast, see *hyperopia*.

myositis (mie-oh-sigh'-tiss) A *chronic* crippling condition resulting from *inflammation* of the muscles.

myotonic dystrophy (mie-oh-tahn'-ik dis'-troe-fee) A type of *muscular dystrophy* characterized by weakness of the fingers, hands, forearms, feet, and lower limbs; does not affect the facial muscles. Also known as *Steinut's disease*, it usually appears in early adulthood.

myxedema (mik-seh-dee'-muh) A skin condition, caused by a deficiency in *thyroid* function, that is marked by dryness and swelling of the affected surfaces.

N

narcolepsy (nar'-coe-lep-see) A condition in which an individual experiences brief involuntary episodes of deep sleep at irregular times; the person has an uncontrollable desire to sleep.

narcotic Any drug or agent that produces insensitivity or *stupor*.

nasal (n., **nasality**) Refers to a voice quality of excessive, unique *resonance* that can be described as "speaking through the nose," as in *cleft palate* speech.

nasopharynx (nay-zoe-fair'-inks) The part of the throat above the level of the base of the *uvula*, or the place at which the nose and throat connect.

natal (nate'-uhl) Pertaining to birth, at the time of birth. A frame of reference, as in *prenatal*, *postnatal*, *perinatal*.

natural environment 1. Refers to the use of community, domestic, social, leisure, and vocational settings for the instruction of individuals with *severe disabilities*, as opposed to most teaching environments, which are referred to as *artificial environments*. 2. In preschool and other programming, refers to the environment in which a specific child would usually be enrolled. Thus, any placement that differs from a general preschool or kindergarten would be viewed as an artificial environment.

near-point vision The ability to see at close *range* (usually, normal reading distance).

nearsighted(ness) See *myopia*.

necrosis (neh-crow'-sis) The death of body tissues, as from loss of blood supply, burns, or cessation of breathing.

need achievement A *concept* advanced to explain the variance among individuals in their levels of need to achieve or in their *motivation* to achieve.

negative eugenics (you-jen'-iks) Any program designed to improve the quality of the human race by limiting the reproduction of inferior members of society. The sterilization of persons with *mental retardation* would be one example.

negative reinforcement A *stimulus* that, when removed as a consequence of a response, results in an increase or maintenance of that response.

neglect Failure to act in a way that would reduce or prevent damage whose potential is commonly accepted (for example, the failure to feed a child is commonly recognized to result in starvation if continued for prolonged periods).

negligence The legal *tort* for which teachers are most often charged. To prove negligence, the *defendant* must have a duty to protect, the *plaintiff* must have suffered actual harm, and a sequential connection must be shown between the teacher's conduct and the harm.

neighborhood school The school nearest the student's home; the student would not have to be transported past other schools to attend this school. Also known as *home school*. The *concept* of educating all children in the nearest school with the supports they need is considered an integral part of the practice of *inclusion*.

Nemeth code Originated as a *braille*-based system for teaching and doing mathematical computations. Used by *blind* persons and applied in such areas as science, calculus, and physics.

neo- A prefix meaning new.

neoinstitutionalism A term used in the 1990s to characterize *group homes*, hostels, and supportive living arrangements for individuals with *disabilities*. Although these facilities are not large and isolated as were the *institutions*, the term implies that even small facilities may have some collective disadvantages and maintain individuals with *disabilities* in a dependent role.

neonatal (nee-oh-nate'-uhl) Pertaining to the first month after birth.

neonatologist (nee-oh-nah-tahl'-oh-jist) A specialist in *pediatrics* especially trained to care for the newborn.

nephritis (ne-frye'-tiss) *Acute* or *chronic inflammation* of the kidneys. Same as *Bright's disease*.

nephrosis (ne-froe'-siss) A noninflammatory disease of the kidneys marked by the escape of protein from the blood into the urine, bringing about a reduction of proteins in the body, and by an increase of fatty substances in the blood. The resulting imbalance in body functions may result in serious illness and, if not treated, in severe deterioration of the kidneys.

nerve deafness (neural loss) A form of *hearing impairment* resulting from a defect in the nerve structure of the inner ear or in the *auditory nerve*. High-*frequency* sounds are the most likely to be affected. The condition rarely can be improved by medical treatment. Also referred to as *sensorineural (sensory-neural) hearing loss*.

neura- or **neuro-** Prefix meaning pertaining to the nerves.

neural tube defect Refers to any of the birth defects in which the spine or *cranium* has an abnormal opening (e.g., *spina bifida*). Detected in utero through *alpha-fetoprotein* screening and *ultra-sonography*. (See also *spina bifida*.)

neurasthenia (nur-ass-thee'-nee-uh) A *syndrome* that includes tiredness, headache, dizziness, upset stomach, loss of appetite, and pain in the chest or stomach. Although no *organic* cause has been *diagnosed* for the *symptoms*, they are real to the person, producing mental and physical fatigue and disrupting normal living and adjustment. A form of *psychoneurosis*.

neurobiological brain disorder A term proposed in legislation to replace *attention deficit disorder*. Term adds nothing new except to point out the presumed origin of the condition as *neurological* and/or biological. See also *attention deficit disorder* and *attention deficit hyperactivity disorder*.

neurological impress method An approach to teaching reading in which the teacher reads a selection and the student "shadows" the selection by repeating what the teacher has read. The selection is read and reread until the student assumes a more dominant role. At that point the teacher begins to soften his/her voice.

neurological "soft" signs Diagnostic characteristics that are not as readily linked to *brain injury* as are such *symptoms* as *seizures*, but instead are more subtle and may be reflected in psychological and *perceptual* tests. Examples are coordination problems and awkward gait.

neurologically impaired Pertaining to individuals with any of a number of conditions resulting from injury to or *malformation* of the *central nervous system*. Conditions such as *cerebral palsy*, *epilepsy*, and the *Strauss syndrome* are examples.

neurologist A medical doctor who has special training in the *diagnosis* and treatment of diseases of the nervous system. Such doctors practice **neurology**.

neurophrenia (nur-oh-free'-nee-uh) A term first used in 1951 by Edgar Doll in referring to conditions now called *learning disorders* or *learning disabilities*.

neurosis (adj., **neurotic**) A term applied to mental/ *emotional disorders* with a variety of characteristics including *anxiety*, *hysterical* behavior, unusual mannerisms, *phobias*, and obsessions; usually not serious enough to require hospitalization. No *organic* basis is found in most cases.

neurotogenic (nur-ah-toe-jen'-ik) Contributing to the onset of a *neurosis*.

Nieman-Pick disease A *metabolic disorder* characterized by enlargement of the liver and spleen; often results in *mental retardation*, *deafness*, and *visual* problems.

night blindness See *nyctolopia*.

non- A prefix meaning not, absence of, reverse of.

nonambulatory Unable to walk or move about independently; may be bedridden or in a wheelchair.

noncategorical Refers to programs or philosophies that do not *label* or differentiate among the various *disabilities* in providing services. (See *interrelated*.)

nondevelopmental approach With regard to *language* instruction, a *concept* holding that individuals with *mental retardation* do not learn language in the same way that average children do. Because their language is assumed to be *deviant*, not merely delayed, little emphasis is placed in language instruction on developmental sequences. Instead, the training emphasizes language forms and skills that are perceived to be most useful to the child for interaction with and control of the environment. This approach is used with those who have *severe disabilities* and involves imitation and *reinforcement* techniques to establish the desired responses. For comparison, see *developmental approach.*

nondirective therapy (approach) A counseling method that is client-centered and emphasizes client selection of solutions. The *therapist* serves as a catalyst but refrains from directing or *evaluating* the *therapy.*

nondiscriminatory testing The administering of measures that are not prejudicial against *minority groups* or individuals. Such testing has been a provision of certain court decisions for cases brought because higher percentages of minority than majority children had been placed in *special classes.* In these decisions the courts ruled that children must be tested in their primary *language* and that *psychologists* must develop *assessment* procedures that do not discriminate against minorities. Further, according to these decisions, the *evaluations* must be comprehensive, using instruments that *accommodate* culture, *language*, and adaptive factors as much as possible.

nondisjunction The incomplete splitting of *chromosome* pairs, resulting in a cell with more than the normal amount of *chromosome* material; often identified with certain forms of *mental retardation* (e.g., *Down syndrome*).

nonfluency Deviations in the normal rhythmical patterns of speech.

nongraded class A group of students in which each pupil is functioning at his/her individual performance level without regard to *grade level*, and each is allowed to progress at his/her own rate of individual achievement.

nonjudgmental Describes an attitude and the resulting behavior on the part of personnel who show neutrality toward pupils or clients and indicate neither approval nor disapproval of their behaviors or attitudes. Being nonjudgmental

is considered an essential quality, especially for counselors.

nonoral communication Denotes the use of a system of pictorial symbols rather than *vocalizations* as a form of *language* interaction, particularly by *nonverbal* persons with *severe disabilities.*

nonverbal Not speaking, as in a child who for any of a number of reasons has failed to develop verbal *language.* A nonverbal child may have some other language abilities.

nonverbal test A measure that does not require the use of words in *stimulus* items or responses to them (e.g., tests that require only pointing or *motor* responses).

norm 1. An average or typical group score against which individual scores can be compared. 2. An acceptable pattern or standard in society.

normalization A *concept* derived from Scandinavia and introduced in the United States in the 1960s in which persons with *disabilities* are treated and placed in situations that are as nearly like those of nondisabled people as possible. Thus, rather than living in a large *institution*, individuals with *mental retardation* may live in a *group home*, work in the community during the day, and participate in community recreation at night.

norm-referenced testing (tests) Testing that compares an individual's performance to that of a group, in contrast to *criterion-referenced tests*, designed to measure an individual's mastery of specific content.

numeration Arithmetic *concepts* including rote counting, one-to-one correspondence, sets, symbol identification, cardinal numbers, or place value.

nyctolopia (nik-toe-loe'-pea-ah) A condition in which a person sees poorly in the dark but can see well in the light. Commonly called *night blindness.*

nystagmus (nis-tag'-muhs) Continuous, involuntary movement of the eyeball that occurs in both eyes and is associated with *visual impairment.*

O

objective Statement of a specific learning goal for a student. Objectives should be developed from *assessed* student needs and be the basis for the learning activities carried out in attempting to meet them.

objective test An instrument designed so that the correct responses are agreed upon and set in advance by the test developer(s); the scores, therefore, are unaffected by the opinion or judgment of the scorer. (See also *norm-referenced testing.*)

observational training Essentially the same as *behavior modeling.*

obsessive-compulsive Describes a *neurosis* in which an individual seems compelled to repeat certain acts or *verbalizations* over and over.

obstacle perception An ability developed by *blind* persons in which they can sense when they are approaching an object. Certain research conducted with adult blind people has indicated that the ability to hear high-*frequency* sound waves and their echoes is responsible for obstacle perception.

obstetrician (ahb-steh-trish'-un) A medical doctor specializing in treatment during pregnancy and childbirth.

obstetrics (ahb-steh'-tricks) The branch of medicine dealing with treatment during pregnancy and childbirth.

obturator (ahb'-tyew-ray-tore) A device, usually constructed of plastic or Dacron, used to close an opening at the top of the mouth (as in *cleft palate*) to improve *articulation* of speech and/or reduce *nasality.*

occipital (ahk-sip'-ih-tuhl) Referring to the bone that forms the back part of the skull.

occipital alpha training A *biofeedback* technique used for improving *visual attention* in some individuals with *disabilities.* Because alpha waves appear to measure visual attention, this technique can reveal whether individuals are really paying attention and can teach them an awareness of what *attending* is.

occluder (uh-klood'-er) An opaque or translucent device placed in front of an eye to block vision from that eye. Used in vision exams when *visually* testing each eye separately or prescribed to correct specific *visual* defects.

occlusion Obstruction of a passage. Refers to an obstruction of the breath stream during the process of speaking or to the fit of the teeth when the jaws are closed. (See also *malocclusion.*)

occupational therapist A graduate of an *occupational therapy* program who is approved by the Council on Medical Education of the American Medical Association, or an individual who has the equivalent of such education and training. Utilizes *creative*, educational, and recreational activities to promote *rehabilitation.*

occupational therapy (OT) A *rehabilitative* process directed by *occupational therapists* in which clients are instructed in purposeful activities as a basis for improving their muscular control; sometimes referred to as "curing by doing." Physical and mental recovery is the main *objective*, with additional emphasis on helping the individual acquire job or *self-help skills.*

OCR See *Office for Civil Rights.*

ocular (ock'-you-lar) Pertaining to the eyes.

ocular control training Exercises of the eye muscles for the purpose of improving *eye coordination* and vision. (See also *orthoptist*.)

ocular dominance The consistent use of one eye in preference to the other in situations such as sighting, in which fixation is involved.

ocular pursuit Movement of the eyes to *visually* follow a moving target. (See also *visual tracking*.)

ocularist (ock-you-lair'-ist) A medical doctor who specializes in treatment and replacement of the eye with artificial parts.

oculist A medical doctor whose practice deals with the *diagnosis* and treatment of *visual* conditions. The oculist may perform surgery, prescribe drugs, measure *refraction*, and prescribe corrective lenses.

offender rehabilitation The preferred terminology for the area of government charged with the housing and supervision of criminals. This term reflects the change from *custodial* care to training and *rehabilitation* for persons with prison sentences. (See also *probation*.)

Office for Civil Rights (OCR) The federal office responsible for *monitoring* civil rights violations, especially under *Section 504* and under the Americans with Disabilities Act.

Office of Special Education and Rehabilitative Services (OSERS) The division of the U.S. Office of Education that contains most federal *special education* and *rehabilitation* programs.

Office of Special Education Programs (OSEP) The federal office involved with the education of students with *disabilities*. It is a division of the *Office of Special Education and Rehabilitative Services (OSERS)* of the U.S. Department of Education. OSEP was formerly known as the *Bureau of Education for the Handicapped*.

OHI See *other health impaired*.

OJT See *on-the-job training*.

olfactory (ahl-fack'-tor-ee) Pertaining to the sense of smell.

oligophrenia (ah-lig-oh-fre'-nee-ah) A term meaning *mental retardation* or deficiency; used primarily in Europe, usually in a medical *context*.

ombudsman (om'-budz-man) One who investigates complaints for the purpose of achieving more equal treatment or *settlements* for *disabled* individuals.

omission (in speech) An *articulatory defect* in which a sound is left out. Often characteristic of *delayed speech* or speech of individuals who have *severe mental retardation*. Examples are "cu" for cup; "kni" for knife; "acuum" for vacuum.

on remand A reference in a citation to a case that indicates that a lower court entered a judgment, for at least a second time, when it received the case from a higher court with a judgment and order to act in a particular way (e.g., the court's initial judgment is appealed, the appeals court enters a judgment to reverse in part and affirm in part and directs the lower court to change its original order; the lower court does so when the case is "on remand" to it from the higher court).

on-the-job training (OJT) A method of teaching high-school-level students specific work skills by assigning them to employment in competitive jobs for partial days or sometimes for full days. If they are assigned for partial days, the remainder of the day is spent in school; if they are in on-the-job training for a number of full days, this employment period is followed by a period of full-time school attendance. Also referred to as a *work-study program* or community work station.

open campus A school or program usually conducted at night in which individuals not usually enrolled in high school or who work can attain their high school degree or prepare for an occupation. (A newer term is *alternative schools*.)

open court method A *basal* reading program that encompasses a strong *phonetic element* and *kinesthetic/tactile* elements. This program is different enough from that of most *basal* texts to provide an alternative method.

operant behaviors Actions that are voluntary (as opposed to *respondent behaviors*, which are involuntary or *reflexive*).

operant conditioning An instructional method in which rewards are controlled so that a pupil has a *reinforcing* experience for performing acts that the teacher desires and does not receive rewards for undesired acts. The behaviors that are rewarded tend to be repeated, and the behaviors that are not rewarded tend to disappear. (See also *behavior modification*.)

operant level Refers to the behavior pattern of an individual that occurs naturally, prior to training or modification. One must know the operant level to establish a *baseline*.

operations (of thinking) The category of thinking abilities in J. P. Guilford's model (see *structure of the intellect*) that includes *cognition, memory, convergent thinking, divergent thinking*, and *evaluation*.

ophthalmia (ahf-thal'-mee-uh) An *inflammation* of the *conjunctiva* of the eye, occurring during the first few weeks of a baby's life and caused by infection contracted during birth or from contamination after birth.

ophthalmologist (ahf-thal-mahl'-oh-jist) A medical doctor with specialized training (beyond the medical degree) in working with the eyes. The ophthalmologist may conduct *diagnosis*, prescribe medications, perform surgery, measure *refraction*, and prescribe corrective lenses.

ophthalmoscope (ahf-thal'-moe-skope) An instrument used by a physician to observe and examine the interior of the eye.

optacon (ahp'-tuh-kahn) A device for converting print into *tactual* images for the *visually* impaired. Employs 144 pins that are activated to produce vibratory images that can be "read" by the reader's index finger. An optacon that reads print *aurally* is also available.

optic nerve The *cranial* nerve that carries nerve impulses of sight to the brain.

optician A technician who, upon prescription from a physician or *optometrist*, grinds lenses, fits them into frames, and adjusts the eyeglasses to the wearer.

optometrist A licensed, nonmedical person trained to work with the function of the eyes but not the *pathology* of the eyes. The optometrist measures *refraction*, prescribes eyeglasses, and carries out vision training.

optometry The science of *visual* care that involves examining the eye and measuring it for visual defects caused by errors of *refraction* that may be corrected by lenses without the use of prescribed medication.

oral (adv., **orally**) Pertaining to or surrounding the mouth; especially, done by the mouth, as speech.

oral interpretation Translation for another person without the use of the hands, essentially employing the upper part of the body (face, neck, eyes, etc.).

oral method (oralism) A system of teaching children with *hearing impairments* in which communication is carried out through spoken *language*, *speech reading* (*lip reading*), listening, and writing, without the use of *sign language* or *fingerspelling*.

order center A skill area in the *engineered classroom* that includes materials appropriate for the child to learn and obtain practice in *attention*, sequencing, and similar activities.

organic Describes a condition resulting from disease, damage, or *dysfunction* of a body part (as opposed to a *functional* condition).

organic brain damage Destruction of the brain that results from injury to or abnormal development of the brain.

organic hearing loss An *impairment* caused by damage to or abnormal development of the *auditory* pathway of the ear.

organic therapy A term referring to practices of psychosurgery and to *aversive*, classical, or *operant conditioning*. The use of any drugs, electrical shock, or electrical stimulation of the brain in which unpleasant physical sensations are induced for treatment purposes.

organicity (ore-gan-ih'-sih-tee) Refers to any condition resulting from an *impairment* of the *central nervous system*.

orientation (v., **orient**) With reference to *blind* persons, an individual's sense of determining one's position with relation to the environment or to a particular person, place, or thing by utilizing the remaining senses. Orientation of a blind person depends upon retaining a "mental map" of his/her environment.

orifice A natural external opening of the body, such as the mouth, nose, and ears.

originality A trait, usually evidenced in *gifted* or *creative* individuals, characterized by inventiveness and the ability to develop new, novel plans and actions. One of the factors in creative thinking.

orphan drugs Medications needed for the control of rare diseases but considered nonprofitable by pharmaceutical firms because of the low patient populations.

ortho- A prefix meaning corrective.

orthocarintology (ore-thoe-care-in-tahl'-oh-jee) The practice of repeatedly fitting the eyes with differently curved contact lenses to try to change the shape of the eye and thus improve vision. This practice is done primarily by *optometrists* rather than *ophthalmologists*.

orthodontia (ore-thoe-dahn'-chuh) A dentistry practice dealing with straightening the teeth and jaws to correct problems such as *malocclusion* and faulty alignment; includes fitting of appliances (braces). An **orthodontist** is the person trained to conduct this practice.

orthogenic (ore-thoe-jen'-ik) Pertaining to educational, medical, or surgical treatment directed toward stimulating mental growth, developing desirable personality traits, or correcting mental or nervous defects.

orthomolecular psychiatry The practice of treating *learning* and *behavior disorders* through the administration of massive doses of water-soluble vitamins *(megavitamin therapy)*. Linus Pauling coined the term in 1968 to describe the study of the optimum molecular environment of the mind.

orthopedic (ore-thoe-peed'-ik) Pertaining basically to the bones, joints, and muscles. Orthopedic surgery is performed for the purpose of straightening, restoring, or preserving muscles, bones, or joints, thus correcting body *deformities*. A medical doctor who performs this function is called an **orthopedist**.

orthopedic disability A condition caused by a physical *impairment*, especially one related to the bones, joints, and muscles, and resulting in restricted *mobility* or comfort.

orthopedist See *orthopedic*.

orthopsychiatry The study and treatment of mental disorders based on combined contributions from such *disciplines* as psychiatry, medicine, *psychology*, and sociology.

orthoptist (ore-thahp'-tist) A nonmedical technician who directs and supervises *visual* training involving the exercise of eye muscles to develop *eye coordination* and to correct vision. Such visual training is termed *ocular control training.*

orthosis (ore-thoe'-sis) A device that gives function to a part of the body (e.g., a brace that causes the limbs to have increased *rigidity* so the individual can stand upright). (See also *prosthesis*.)

orthoticist (ore-thah'-tih-sist) A skilled technician who works with an *orthopedist* in designing and fitting braces. The orthoticist must have a working knowledge of metals, materials, fabrics, and shoes to be able to interpret prescriptions into *functional* structures.

orthotics (ore-thah'-tiks) The specialty field involved in making limb braces and other *orthopedic* appliances.

OSEP See *Office of Special Education Programs*.

OSERS See *Office of Special Education and Rehabilitative Services*.

ossicles (ahs'-ih-kulz) The three small bones (*malleus*, *incus*, and *stapes*) of the middle ear that transfer sound waves from the *eardrum* to the oval window, which connects the middle ear to the inner ear.

ossification (v., **ossify**, **ossified**) The process of *cartilaginous* substances hardening to form bone.

osteogenesis imperfecta (ahs-tee-oh-jen'-ih-sis im-per-fek'-tuh) An inherited, rare bone disease resulting in fragile bones.

osteomyelitis (ahs-tee-oh-my-ah-lite'-iss) An infectious condition of the long bones resulting in *inflammation* of the bone marrow.

osteopathy (oss'-tee-oh-path-ee) A treatment system of healing disease that emphasizes normal body mechanics and environmental conditions. Generally accepted physical, medicinal, and surgical methods are used if necessary, along with bone and muscle manipulation. A doctor trained in and practicing osteopathy is called an **osteopath**.

ostomy (ahs'-toe-mee) An operation in which a conduit *(stoma)* is made in the abdominal wall to carry urinary or *fecal* matter out of the body.

ostosclerosis (ahs-toe-skluh-roe'-sis) An inherited condition in which the *stapes* bone in the ear is abnormally attached to the ovalwindow and thus does not properly transform mechanical energy into hearing. Surgery may correct the problem.

OT See *occupational therapy*.

other health impaired (OHI) A term encompassing health conditions typified by *chronic* ill health, low vitality, and progressive deterioration, all of which interfere with a child's educational progress.

otitis media (oh-tight'-iss mee'-dee-ah) One of the most common diseases of early childhood, characterized by fluid and infection in the middle ear. Often results in reduced hearing in children, but is one of the more treatable conditions.

otolaryngology (oat-oh-lair-uhn-gahl'-oh-jee) The branch of medicine dealing with the *diagnosis* and treatment of diseases and conditions of the ear and *larynx*. A physician specializing in this area is called an **otolaryngologist**.

otological Pertaining to the ear.

otology The medical specialty that deals with diseases and problems of the ear. A physician who specializes in this area is called an **otologist**.

-otomy (ah'-toe-mee) A suffix that means cutting or removing (e.g., lobotomy: a surgical operation involving an incision in the *cerebral* lobe).

otoplasty (oat'-oh-plas-tee) The rebuilding and correction of the ear by plastic surgery.

otosclerosis (oat-oh-skler-roe'-sis) A *hereditary* disease affecting the bony capsule that surrounds the inner ear; causes *chronic* and progressive *hearing loss*.

otoscope (oat'-oh-skope) An instrument with a light, designed specifically for examining the ear.

ototoxic (oat-oh-tock'-sick) Describes drugs that can have harmful effects on the organs that control hearing and balance.

outcome-based education The current term for educational programs based on predetermined goals. Instructional activities and *assessments* are designed with these goals in mind.

outdoor education A term that encompasses all learning activities involving performance in the *natural environment* "laboratory"; current terminology has shifted to *leisure life skills*.

outreach worker An individual who has special training in locating, identifying, and collecting information on human problems and in referring individuals with problems to services within their neighborhood settings.

overachiever A pupil who achieves at a level above that predicted from his/her prior performance and testing.

over-age Describes a pupil who is older chronologically than is usual for his/her *functional* level or educational placement.

overattention A characteristic of some individuals in which they fix their *attention* on a particular object and seem unable to break the focus. Often noticed in *autistic* children.

overcompensation A reaction in those who feel a deep-seated sense of inferiority and inadequacy in certain areas, characterized by overinvesting energy in an endeavor at which one can achieve. For example, a short, overweight boy who cannot successfully compete in baseball may learn the names and playing records of every major league player.

overcorrection A procedure used to help a student correct misbehavior; involves having the student practice more appropriate behavior or improving the environment in which the student misbehaves.

overgeneralization The application of a *language* rule without regard for exceptions, such as "goed" for "went."

overlearning Learning that results from additional practice, to the level necessary for immediate recall, after something has been learned. Overlearning helps many individuals with *learning disorders* overcome *short-term memory deficits* and learn academic and other materials to the level that facilitates *long-term memory*.

overloading An inability to handle all the information coming in through all the senses. Learning may be improved if one or more *sensory* modalities is eliminated or masked.

overprotection The sheltering of an individual by another to the extent that the sheltered individual is denied experiences necessary for normal development. This behavior is sometimes shown by parents of students with *disabilities*.

overt Describes an action that can be objectively observed. Opposite of *covert*.

oxycephaly (ok-sih-seh-fah'-lee) A *congenital* condition in which the top of the head is pointed, the eyes are large and widely set, the hands and feet are webbed, and *mental retardation* is typical. Same as *acrocephaly*.

P

pacing An instructional procedure in which the teacher directs a pupil's activities by giving an example or indication of the speed at which the activities are to be achieved; often used in teaching reading. Also applied to the *gifted*, who benefit from rapid pacing.

paired-associate learning A teaching or research technique wherein a *stimulus* and a desired response are presented simultaneously and the learner is *conditioned* to give the desired response when the stimulus is presented by itself. In teaching, one member of the stimulus-response pair is known to the student and is used to facilitate learning the other.

palate The roof of the mouth, consisting of a hard part in the forward portion of the mouth and a soft part in the back of the mouth (hence, *hard palate* and *soft palate*).

palsy A *neurological* condition that causes an individual to be unable to hold affected body parts steady without support; as a result, the condition is accompanied by a shaking or reciprocating action.

pancreas The gland located behind the stomach that produces digestive *enzymes* and *insulin*. *Inflammation* of the pancreas is termed **pancreatitis** (pan-kree-ah-tie'-tiss).

paperless braille A term applied to the Versabrailler and other equipment that electronically records *braille* on an audiotape, which can be read *tactually* when an individual places his/her fingertips on the machine. Some types of more advanced equipment will also produce paper braille tapes.

papillomavirus (pap-pi-lo'-ma-vie-rus) A *virus* that can affect the vocal folds, resulting in excess growth of the folds, *hoarseness*, and difficulty in breathing. The excess growth can be surgically removed. The condition usually does not occur past age 12.

paradoxical reaction A condition that results when a drug or treatment has an effect opposite to the one expected (e.g., a medication given as a sedative produces stimulation and overactivity).

parageusia (pair-ah-gyew'-see-ah) *Impairment* of the sense of taste resulting in the individual experiencing a bad taste in his/her mouth.

paragraphia (pair-ah-graf'-ee-ah) A *language disorder* in which the individual misspells words or writes one word in place of another.

paralalia (pair-ah-lay'-lee-ah) A disturbance in the production of speech, especially one in which the vocal sound produced is different from the desired sound.

parallel curriculum A type of *curriculum* often used for students with *severe disabilities*; the term indicates that the curriculum will not be the same as that offered for general education students but may have elements or subject matter related to the general curriculum. Thus the general education students might be studying division of fractions while students with *severe disabilities* are separating objects into sets.

parallel instruction An educational practice of the 1990s in which students with *severe disabilities* in general education classrooms are offered a *curriculum* or instruction that is tangentially related to, but at a much lower developmental level than, that of the remainder of the class. An example that has been used is when a student with *disability* is exposed to differences in shapes (e.g., diamond versus triangle) while the rest of the class is studying geometry.

parallelism Occurs when a person is *proximal* to a group without being *assimilated* into full membership; primary interaction is observation.

paralysis (adj., **paralytic**; v., **paralyze[d]**) Partial or complete loss of the power of voluntary motion or sensation.

paranoia (pair-ah-noy'-ah) A *chronic* mental disorder in which the affected individual has *delusions of persecution*. Such individuals are said to be **paranoid**.

paraplegia (pair-ah-plee'-juh) (adj. or n., **paraplegic**) *Paralysis* of the lower half of the body, including both legs.

parapro Shortened form of the term *paraprofessional*; often used for a *teacher aide*.

paraprofessional An individual such as a *teacher aide* who performs some of the functions of a professional under the general supervision of a professional but who, because of insufficient training, insufficient experience, or legal reasons, is not allowed total responsibility.

PARC case See *Pennsylvania Association for Retarded Children (PARC) v. Commonwealth of Pennsylvania*.

parens patriae A Latin term that means, literally, "father of the country," and that refers today to the doctrine that a state may act in a paternalistic way on behalf of its citizens, especially children or those who have mental *disabilities* and therefore are less effective than other people in protecting themselves. The parens patriae doctrine justifies, for example, compulsory education, which the state requires of all children for their own good.

parent education Educational programs designed to improve parents' or caregivers' knowledge about child care, disabling conditions, their child's educational program content and goals, family living, and similar topics. (See also *parent training*; *parent involvement*.)

Parent Effectiveness Training (PET) Title of one of the largest and most systematic training programs for parents on the management of children.

parent involvement A term used to describe a wide *range* of programs (e.g., parent counseling, volunteer service, *parent education*, *advocacy* training) in which parents are active participants in planning and the education of their children.

parent training A term used since the 1980s that is equivalent to *parent education*. Parent training programs seek to train parents in skills that will augment and extend that which is taught to their children at school.

parental rejection A reaction in which parents openly repudiate a child, expressing undisguised hostility and *neglect*. Parental rejection is more common among parents of students with *disabilities* than among the general population.

parent-teacher conference A planned meeting between parents and their child's teacher, usually held at the school at a specified time, in which the *objectives* are to discuss the student, the school program, the child's achievements in the program, *reinforcement* that might be carried out at home, and any problems; also a time to encourage parental questions, suggestions, and general communication. Some of these functions are more formally addressed in the *individualized education program* or *placement team* meetings.

paresis (pair-ee'-siss) Mild *paralysis* that inhibits movement but not sensation. Often accompanies *cerebral palsy*.

Parkinson's disease A progressive condition, generally found in older adults, that is characterized by *tremors*, slow voluntary movements, weakening of muscles, and poor coordination, especially when walking.

partial participation An educational practice in which individuals with *severe disabilities* are engaged in the activities or tasks of the general education *curriculum* to the level they are capable of, which at times may be very limited. If a student with *disabilities* could hold up the *experience chart* that the class is studying, for example, that would be referred to as partial participation. The *concept* has been applied especially where placement in general education has been accomplished through *inclusion* (see also *full inculsion* and *total inclusion*). A related concept is *parallel instruction*. In parallel instruction, however, the relationship to the general education curriculum would be more direct.

partially sighted Describes an individual whose vision is impaired, usually to the extent of having between 20/70 and 20/200 central *visual acuity* in the better eye with correction. Various aids and educational techniques allow most partially sighted children to be educated as sighted rather than as *blind* children.

passive aggression (adj., **passive-aggressive**) Hostility or antagonism expressed as uncooperative, inefficient, obstructive behavior, but without outright defiance or visible anger.

passive learner A student, usually considered to have a *learning disability* or *mental retardation*, whose learning problems result more from a lack of *cognitive attention* or *vigilance* than from a *deficit*. When passive learners are taught *metacognitive* and *active listening* skills, their learning sometimes improves.

passive motion A *modality* of *physical therapy* in which the *therapist* moves a client's bodily *extremity* back and forth through its full *range* of movement. Stretching and contracting the muscles improves circulation and nutrition to the joints and muscles. Passive motion implies that the client is not an active participant in the exercise.

passive resistance (adj., **passive-resistive**) A behavior characteristic of persons with *passive-aggressive* personalities in which the individual appears to do as little as possible to learn or be part of the group, but without outright defiance or visible anger.

passive responding A term used in *effective instruction* to indicate that a child is not actively responding to instruction but may be benefiting from it, as from listening to other students involved in the instruction.

passive-dependent children Children who present or promote themselves as helpless.

pathogenic (path-oh-jen'-ik) Causing a disease or marked *symptoms* of a disease.

pathological Describes a *diagnosed* condition of the body that is indicative of disease or physical damage.

pathologist A medical doctor who specializes in studying the structural and *functional* changes caused by disease, conducts postmortem examinations, and studies tissues removed during operations for positive or negative indications of disease.

pathology The science or branch of medicine concerned with studying diseases and their nature, causes, and treatment.

pathsounder An electronic device, worn around the neck, that emits a sound when an individual approaches an object. The device aids *blind* persons in *mobility*.

patterning See *Doman-Delacato method*.

PC See *politically correct*.

PCMR See *President's Committee on Mental Retardation*.

pedagogy (ped'-ah-goj-ee) (adj., **pedagogical**) The science or profession of teaching.

pediatric(s) Pertaining to the medical specialty involved in the treatment of children.

pediatric neurologist A physician trained in the *neurological* disorders of children.

pediatric psychiatry The branch of medicine that deals specifically with mental disorders in children.

pediatrician A physician who specializes in treating children.

pediculosis (peh-dik-you-loe'-siss) Infestation of the head and/or body with crab lice.

pedometer (peh-dah'-meh-turr) A mechanical device used for measuring movement of the lower *extremities*. Gives a quantitative measure of walking distance and has been used in research to determine the activity of children with various *disabilities*.

peer accounting A system in which students set up and *monitor* the consequences of inappropriate and appropriate classroom behaviors. Usually more effective at or above the fourth-grade level.

peer group People who are of equal standing with one another in society, as defined by age, grade, or status.

peer support group A technique fostered by teachers to assist the *integration* and further *inclusion* of students with *disabilities* into the general education classroom environment. The approach works like "The Circle of Friends," which was developed in Toronto.

peer tutoring Describes academic assistance given to a student by another student of approximately the same age or grade, except in *cross-age tutoring*, in which an older student may teach a younger student or a younger *gifted* student may instruct an older student who has learning problems.

pellagra (peh-lah'-grah) A condition characterized by *dermatitis*, gastrointestinal problems, diarrhea, and *central nervous system* disorders; caused by a lack of niacin and protein in the diet.

Pennsylvania Association for Retarded Children v. Commonwealth of Pennsylvania case (PARC case) A landmark lawsuit brought in 1971 by the Pennsylvania Association for Retarded Children (PARC) against the Commonwealth of Pennsylvania in which the court ruled in favor of PARC and ordered extensive *due process* procedures that provided, in essence, that a student with *mental retardation* could not be expelled, transferred, or excluded from a public education program because they have retardation.

people-first language The practice in the United States and many other countries of using *language* that emphasizes the people first and the *disability* second, as in "individuals with *cerebral palsy*." This terminology is not favored in Britain.

per curiam A Latin term in a citation to a case that refers to the judgment of a court entered "by the court" (rather than by a judge who writes the opinion for the court). A per curiam judgment normally does not include the opinion of the judge, only the court's disposition of the case (e.g., affirmed, petition denied, etc.).

percentile A rank in a distribution at or below which falls the percent of cases indicated by the percentile. Thus, a score in the 35th percentile means that 35% of the scores fall at or below the specified score.

perception Awareness of one's environment through *sensory* stimulation. Perception is an important part of *cognition* and understanding. A child who has faulty perception may experience difficulty in learning.

perceptual Involving perception; refers to any combination of sensations automatically retained and integrated by the brain, providing an organism with the ability to be aware of the unity of things.

perceptual disorders Difficulties or deficiencies in using the sense of sight, touch, smell, taste, or hearing to correctly recognize the various objects or situations within the environment. This type of disorder may become apparent through an individual's poor performance in such activities as drawing, writing, and recognizing forms, sizes, or shapes.

perceptual-motor A term used to refer to the interaction of the various aspects of *perception* with *motor* activity. *Perceptual* areas that commonly affect motor activities are *visual, auditory, tactual,* and *kinesthetic.*

perceptual-motor match A *concept* advanced by Newell C. Kephart in which *motor* development is said to occur prior to *sensory* development and learning is based on the match of sensations and

motor responses; hence, Kephart's heavy reliance on motor training.

performance assessment A practice developed in the 1990s to judge the success of students in an educational program with *disabilities.* Performance assessment does not require the students to undergo *formal* or *norm-referenced testing* but does require that the students do something (e.g., produce, demonstrate, perform, create, construct, apply, build, solve, plan). Performance assessments may be built into *individualized education program* goals and *objectives.* *Performance assessment* is one of the alternative forms of *assessment.*

performance standards According to the *Goals 2000* program, refers to "*concrete* examples and explicit definitions of what students have to know and be able to demonstrate, and that such students are practiced in the skills and knowledge framed by content standards." This term and *performance assessment* may have a great impact on students with *disabilities* in the future, for it sets out performance expectations based on what should have been taught and mastered by most students.

performance test A measure involving some *motor* or manual response on the examinee's part, generally the manipulation of *concrete* materials.

peridontia (pair-ih-dahn'-tshuh) The study of dentistry specializing in the treatment of the tissue and other supporting structures that surround the teeth.

perinatal (pair-i-nay'-tul) Refers to the general time period of birth.

perinatologist (pair-i-nay-tol'-o-jist) A specialist in *obstetrics* and *gynecology* trained to care for high-risk maternal and *fetal* patients.

periosteum (pair-ee-ahs'-tee-um) The thick, vascular connective tissue that covers all bones and possesses bone-forming potential. *Inflammation* of this tissue is termed **periostitis** (pair-ee-ahs-tite'-iss).

peripatology (pair-ih-pah-tahl'-oh-jee) The art of teaching *orientation* and *mobility* to *blind* persons. An instructor in these skills is called a **peripatologist** or *mobility specialist* (preferred).

peripheral (purr-if'-er-ul) **vision** The *perception* of objects, color, or motion by portions of the eye other than the *macula*. The images perceived are not in the center of vision but are seen by the outside parts of the *retina*.

peritoneum (pair-ih-toe'-nee-uhm) The membranous tissue lining the abdominal wall and covering most of the internal organs of the abdominal cavity. *Inflammation* of this lining is termed **peritonitis** (pair-ih-toe-nye'-tiss).

Perkins brailler The most commonly used typing machine for producing *braille*. Has six keys and a spacer bar for the production of braille letters and numerals.

permanency planning A stipulation of PL 96–272, the Adoption Assistance and Child Welfare Act; requires the planning and implementation of programs at the state level for more stable living arrangements for students with *developmental disabilities*.

permissive legislation Laws enabling changes in or the implementation of programs for students with *disabilities* but not requiring them; this type of legislation became obsolete with *PL 94–142* and *IDEA*.

per-pupil cost The amount of money required (usually figured on an annual basis) to educate a student in a given situation. It is computed by dividing the total expenditure for that situation by the stated pupil figure (e.g., pupils enrolled, pupils in *average daily membership*, pupils in *average daily attendance*, or other defined terms).

Perry project Perhaps the most famous early *intervention* project, in which disadvantaged high-risk children were given earlier schooling than their age peers. Students who attended the program grew up to have fewer *disabilities* and fewer encounters with the law, and they demonstrated a highly cost-effective benefit for the program. Also called the *Ypsilanti project*. Many consider the project to be the forerunner of *Head Start*.

perseverate (n., **perseveration**) To persist in an action, word, idea, or mental process, even though the result may not be goal-directed and the response has lost its initial meaning or usefulness. Perseveration may interfere with learning because it tends to inhibit goal-directed activities.

personal adequacy One's ability to function in society; considered one of the goals for persons with *disabilities*.

personality problem Any trait that reduces an individual's *rapport* with people or interferes with his/her adjustment in society but is not serious enough to be considered a severe mental problem.

Perthes disease See *Legg-Calve-Perthes*.

pervasive mental retardation A term in the 1992 American Association on Mental Retardation definition scheme that is for practical reasons the same as *profound mental retardation*. It implies the extensive need for support and represents the most severe level of retardation. This term has not been generally accepted by the field.

PET See *Parent Effectiveness Training*.

petit mal (pet'-ee mahl) A mild form of *seizure* occurring in *epileptic* conditions that is characterized by a momentary lapse of consciousness. These seizures can vary in frequency from 1 to 200 times a day and last from 5 to 20 seconds each. Sometimes referred to as *absence seizures*.

phantom pain An experience of *amputees* in which sharply felt sensations seem to come from the absent, amputated *extremity*.

pharmacology (far-mah-kahl'-oh-jee) The science of the uses of drugs and their relationships to the body.

pharynx (fair'-inks) The passage in the alimentary canal that connects the mouth and *nasal* cavities with the *larynx* and *esophagus*; the throat.

phenocopy (fee'-noe-kah-pea) A *phenotypic* variation that develops in some special instances through environmental factors that are different from those normally operating; the trait that is expressed resembles a *genotype* other than its own. The same *intellectual* condition, for example, may be attributed in one instance to distinct *genetic* characteristics and in another to a unique environment.

phenotype (fee'-noe-tipe) (adj., **phenotypic**) The outward, visible properties of an organism, which are determined by both its *hereditary constitution* and the environment. Thus, the phenotype may vary considerably from the *genetic* structure. A dog that appears phenotypically to be purebred may actually not be.

phenylketonuria (fen-uhl-kee-toe-noor'-ee-ah) **(PKU)** A *hereditary* condition in infants in which the absence of an *enzyme* essential for digesting protein affects the *metabolism* of the body and results in a gradual buildup of *toxic* substances in the blood and urine. Interferes with the normal development and function of the brain and is possibly the most widely known abnormality of metabolism that causes *mental retardation*.

phobia A persistent and unreasonable fear; may be directed at fire, heights, animals, etc.

phocomelia (foe-koe-mee'-lee-ah) A developmental *deformity* characterized by the absence of a portion of a limb or limbs at birth, so that the hands or feet are attached to the torso by a single small bone, creating a flipper-like appearance. Mothers who took the drug thalidomide often produced children with this condition.

phonation (foe-nay'-shun) The functioning of the *larynx* to produce vocal sounds.

phoneme (foe'-neem) One of the 36 sound families recognized in the modern English *language*. Spoken English contains 24 *consonant* phonemes and 12 *vowel* phonemes. A phoneme is the minimal *linguistic* unit of sound.

phonetic Pertaining to speech sounds.

phonetic alphabet A means of representing speech sounds in which each sound is symbolized by a single written character. Examples of this system are the *initial teaching alphabet* and the *international phonetic alphabet*.

phonetic elements Parts of words, which may be syllables, letter combinations, or single letters, that represent sounds. *Blended* together, they form words.

phonetics The study of speech sounds involving the breakdown of words into separate sound elements.

phonetype A communication device for persons with *hearing impairments* that incorporates a telephone and teletype. Messages are typed, using this equipment, and transmitted to an individual having the same type of device; a flashing light rather than a sound indicates that a message is being sent. The terminology has changed most recently to *telecommunication device for the deaf (TDD)*.

phonics The area of *linguistics* dealing with speech sounds and their relationship to symbols. As applied to teaching reading, syllables, letter combinations, and letters that consistently represent specific sounds are taught to enable the reader to be more independent in sounding out and recognizing words.

phonological disorders Deficiencies in the production and *articulation* of speech sounds, traditionally known as *articulatory defects* (*omissions*, *substitutions*, and *distortions*). The term phonological disorder is preferred because the problem involves more than just articulation.

phonology (foe-nahl'-oh-jee) The science or study of *language* structures and their relationship to the sound system of *oral language*.

photophobia An extreme sensitivity to and dislike of light. This condition is most often observed in individuals with *albinism*. (See also *albinism*.)

physical disability A bodily defect that interferes with education, development, adjustment, or *rehabilitation*; generally refers to crippling conditions and *chronic* health problems but usually does not include single *sensory disabilities* such as *blindness* or *deafness*.

physical reinforcer A reward utilizing body contact or sensations that are pleasant to a pupil. May consist of hugging, shoulder pats, etc.

physical therapy (PT) The treatment of *disabilities* by using massage, exercise, water, light, heat, and certain forms of electricity, all of which are mechanical rather than medical in nature. Physical therapy is practiced by a professionally trained **physical therapist** under the *referral* of a physician.

physiological method An approach to educating children with *mental retardation* first advocated by Edward Seguin in the mid-19th century; emphasizes the development and training of neuromotor and *sensory* skills followed by coordinated academic and occupational training.

Piagetian (pea-ah-gee'-tyan) Refers to any *concept* that incorporates Jean Piaget's sequential development theories.

Pidgin Signed English A communication system for individuals who are *deaf* employing a combination of *Signing Exact English* and *American Sign Language*, in which verbs are conveyed with the eyes or facial expressions.

piecework Refers to tasks done in *sheltered workshops* by individuals without the benefit of assembly-line techniques. **Piece rate** refers to the amount paid per unit produced, or the number of units produced or serviced in a specific time period.

pinna The outer, external portion of the ear.

PIP See *prescriptive instructional plan*.

pitch The subjective impression of the highness or lowness of a sound; the psychological equivalent of *frequency*. Pitch is a factor in *voice disorders* in which speech is too high, too low, monotonous, *stereotyped*, *inflectional*, or has pitch breaks.

pituitary (pih-too'-ih-tare-ee) **gland** An *endocrine* gland that produces secretions contributing to the regulation of most basic body functions.

PKU See *phenylketonuria*.

PL An abbreviation for "Public Law," referring to a statute passed by Congress as a public law. Every public law has a number that follows the PL designation; thus, *PL 94–142* refers to Public Law 142 of the 94th Congress.

PL 94–103 The Developmental Disabilities Act of 1975.

PL 94–142 See *Education for All Handicapped Children Act of 1975*.

PL 98–199 Education of the Handicapped Amendments, the 1984 amendments to *PL 94–142*.

PL 99–372 Federal act to assist parents in obtaining rights for children with *disabilities* by providing financial assistance.

PL 99–457 Known as the Early Childhood and Infant Act, PL 99–457 reauthorized the provisions of *PL 94–142*.

PL 101–476 The *Individuals with Disabilities Education Act*, the extension of *PL 94–142* and subsequent acts.

placebo (plah-see'-boe) A substance that has no biological effect on an individual but is given to satisfy that person's perceived need for medication. In research, placebos are sometimes used for comparison to the drug under study.

placement team The current term for the type of group formerly called a *screening committee*. *PL 94–142* calls for such a group or team to review *diagnostic* and instructional data concerning a student with *disabilities* with that student's parents when planning an *individualized education program*. The general education teacher, *resource teacher*, *diagnostician*, counselor, and other professionals may be involved. This group is also variously called a child study team, pupil *evaluation* team, *staffing* committee, or *eligibility* committee.

placenta previa (plah-sen'-tah pree'-vee-ah) Separation of the placenta from the *uterine* wall, which results in the loss of oxygen and food for the *fetus*.

plaintiff A person who brings a lawsuit to redress a violation of one or more of his/her legal rights.

plasma The fluid part of the blood in which corpuscles and other components are suspended. Plasma transfusions are sometimes needed in medical treatment.

plateau In the *context* of *special education*, refers to a level of learning or physical growth at which the pupil no longer is showing improvement or advancement.

platelets Tiny plate-like disks in the blood that control coagulation, or clotting.

play audiometry An approach to testing young children's hearing in which the child being tested responds to spoken signals in a game situation.

play therapy A technique used with children who have emotional problems that allows them to express fear, hate, *aggression*, *anxiety*, and other emotions through activities with toys and games.

pleoptics (plee-ahp'-tiks) A Swiss-developed procedure for improving the function of suppressed vision; involves stimulation of the eyes by a blinking light.

plosive (ploe'-siv) Any of the six *consonant* sounds (*p, b, t, d, k,* and *g*) that are formed by a blocking of the breath followed by a sudden release of air.

plumbism See *lead poisoning*.

pneumoencephalography (new-moe-en-sef-ah-lah'-grah-fee) A medical *diagnostic* procedure in which *cerebrospinal fluid* is withdrawn from the brain, air or gas is injected into the ventricular spaces, and then *X-ray* techniques are used to obtain a picture of the ventricles of the brain. (See also *encephalography*.)

pocket brailler A device for the electronic production and storage of *braille*. This device, produced by the American Printing House for the Blind, can store up to 200 pages of braille, provide *tactile feedback*, and, through a separate printer, provide a braille hard copy.

poliomyelitis (polio) An *acute viral* disease that causes *inflammation* of the nerve cells of the spinal cord or brain stem and results in *paralysis* or muscular *atrophy*. Formerly caused many individuals to have physical *impairments*, but now most people receive vaccinations to prevent the disease.

politically correct (PC) Views and actions that without *objective* analysis conform to current agendas and initiatives of political authorities.

poly- Prefix meaning excessive or many.

polydactylism (pah-lee-dak'-tih-lizm) A condition in which a child is born with more than the normal number of fingers or toes.

polygenic inheritance A *genetic* hypothesis that describes the biological phenomena that occur when a characteristic is determined by the combined action of a large number of randomly assorted genetic influences working together.

Portage model A specific type of *preschool education* program for children with *disabilities* that uses parents as the teachers, with once-a-week *monitoring* and *modeling* by a traveling teacher-instructor.

portfolio assessment The use of records of a student's work in a variety of modes over a period of time to describe the student's strengths and weaknesses and to reflect his/her accomplishments toward a goal(s). Such work products include, for example, class papers and classroom tests. Portfolio assessment is an alternative form of *assessment* being used in the 1990s. Other types of *alternative assessment* are *authentic assessment*, *performance assessment*, and *direct assessment*.

positioning Moving or arranging an individual's body and limbs in ways that are helpful or *therapeutic* to the person. Usually applies to individuals with *severe* or *multiple disabilities*.

positive reinforcement Rewards given for a specific desired behavior. (See also *reinforcement*.)

possum device An *autotelic* system developed in England for teaching *nonverbal language* to persons with *severe disabilities*.

post- A prefix meaning coming after.

post-polio syndrome A muscle deterioration in individuals who were previously afflicted with *poliomyelitis*. Usually appears in later life as the affected muscles show the effects of their use over the years.

posterior Toward the rear or back side, as of the body. Opposite of *anterior*.

postictal state (poe-stik'-tahl) One's condition after having a *stroke* or a *seizure*.

postlingual deafness Loss of hearing that occurs after an individual has developed speech and *language*.

postnatal Pertaining to the time period after birth. Used in reference to the newborn.

postpartum Refers to the time period following childbirth. Most often used in reference to the mother, as in "postpartum *depression*."

Prader-Willi syndrome A *genetic* disorder resulting in *mental retardation* and a shortened life expectancy (generally not beyond age 30); usually characterized by an uncontrollable appetite and obesity.

pragmatics The rules governing the use of *language* in *context*, including the speaker's communicative intent—e.g., to inform, persuade, entertain, describe, control. Also includes a child's knowledge of how to use language in social settings and his/her knowledge of how to use language to communicate.

pragmatism A practical approach to problem solving with the premise that truth is tested by consequences of belief.

pre- A prefix meaning coming before or prior to.

preassessment See *prereferral system.*

precedent A previous decision by a judge or court that serves as a rule or guide to support other judges in deciding cases involving similar or analogous legal questions. In the early right-to-education cases, courts cited some famous education decisions as precedents, including *Brown v. Board of Education*, outlawing *segregated* schools, and *Gobson v. Hansen*, outlawing the track system in the District of Columbia. Just as *PARC* and *Mills* were cited as precedent by other courts for finding a constitutional right to education, so *Rowley* is now cited on various legal issues.

precision teaching A systematic instructional procedure that involves the continuous and direct recording of behavior, espoused by Ogden Lindsley and others. Precision teaching employs the techniques of *behavior modification* and *task analysis* for the management of instruction and behavior. Now more likely referred to as *direct instruction* or *curriculum*-based instruction.

precocious (prih-koe'-shus) (n., **precociousness**) Exhibiting development that is advanced beyond the usual, mentally and physically. Frequently used in reference to young *gifted* children.

predictive validity A measure of the ability of a test to forecast an outcome. If, for example, a test were to be given to predict good teachers, we would be interested to know how successfully that test predicts which persons were good teachers.

predisposition An inherited potential for the development of certain characteristics.

prelingual deafness An absence of hearing at birth, or *hearing loss* that develops early in life before *acquisition* of speech and *language.*

prelinguistic Refers to skills that are *prerequisite* to *language* learning. These include various sensorimotor and *cognitive* skills that lead to the *acquisition* of the *symbolic function* of language.

Premack principle A *concept* effective in *reinforcing* the classroom environment whereby pupils are motivated to do low-frequency or less desirable activities by being assured that upon completion of the activities, they will be able to do high-frequency or highly desired activities. The principle operates regardless of students' awareness of the contingencies; simply following a low-probability behavior with a high-probability behavior increases the probability of the low-probability behavior in the future.

premature baby Any infant weighing less than 5 pounds at birth. Research has indicated that the lower the birth weight in premature babies, the greater is the potential for a *disability.*

prenatal Pertaining to a time period prior to birth.

prereferral system A procedure that occurs before *referral* to *special education* in which general educators attempt alternative programs. (See also *teacher assistance team* and *student support team.*)

prerequisite skills Abilities that must be developed before proceeding to a given task or *objective. Early childhood education*, for example, focuses on skills prerequisite to academic learning.

presbycusis (prez-bih-cue'-sis) Deterioration in hearing as a result of aging.

presbyopia (prez-bee-oh'-pea-ah) A gradual lessening of the ability of the eyes to *accommodate*, because of physiological changes occurring after age 40.

preschool education A training program, usually in the development of social behavior and *language*, that is available to children prior to enrollment in kindergarten or a formal school program. Preschool education is important for children with *disabilities* because they generally need early stimulation, experiences, and direction to aid necessary development that might not occur incidentally. (See also *early childhood education*.)

prescriptive education See *prescriptive teaching*.

prescriptive instructional plan (PIP) A plan used in some states as the equivalent of an *individualized education program (IEP)*.

prescriptive teaching Educational terminology referring to the process of planning individual educational activities as a result of needs concluded from *diagnostic test* information.

President's Committee on Employment of People with Disabilities A panel appointed by the President to promote and encourage a positive action program of jobs for persons with *disabilities*; includes promotional activities and the recognition of outstanding people with disabilities.

President's Committee on Mental Retardation (PCMR) A panel first appointed by President John F. Kennedy to study the problems experienced by individuals with *mental retardation* and to make recommendations on how to deal with mental retardation on a national basis.

presumptive disability A term used in conjunction with an administrative provision that allows the Social Security Administration to make an immediate determination of *disabilities* based on the nature of certain disabilities. Under this provision, individuals with more severe cases of *developmental disability* can obtain *supplemental security income (SSI)* almost immediately rather than waiting.

prevalence How common a condition is in the population (e.g., about 3% of the population is *mentally retarded*; therefore, the prevalence of mental retardation in the population is about 3%). See also *incidence*.

preventive physical education A program that involves specific activities or exercises selected to promote proper body use as a protection against injury or to prevent the occurrence of predictable anomalies.

prevocational level Pertains to beginning programs for students with *disabilities* that emphasize skills necessary for employment. Such programs emphasize skills other than direct job skills, such as social and work attributes.

prevocational teacher (PVT) An instructor trained in coordinating the school activities and job placements of students with mild *disabilities* at the *prevocational level*.

prevocational deafness The loss of hearing prior to age 19. Persons deafened after that age are not expected to have as severe vocational problems or as great a need for special *vocational education*.

primary disability The condition that is considered the overriding *disability* as far as education, medicine, *rehabilitation*, or employment is concerned. In some cases the primary disability may vary based on the situation. With *cerebral palsy*, for example, medical personnel may consider the *physical disability* as primary, whereas in education the same child's *mental retardation* may be viewed as primary.

private action A case brought on behalf of one or more individuals to vindicate violation of their own legally protected interests. As distinguished from a *class action*, where the relief applies to all persons similarly situated or within the class represented by the plaintiffs (e.g., *PARC*), any *relief* granted in private action applies only to those *plaintiffs* actually before the court (e.g., *Rowley*).

private speech A person's speech, vocal or subvocal, that is directed to the self. Before age 6 or 7 it is usually *overt*; after 8 to 10 years of age, most is *covert*.

PRN *Acronym* for the Latin **pro re nata**, a term in medicine meaning "to use as needed or required."

pro-social skills Those skills which facilitate social acceptance across a broad *range* of settings but specifically those skills which facilitate acceptance by peers and teachers in the school culture. Many schools and some systems are using a pro-social skills *curriculum* to produce a common school culture, thus reducing social *rejection* and *screening* for *special education* services. Most curricula include both a *cognitive* and behavioral component using frequent practice, *role playing*, and attention to *generalization* across settings to strengthen skills. Many also include events like accepting criticism and expressing disagreement with authority figures appropriately.

proactive inhibition Greater difficulty in learning or recalling knowledge as a result of prior learning (e.g., hesitating to cross the street on a green light after learning that cars can run over you). For comparison, see *retroactive inhibition*.

probation A provision applied to a convicted law offender (*delinquent*) whereby he/she is released on a suspended sentence under supervision and with an agreement to report regularly to the court or to a representative of the court, such as a *probation officer*. (See also *offender rehabilitation*, the preferred term.)

probation officer A person appointed by the court to supervise and receive regular reports from a law offender (*delinquent*) whose sentence has been suspended or who has been released from a penal *institution* but is required to serve out his/her term on *probation*. Same as *correctional counselor*.

procedural due process The right to a hearing, to be notified of the hearing, to be represented by counsel, and to be given the opportunity to present evidence and confront witnesses. This is one of the *concepts* inherent in *IDEA*.

procedural noncompliance Any situation in which a *local education agency* or *state education agency* does not carry out the required procedures of *due process*, *nondiscriminatory testing*, *least restrictive environment*, native *language* considerations, or *confidentiality*.

procedural right A right that relates to the process of enforcing substantive rights or to obtaining *relief*, such as the right to a hearing, the right to present evidence in one's defense, and the right to counsel.

procedural safeguards Specific procedures designed by law to protect the rights of children and parents, which include *due process*, *nondiscriminatory testing*, *least restrictive environment*, native *language* considerations, and *confidentiality*.

processing The use of internal thinking skills such as generalizing, abstracting, classifying, and integrating to carry out thought.

prodigy A person who expresses advanced abilities at an early age and whose *precociousness* indicates *giftedness* or special talent. These abilities are expressed in *intellect*, the performing arts, or *creativity*.

products (of thinking) In J. P. Guilford's model (see *structure of the intellect*), the elements of thinking that are cognized, memorized, or *evaluated*.

professional judgment A *concept* involving one's use of a reasonable collection of data to arrive at a decision. In recent years, courts have given greater credence to the testimony of those skilled in *diagnosis*. In rendering legal decisions, judges have been reluctant to overturn or "second guess" the professional judgment of educators.

profile A graphic representation of the results of several measures for either a group or an individual, with the results expressed in terms of uniform or comparable scores.

profound mental retardation A term introduced by the American Association on Mental Retardation that refers to a level of *intellectual* functioning comparable to the educational classification of *severe mental retardation*. The individual with profound mental retardation requires supervision throughout life. The intellectual level, when *assessed* with an individual *intelligence* test, is estimated at *IQ* scores below 20.

progeria (pro-jare'-ee-ah) A rare form of *dwarfism* that is accompanied by premature *symptoms* of aging including wrinkled skin and gray, thinning hair. Children with this condition have a shortened lifespan, and no cure has been found.

prognosis A projection of outcome for the future; a prediction of the probable result of an illness or disease or the probable status of behavior in terms of achievement or adjustment (e.g., prediction of a child's educational and independence level as an adult or the expectancy for a *rehabilitation* client to become employed successfully).

programmed instruction The provision of learning materials that are designed to present knowledge and skills to pupils in a way in which they can learn independently.

programmed reading An approach to teaching reading that uses materials designed for students' self-instruction and self-correction of errors.

Project Re-Ed A program for educating and helping children with emotional problems that was originated at George Peabody College; emphasizes ecological and *psychoeducational* elements and depends heavily upon teacher-counselors to serve in a limited way as teachers, *social workers*, *psychologists*, and recreation workers combined.

projective technique A relatively unstructured approach to studying and diagnosing certain problems of personality in which a product or response (such as a drawing, an interpretation of a picture, or the completion of a sentence) is secured from an individual and analyzed in an effort to gain an understanding of the total personality.

proleptic Describes a *concept* in Leo Vygotsky's theory of social *context* in learning that teaching should contain enough of the message or meaning so that the students can construct their own extended meaning.

prompting A form of teacher assistance provided to aid the student in making correct responses. *Antecedent prompts* consist of modifications to the instructional material to assist the student in attending to the relevant dimensions of the task. Response prompts consist of the teacher assisting the student in making the correct response (e.g., physically guiding the student).

prompts Cues or assistance provided by a teacher to facilitate learning. These cues are *faded* or removed as learning is accomplished.

pronation (proe-nay'-shun) A physical condition in which inadequate muscle strength or improper bony structure allows the ankle to roll inward, placing the body weight on the inner side of the foot.

prone A position of lying on one's stomach with the face downward. Opposite of *supine*.

prophylaxis (proe-fih-lack'-siss) Any preventive treatment of disease.

proprioceptors (proe-pree-oh-sep'-tores) *Sensory* nerve endings that give information concerning movements and positions of the body. These endings occur in muscles, tendons, and the canals of the inner ear.

prosody The rhythm of speech, including its patterns of stress and rate, which helps give meaning to speech.

prosthetic (prahs-thet'-ik) **device** (n., **prosthesis**) An artificial part attached to one's body following the loss of the natural part, such as an arm or leg. It may provide the individual with some of the function of the natural part, as in the most common artificial hands.

prosthetics (prahs-thet'-iks) The branch of medicine that deals with the application of artificial body parts to *amputees*; includes *evaluation*, treatment, and prescription.

protective services The assumption of temporary or partial *guardianship* to assure the safety and well-being of a minor person with a *disability* or of another individual deemed in need of such protection.

protege (proe'-teh-zhay) In *advocacy* circles, refers to the person for whom the *advocate* intercedes.

proximal Near to something. Opposite of *distal* or lateral.

pseudo mental retardation A condition in which a child appears to have *functional mental retardation*, but *diagnosis* and educational program *evaluations* give evidence that the performance results from factors other than *mental retardation*, such as *environmental deprivation* or low vitality.

pseudohypertrophy A name applied to *Duchenne disease* (a form of *muscular dystrophy*), but really refers to the enlargement of cell muscles caused by fat deposits.

psyche (sigh'-key) The sum of the psychological processes of the human mind and soul.

psychiatric outpatient services Alternative treatment programs that enable individuals to obtain psychiatric help for emotional, mental, or behavioral problems without disrupting the pattern of their daily lives. The usual procedure involves periodic visits of a relatively short duration.

psychiatrist A medical doctor who specializes in the *diagnosis* and treatment of mental/*emotional disorders*.

psychic energizers Drugs (e.g., Ritalin, Dexedrine) used to treat *behavior* and *learning disorders*.

psychoanalytic Refers to an approach to psychiatry based on the method of **psychoanalysis** developed by Sigmund Freud. Psychoanalytic methods (e.g., *free association* and dream interpretation) are used to investigate and understand a patient's *psychodynamics*.

psychodrama A *group therapy* method of counseling in which patients dramatize their individual problems.

psychodynamic (n., **psychodynamics**) Describes an approach to psychiatry that grew out of the *psychoanalytic* theory of Sigmund Freud; views the cause of behavior to be ideas and impulses, either conscious or unconscious, that are emotionally charged (psychic energy). *Therapeutic* methods based on this *conceptualization* vary according to the school of psychodynamic thought.

psychoeducational Refers to a *service delivery system* that has a *psychodynamic* orientation with an emphasis on the reality demands of the school and everyday functioning.

psychoeducational approach One of the theories that has been applied to the treatment of children with *behavior disorders*; utilizes ideas from the *psychoanalytic* approach and the *therapeutic* process of education.

psychoeducational diagnostician A specialist who *assesses* the educational status of the learner, provides meaningful, educationally relevant *evaluations*, and outlines specific and long-range educational goals.

psychogalvanic (sie-koe-gal-vahn'-ik) **skin response** The *dermal* response to a *stimulus*. This response is measured in *audiometry* to detect *hearing loss.*

psychogenic (sie-koe-jen'-ik) Describes conditions resulting from psychological or *psychosomatic* causes. A person with psychogenic *deafness*, for example, has no physical or physiological basis for the *hearing loss.*

psycholinguistics Commonly used in reference to programs, services, or *assessments* involving a combination of psychological aspects and the study of *language* or speech.

psychological autopsy A technique used by *psychologists* in which all acquaintances of suicide victims are interviewed to determine possible reasons for the suicide. This technique is similar to the investigative work done by detectives and has proved more successful than any previous methods of getting at causative factors.

psychologist A professional who has had specialized training in **psychology** and in practice does research or *evaluates* and treats individuals in any of the areas of mental functioning.

psychometry (sie-kah'-meh-tree) (adj., **psychometric**) The *evaluation* or measurement of psychological functioning by means of mental tests. A person qualified to do this work is called a **psychometrist**; he/she usually is a college graduate but does not have as much professional training as, or the certification of, a *psychologist.*

psychomotor Pertaining to psychological effects on physical skills, especially *sensory* and *perceptual* effects on *motor* coordination.

psychomotor seizure An *epileptic* activity in which the individual appears to be conscious during the attack but behaves in an unusual or a bizarre way; following the attack, he/she does not remember what happened during the episode. Some indications of psychomotor *seizure* may be chewing, lip smacking, ringing in ears, abdominal pains, and dizziness.

psychoneurosis (adj., **psychoneurotic**) A minor mental disorder in which physical manifestations such as *anxiety* are displayed. (See also *neurosis*.)

psychopath (adj., **psychopathic**) An individual having an instability of character represented by such traits as undue conceit, suspiciousness, and perversity of conduct or having a lack of emotional stability, self-control, social feeling, honesty, and persistence. In many cases, such individuals have no *impairment* of *intellectual* functions.

psychopathology The scientific study of the more serious mental disturbances from a psychological viewpoint.

psychopharmacology (sie-koe-far-mah-kahl'-oh-jee) The science of the use of drugs to influence behavior. Drugs prescribed to influence behavior are broadly classified as *stimulants, tranquilizers,* and *antidepressants.*

psychophysiologic (sie-koe-fiz-ee-oh-lah'-jik) **disorders** Conditions in which emotional and physical elements combine to produce physical *symptoms,* without the individual being aware of the emotional relationship. *Eczema* and *asthma* may be examples of such disorders. The preferred descriptive term at present is *psychosomatic.*

psychosis A broad classification covering severe mental/*emotional*/*behavior disorders* that are characterized by a persistent ignoring of reality, a lack of order in behavior, and an inability to function adequately in daily living.

psychosomatic Describes physiological disorders induced by mental or emotional pressures or disturbances.

psychotherapy An approach to treating mental disorders by psychological methods using the influence of suggestion, *nondirective therapy* methods, *psychoanalysis,* and *reeducation* of the mind.

psychotic (adj.) Describes any of the psychoses; *schizophrenia* is one example.

psychotropic drugs Medications used primarily for their behavioral effects; may be used to control *attention* and activity level in children.

PT See *physical therapy.*

ptosis (toe'-siss) A condition characterized by drooping of the upper eyelid; caused by faulty development or *paralysis* of a muscle. The condition sometimes can be corrected by surgery, but if it is not corrected, the eyelid may grow attached to the eye.

puberty (pyew'-burr-tee) The period in a person's development at which time secondary sex characteristics appear and the reproductive organs mature to the capability of bearing offspring; the period marking the beginning of adolescence.

Public Law 94–142 See *Education for All Handicapped Children Act.*

Public Law 101–476 See *Individuals with Disabilities Education Act.*

pull-out program Any program that removes students from their general education classes for either *therapy* or specialized instruction. The best examples would be programs involving the assistance of *resource teachers* or *speech/language pathologists.*

pulmonary Associated with or pertaining to the lungs.

punctographic symbol An element in a raised, *tactile,* graphic system, such as *braille,* used by *blind* persons.

pupil (of the eye) The contractible opening in the center of the *iris,* through which light enters.

pure-tone audiometer An instrument for measuring the *acuity* of hearing by testing at selected *frequencies* at a number of different loudness levels, usually graduated in 5-*decibel* steps. The sound is produced in a receiver or an earphone held snug against the subject's ear, and the subject gives a signal for the sounds that he/she can hear.

PVT See *prevocational teacher.*

pyorrhea (pie-uh-ree'-ah) *Inflammation* of the gum tissues surrounding the teeth. If not treated, this condition results in *degeneration* of the gum tissues.

Q

qid Abbreviation for the Latin quarter in die, a term used in medicine to denote "four times daily." Frequently seen on prescriptions for medications.

quadriplegia (kwad-rih-plee'-jah) (adj., **quadriplegic**) *Paralysis* involving all four of the body *extremities* (arms and legs).

quality control The *random sampling* of product or services to ensure that the production meets or is better than minimum requirements set by those for whom the work is being done. Quality control is conducted in *sheltered workshops*, among other working environments.

quality disorder A voice defect that may be described as *nasal*, strident, falsetto, *breathy*, *hoarse*, or similar terms.

quality of life A subjective *concept* that should drive all services for adults with *disabilities*. This concept can be considered an extension of the *normalization* concept. Quality of life emphasizes personal choice and personal satisfaction with adult life experiences.

quartile One of three points that separate the four equal parts of a whole. If a person is said to be in the upper quartile, he/she is in the top 25%.

quid pro quo A Latin term that means, literally, "something for something" and indicates an exchange of money and/or goods (e.g., a school district provides *inservice training* in exchange for—as a quid pro quo for—state aid to defray expenses).

R

radio reading A procedure used in teaching reading in which the teacher encourages a child to read a passage like a radio announcer would, telling the child that he/she does not have to read each word as it is written but instead may paraphrase or give the gist of the text.

radius The smaller of the two bones in the forearm, located on the thumb side of the arm. The other bone is the *ulna*.

RAID An *acronym* for rules, approval, ignoring, and disapproval. RAID is a *behavior management* system employing these elements to improve behavior.

ramp A sloping passageway built to connect varying levels of buildings or terrain. Ramps are built to allow greater *mobility* for individuals in wheelchairs or on crutches who have difficulty climbing or cannot climb stairs. Ramps are becoming increasingly used because of various codes enacted to reduce *architectural barriers*.

random sample (random sampling) A selection of a certain percentage of individuals from a defined group in which each member has an equal chance of being drawn for study. The subgroup is representative of the larger group, and, therefore, study results are generalizable to the larger population.

range The continuum from the lowest to highest scores for a specified group; shows the extent of variation within the extremes.

rapport (rah-pore') A relationship between two individuals that is harmonious, understanding, and involves mutual confidence. Such a relationship is desirable between teacher and student for creating a good learning climate.

rationalization A psychological *defense mechanism* in which one justifies illogical behavior by thinking of motives that seem plausible; rationalization hides the true motives or desires that might be causing *anxiety* or *distress*.

raw score The number of items answered correctly on a test.

readability level A measure of the difficulty of specific instructional material expressed in terms of the *grade level* at which it can be read best and most appropriately. Readability level is one consideration in selecting materials for individuals or classes.

reader services *Rehabilitation* teaching services such as readers, note-taking services, and *orientation/mobility* services for *blind* persons.

readiness The point in a child's maturation at which he/she has developed the necessary *sensory* and *intellectual* skills to be able to learn a specific task or skill.

reading comprehension The ability to understand the meaning of what one has read.

reading disability An inability to read at the *achievement level* for one's *chronological age*; usually considered as being a significant *disability* if reading is more than one level below grade-level placement. Children with *mental retardation* read below their chronological age, but their reading achievement usually is compared to their *mental age*.

reading readiness The stage in a pupil's development at which he/she is ready to learn to read. Reading readiness requires a combination of physical, emotional, *sensory*, and mental maturation.

reality therapy A treatment method, originated by William Glasser, that emphasizes behavior in the real world and the client's responsibility for his/her behavior. The *therapy* teaches *coping behavior* and is carried out in the client's environment, without removal of the client to another setting for treatment.

reasonable expectation of benefit One of several *criteria* used by courts to determine *least restrictive environment.* See also *inclusion philosophy* and *maximum benefit*.

reauditorization The ability to retrieve *auditory* images; the capability of experiencing or re-creating auditory experiences simply by thinking about them. In some children with *learning disorders*, this ability is impaired or lacking, and they are not able to recall auditory images that could be of great value to them.

rebus (ree'-bus) A representation of a word or phrase by pictures that suggest the syllables or words. The Peabody Rebus Reading Program is an example of a *programmed reading* approach to *reading readiness* and beginning reading utilizing a vocabulary of rebuses.

receptive aphasia See *sensory aphasia*.

receptive language The aspect of communication that involves an individual's reception and *comprehension* of information from others. In contrast, see *expressive language*.

recessive genes See *autosomal recessive inheritance*.

recidivism (reh-sid'-ih-viz-uhm) The return to lawlessness by an individual who had been released or paroled from institutional confinement and, as a result, is returned to an *institution*.

reciprocal inhibition J. A. Wolpe's *conceptualization* involving *counter-conditioning*, in which an *anxiety* response is eliminated by training an individual to make a different response.

reciprocal teaching A method of teaching based on the Russian *psychologist* Leo Vygotsky's theory of social *context* in learning in which the teacher begins by using considerable structure, but the structure is gradually reduced as students are able to *monitor* their own work. The four main activities are summarizing questions, generating, clarifying, and predicting.

reciprocation (adj., **reciprocal**) In *physical therapy*, an approach in which joints or limbs are *flexed* backward and forward; also, the movement of both arms and/or both legs at the same time but in opposite directions.

recreational therapy (RT) The use of games and other activities of a pleasant nature as a form of treatment.

redundancy A teaching technique in which the same information is presented over and over, each time with a different format. Thus, math facts could be taught by counting blocks, using ditto masters, counting to music, etc.

reeducation Presenting already learned material for the purpose of establishing new understandings and relationships; necessitated by the *inhibition* of the use of the original learning resulting from *physical*, mental, or emotional *disabilities* or improper application of the original learning.

referral The process of informing a *clinic*, school, medical doctor, or other appropriate specialist about an individual for the purpose of *evaluation* or treatment.

reflex A consistent, involuntary muscular or *neurological* response resulting from *sensory* stimulation. A commonly referred to reflex is the knee jerk.

reflex audiometry Testing one's responses to sounds by observing *reflex* actions such as the *Moro reflex*.

refraction The bending or deflection of light rays within the eye; measured by an eye specialist to *assess* and correct vision.

regression A behavioral reaction to frustration in which the individual returns to an earlier, more immature form of behavior.

regression effect The tendency for scores on a test to move toward the true *mean*. The implication for *special education* is

that disproportionately high or low scores will tend to move more toward the *norm* on future tests.

regression/recoupment syndrome Refers to a loss of learned academic, social, and *motor* skills during the summer months and the resultant time required to relearn the same skills when the child returns to school. The term came into use in the 1980s in relation to extended-school year litigation for individuals with *severe mental retardation*.

regular education initiative (REI) An effort starting in about 1985 to combine general education and *special education* into one system. REI would provide maximum *mainstreaming* for students with all types of *disabilities*. The term has now been replaced by use of the term *inclusion*.

rehabilitation The process of helping a nonproductive or *deviant* person whose performance deviates markedly from the *norm* toward restoration of the desired standard through education or retraining. *Rehabilitative services* are often vocational or physical in nature.

Rehabilitation Act of 1973 (PL 93–112) A comprehensive piece of federal legislation that expanded federally funded *rehabilitation* services to persons with *severe disabilities*. This law contains *Section 504*, which prohibits *discrimination* on the basis of disability in all federally assisted programs and *mandates accessibility* of these programs to people with disabilities.

rehabilitative services More recent term for *vocational rehabilitation*.

REI See *regular education initiative*.

reinforcement (v., **reinforce**) Any consequence of a behavior that increases the probability of that behavior recurring. A **reinforcer** is any event or reward that, when given following a behavior, increases the probability of that behavior being repeated in the future.

rejection Expressing attitudes and behavior toward another person that lead that person to believe he/she is not accepted, loved, or appreciated. These attitudes may be conscious or unconscious.

related services Those services other than *special education* services that are necessary for a student to benefit from special education. Examples of related services are often considered to be *speech therapy*, *physical therapy*, and *occupational therapy*. Other related services have included auxiliary services, computers, wheelchairs, summer *music therapy*, *catheterizations*, and toileting assistance, to mention only a few. *PL 94–142* describes related services as those that are supportive of and may or may not be part of classroom instruction, including transportation, occupational therapy, and so forth. Also called *support services*. These provisions are continued in the *Individuals with Disabilities Education Act*.

related vocational instructor (RVI) An educator authorized in some states through *vocational education* funds to assist students with regular vocational and technical education curricula. Usually not associated with or funded as part of *special education*.

relatively profoundly disabled A term that came into use in the late 1980s to denote that group of students with profound *disabilities* for whom instructional methodology can produce a measurable difference, as opposed to those *labeled absolutely profoundly disabled*.

reliability The consistency with which a test or method measures something. In behavior observation, the degree to which independent observers agree on what they have observed during the same observation session.

relief A remedy for some legal wrong. Relief is requested by a *plaintiff* and is granted by a court against a *defendant*.

religious interpreter A slang term referring to an *interpreter for deaf persons* who tells them what he/she wants that person to hear rather than translating literally.

remedial reading Corrective instruction offered to students whose reading achievement is a level below that expected for their *chronological age*.

remediation (adj., **remedial**) The process of correcting inappropriate behaviors or skills; any methods or exercises designed to correct deficiencies and help a student perform nearer the level expected of his/her *chronological age*.

remission A reduction in the *intensity* of a disease; or the period during which the intensity of a disease abates, or lessens.

renal Pertaining to the kidneys or kidney function.

repression An unconscious or conscious *rejection* or *blocking* out of desires or impulses, in order to prevent the natural expression or development of something having disagreeable content.

residential Refers to a living arrangement in which individuals are housed 24 hours a day in a protective environment.

residential alternatives See *alternative living*.

residential institution A facility, either private or state-supported, that is designed to provide designated care and other services on a 24-hour basis to those housed there. People with *mental retardation* and *mental illness* constitute the largest groups of people with *disabilities* in residential institutions.

residential services Amenities and functions necessary to maintain persons with *disabilities* in *residential* facilities. These services may extend to *institutions*, *group homes*, and other community living arrangements.

residual hearing The remaining hearing that can be measured in or is usable by a *hearing impaired* person.

residual vision The remaining *visual acuity* of *partially sighted* persons; usually refers to individuals' using or learning to use their remaining vision.

resistive motion A mode of *physical therapy* wherein the patient moves a bodily part against something, which may be weights or pressure by the *therapist*.

resonance The quality of the sound imparted by vibrations in the vocal tract; affected by the size, shape, and texture of the organs in the vocal tract.

resonator Any of the bodily cavities—*oral*, *nasal*, *pharynx*—that affect voice quality and *pitch*.

resource center See *instructional materials center*.

resource room A specially equipped and managed setting in which a teacher with special training instructs students who are assigned to report to him/her at designated times for assistance in some aspect of learning or guidance. Resource rooms are one of the *service delivery system* options in *special education*.

resource teacher A specialist who works with students who are having difficulty learning in the general education classroom setting. This teacher serves as a *consultant* to the general education classroom teachers and searches to secure appropriate materials to use in teaching these children. The resource teacher also may function in a *resource room* where students report for specialized instruction. (See also *consultant*.)

respiratory Pertaining to breathing.

respite (res'-pit) **care** Temporary measures taken to care for a child with a *disability* by someone other than the child's parents in order to relieve the parents of this responsibility for a short period of time. Respite care may be in the home, in a special home outside the child's home, or in an available bed in a *residential* facility.

respondent behavior Actions produced by classical *conditioning*.

retardate A term of *institutional* origin that is not generally acceptable today in social or professional circles. The correct term would be an individual with *mental retardation*.

retardation (adj., **retarded**) See *mental retardation*.

retention Holding or being able to recall knowledge acquired previously.

retina (adj., **retinal**) The innermost component of the eye, which contains sensitive nerve fibers that connect to the *optic nerve* to produce sight. **Retinal detachment** is the loosening or pulling away of the retina from its normal position in the eye. In children, this condition usually is caused by an accident; the initial *symptom* may be a slight loss of vision, but the symptoms might progress to almost complete *blindness*.

retinitis pigmentosa (ret-ih-ny'-tiss pig-men-toe'-suh) A condition of reduced *peripheral vision*, where an individual retains the ability to see in the central *visual* area but has tunnel-like vision.

retinoblastoma (ret-ih-noe-blas-toh'-mah) A *malignant* tumor originating in the *retina*. The condition occurs in childhood, and surgical removal of the eye usually is successful in removing the malignancy.

retinopathy of prematurity The term, which has replaced *retrolental fibroplasia*, for a condition of the eyes resulting from too much oxygen being administered to infants after birth (in an incubator). This condition can cause *blindness*.

retroactive inhibition Difficulty in recalling knowledge or activities because of learning that takes place after that which is being recalled (e.g., difficulty recalling a word learned on Monday because of being taught a similar word on Tuesday). For comparison, see *proactive inhibition*.

retrolental fibroplasia (reh-troe-lent'-uhl fie-broe-play'-zee-ah) **(RLF)** See *retinopathy of prematurity*, now the preferred term.

reversal In reading and writing, an irregularity in which the order of the letters in words is misperceived, resulting in a tendency to read from right to left, to confuse letters with each other, or to mix the order of letters in writing.

reverse chaining See *backward (reverse) chaining*.

reverse mainstreaming A procedure in which children without *disabilities* are placed in *special education* for a limited time. May involve general education children visiting a *special class* or a *residential* school.

reversed (rev'd) A word in a citation to a case that indicates that a higher court has overturned the result, and usually the reasoning, of a lower court and entered (or ordered the lower court to enter) a different judgment. Sometimes a higher court can reverse part of a lower court's judgment and affirm part of it; whether that is possible depends on the nature of the judgment.

revisualization (v., **revisualize**) The ability to retain and recall a mental picture in the mind's eye; an extremely important characteristic that often is impaired in individuals with *mental retardation* and *learning disabilities*.

Rh factor An element in the blood that determines the compatibility of the mother's blood and the developing *fetus's* blood during the *prenatal* period. An incompatibility causes an *allergic* reaction in the fetus that results in a breakdown of red blood cells and the release of large amounts of *bilirubin* (the red pigment in the red blood cells); at birth, *degenerative* changes cause the infant to show *jaundice*, drowsiness, listlessness, muscle twitching, and possibly *flaccidity*, and later may result in *severe disabilities*. (See also *erythroblastosis*.)

rheumatic (roo-mat'-ik) **fever** A disease that usually follows a *streptococcus* infection and is characterized by *acute inflammation* of the joints, fever, *chorea*, skin rash, nosebleeds, and abdominal pains. The disease is considered serious because it often damages the heart by scarring its tissues and valves. **Rheumatic heart** is a general term referring to heart murmurs or irregular heartbeat that occurs as a residual effect of rheumatic fever.

rheumatism (roo'-mah-tiz-uhm) An *inflammation* of the muscles, joints, or nerves that causes stiffness of joints and muscle pain during motion.

rheumatoid arthritis See *juvenile rheumatoid arthritis*.

rhythm disorder A speech problem characterized by a breakdown or interruption in the normal outflow of speech sounds affecting or affected by breathing rate, tension, and emotional set.

ribonucleic (rye-boe-new-klee'-ik) **acid (RNA)** An element of body cells that is the means by which *chromosomal DNA* exerts control over protein synthesis.

rickets A childhood condition caused by a deficiency in vitamin D or sunlight, which results in softness of the bones and, consequently, their bending and distortion under muscular action.

right to education A principle supporting the obligation of the state to provide an *appropriate education* to all children; defined by the *Pennsylvania Association for Retarded Children (PARC)* court decision and spelled out with specific reference to persons with *mental retardation.*

right to treatment A principle set forth by the Alabama court case *Wyatt v. Stickney*, in which the judge ruled that if an individual is placed in an *institution*, the state has the moral responsibility to provide that person with adequate educational treatment.

rigidity 1. A manifestation of *cerebral palsy* in which *hypertension* of the muscles creates stiffness; both the contracting muscles and their paired relaxing muscles are affected. 2. An inability or inflexibility in shifting from one task, activity, or behavior to another, particularly observable in some persons with *mental retardation* and *brain injury.*

RLF An *acronym* for *retrolental fibroplasia.* See *retinopathy of prematurity*, now the preferred term.

RNA See *ribonucleic acid.*

Rochester method A communication system for *deaf* people based on *fingerspelling*; the method originated at the Rochester School for the Deaf. *Total communication* is now the preferred approach.

role play A technique used in teaching and counseling wherein individuals act out or walk through a desired role for the purpose of learning it or better understanding any problems they have had with it.

role tutor A student with a *disability* who teaches a younger general education student in an attempt to improve the tutor's self-image and to give the tutor added practice in basic skills; this technique is especially employed with students with *behavior disorders.*

Rood therapy A form of physical treatment applied to those with *cerebral palsy* that emphasizes the use of pressure to activate hard-working muscles and the use of light brushing to activate light-working muscles.

rote drill Numerous repetitions of a specific activity without applying the skills to problem-solving situations.

rote learning Knowledge acquired by memorization with little *attention* to its meaning.

RT See *recreational therapy.*

rubella See *German measles.*

rubeola The "old-fashioned" 10-day *measles*, or red measles, a disease accompanied by a red rash and fever. The disease can be prevented with a vaccine, but it is far less threatening to the unborn *fetus* than is *rubella.*

RVI See *related vocational instructor.*

S

Santa Monica Project A program developed at a school in Santa Monica, California, that serves students who are educationally *disabled* in a highly structured and individualized learning environment. Terminal goals are achieved through the use of *behavior modification* principles. See also *Madison Plan.*

satiation Satisfaction, often to the point of excess. One specific situation of satiation being to the point of excess would be in offering unlimited amounts of a *reinforcer* that has been maintaining a behavior; often the reinforcer will no longer stimulate the behavior.

savant syndrome A condition in which an individual with generally low *intelligence* displays a specialized area of extraordinary ability. For example, a person with *severe mental retardation* or *autism* may be able to add extremely large numbers in his/her mind or may be able to paint or play a musical instrument with great proficiency. The term savant syndrome is now more acceptable than the historical term *idiot savant.*

schedule of reinforcement The ratio or interval at which responses are rewarded.

schizophrenia (skit-so-fren'-nee-ah) (adj., **schizophrenic, schizoid**) A severe mental disorder *(psychosis)* characterized by a fragmented personality, fantasies, illusions, *delusions*, and, in general, being out of touch with reality.

school phobia A general fear of school or of some specific aspect of school, which causes an individual to resist attending school. Current theories suggest that the young child with school phobia really fears separation from parents rather than fearing school.

school-to-home telephone program A learning arrangement that enables a mature student with a *physical disability* to remain in complete contact with the general education classroom while doing schoolwork at home (or in the hospital). The school-to-home telephone program usually is supplemented by *home-based instruction* or by visits from someone from the hospital. Most recently called *teleschool.*

school-within-a-school Describes the organization of a school or class so that a particular segment such as *special education* operates as an integral part of general education.

scissor gait A manner of walking in which one foot passes in front of the other because of *spasticity* of the thigh muscles. Common in *ataxic cerebral palsy.*

sclera (skler'-uh) The tough protective covering of the eye.

sclerosis (skler-oh'-sis) Thickening and hardening of body tissue or part of an organ.

scoliosis (skoe-lee-oh'-sis) A lateral curvature of the spine. Bracing and surgery are both methods of treatment. The condition is most commonly first noted in girls between the ages of 10 and 13.

screening Abbreviated testing procedures conducted by a variety of *disciplines* on a large scale to locate individuals requiring more detailed testing or specialized teaching. The procedures have become quite elaborate to protect the rights of students and to ensure that proper decisions are made on placement in the *least restrictive environment.*

screening committee See *placement team.*

scurvy (skur'-vee) A disease caused by a deficiency of ascorbic acid (vitamin C) in the diet and characterized by *anemia*, low vitality, spongy gums, and bleeding into the skin and mucous membranes.

SDD See *significantly developmentally delayed.*

SEA See *state education(al) agency.*

second injury clause A provision that allows workers with *disabilities* to be protected by *workmen's compensation* while not requiring the employer to assume all the responsibility. This clause helps persons with disabilities to get jobs, because a special fund assumes much of the risk. Also called *subsequent injury clause.*

secondary drives Forces present in most humans but having little or no influence on animals or humans who function in the lower levels of *mental retardation.* Examples of these drives are desires for wealth, social prestige, and beauty.

secondary disability A condition, or conditions, of lesser severity than the major or *primary disability*, but that contributes to the total condition.

secondary reinforcer A *stimulus* that when paired with a primary *reinforcer* takes on the reinforcing properties of the primary reinforcer. (See also *reinforcement*.)

Section 504 The last section of the *Rehabilitation Act of 1973*; prohibits discrimination against persons with *disabilities* in employment and other fields. Part of a set of regulations (published in the *Federal Register*, May 4, 1977) established in an effort to assure the civil rights of these individuals.

SED See *seriously emotionally disturbed*.

SEE See *Signing Exact English*.

seeing eye dog An animal that is specially trained to aid *blind* persons in *mobility* and to protect them. The terms *lead dog* and *guide dog* are preferred.

segregation In the *context* of *special education*, the placement of individual children with *disabilities* in programs in which they relate only to other students who are *disabled* and do not have an opportunity to interact with general education students. This term represents the opposite of *integration*.

seizure An outward expression of abnormal brain discharges; may be characterized by several forms of behavior, from mild to severe in *intensity*. Associated with *epilepsy*. (See also *grand mal*, *petit mal*, *akinetic*, *myoclonic seizure*.)

self-as-a-model videotapes Used especially with students who have *emotional/behavior disorders* to facilitate improved behavior and better self-esteem. The students are videotaped in an activity and all inappropriate behaviors and comments are edited out to produce a 4–6

minute tape that the students view for 10 days in a row.

self-contained class (program) One in which students with similar needs and skills are assigned and taught by a *special education* teacher throughout the school day.

self-control curriculum A program taught to students with *behavior disorders* that emphasizes *metacognition* and the use of conscious and unconscious thought to help the students control their own behavior.

self-fulfilling prophecy The theoretical belief that an individual will become what is expected of him or her; also refers to the effect that *labeling* may have on how a person performs.

self-help (self-care) skills Knowledge that allows one to carry out daily living tasks without assistance or with a minimum of assistance. Teaching these skills is included in curricula for students with *disabilities*.

self-injurious behavior (SIB) Harm an individual inflicts on him- or herself that may result in tissue damage, may be life-threatening, or may be anything in-between. Examples are face slapping, eye gouging, head banging, and scratching.

self-injurious behavior inhibiting system (SIBIS) An electrical device that shocks an individual when he/she engages in head banging; used to reduce the occurrence of the unwanted behavior. However, this use of shock is controversial.

self-instructional training Describes the process in which a learner carries out problem orienting and emits a problem-solving statement to guide him- or herself through specific tasks. Students are taught to use *overt* and *covert verbalizations* to help maintain their *attention* or behavior. They may repeat to themselves "eyes on my work," "think before speaking out," etc. The procedure was developed by Donald Meichenbaum to help individuals use their own thought processes to control behavior. The procedure is now known as *cognitive behavior modification*.

self-mutilation A characteristic of some forms of *pathology* in which the individual does harm to his/her own body. (See also *self-injurious behavior*.)

self-stimulatory behavior Mannerisms frequently encountered in individuals with *autism* and *severe retardation*; consists of repeated rocking, flapping of the arms, and other movements. (See also *blindism* and *stereotypic behavior*.)

semantics (seh-man'-tix) The study of the significance or meaning of words.

semantography (seh-man-tog'-ruh-fee) An international system of symbols developed by Charles Bliss, who was born in Old Austria in 1877, where 20 different *languages* were spoken. Currently being used with individuals with *severe mental retardation*. (See *Bliss method*.)

semicircular canals The loop-shaped tubular parts of the labyrinth of the inner ear that function in determining one's position in space and in maintaining equilibrium and balance.

semi-independent living arrangement (SLA) A *group home* for adults with *disabilities* who require assistance with some minimal needs in order to live nearly independently.

semiskilled Describes a job or worker that requires some specialized training and usually does not require close supervision.

sensorimotor (sensory-motor) training The use of activities involving a transition from gross *stimuli* to refined ones, for the purpose of eliciting specific *motor* responses useful in problem solving.

sensorineural (sensory-neural) hearing loss See *nerve deafness (neural loss)*.

sensory Pertaining to any of the senses (sight, hearing, taste, smell, touch) or to sensations.

sensory aphasia (ah-fay'-zyuh) An inability to understand the meaning of written, spoken, or *tactile* speech symbols because of disease or injury to the *auditory* and *visual* brain centers.

sensory disability An *impairment* in one, or both, of the main senses (vision and hearing) such that *sensory* input is restricted through that channel(s).

sensory vocabulary Words, such as "cold" and "loud," that relate to any of the five senses.

SEP See *Office of Special Education Programs*.

separation anxiety disorder One of the classifications of the *DSM*-IV System. Individuals with this condition express excessive *distress*, withdrawal, *apathy*, or sadness when separated from a person to whom they feel an attachment.

sequenced instruction The logical, step-like succession of educational activities taught to students over time. The activities form a continuum of educational experiences based on the learning potential and needs of students at various *chronological ages*.

seriously emotionally disturbed (SED) A term used in U.S. laws referring to children with *behavior disorders* or disturbances. "Seriously" was added in the hope of limiting programs to those who are most severely disturbed. Recent legislation has changed the term to *emotional/behavior disorders*.

service delivery system The *range* of possible types of programs offered in *special education*, involving a gradient from full-time placement in general education classes to the most restrictive environments of a *special day school* and *institutionalization*. The preferable term in the 1990s is *service options*.

service options An administrative arrangement to provide services. *Special education* models include *resource room*, *special class*, itinerant program, and others. (See *service delivery system*.) This term has gained preference over the term *service delivery system*.

setting event An environmental condition more complex than a single *stimulus* event that, simply by occurring, will affect subsequent stimulus-response relations. For example, giving instruction to a fatigued child (the stimulus event) may result in disruptive behaviors such as *tantrums* (subsequent stimulus).

settlement An out-of-court agreement among parties to a lawsuit, which resolves some or all of the issues involved in a case.

severe disabilities (adj., **severely disabled**) A term applied to individuals having physical, mental, or emotional problems that require educational, social, psychological, and/or *medical services* beyond those traditionally offered by general and *special education*. Also known as **severely handicapped**. Current preferences are against using this term as a noun ("the severely handicapped").

severe discrepancy A *concept* closely tied to determining *eligibility* for service for students with *learning disabilities*. School systems must establish a significant difference (or severe discrepancy) between the potential and the measured achievement of such individuals to determine them eligible for service. This is probably the most used characteristic in this regard.

severe mental retardation (adj., **severely retarded**) 1. A term of educational origin that refers to an *intellectual* level of functioning lower than *trainable mentally retarded*. These individuals usually have an *IQ* 4 *standard deviations* below the *mean*. Individuals with severe mental retardation may be able to live in a *group home* or *alternative living* system but require supervision throughout life. 2. One of the levels of retardation in the American Association on Mental Retardation's (AAMR) classification system (now called *extensive mental retardation*). It is the next-to-lowest category, characterized by IQs in the 20 to 39 *range*.

shape vocabulary An educational term referring to words identified with the physical attributes of configurations— e.g., square, circle.

shaping A procedure of *reinforcing* specific behavior that requires the individual to make ever closer approximations to the desired terminal behavior. Shaping involves the reinforcement of desired behavior and the *extinction* of undesirable behavior.

shared services An arrangement whereby a number of school districts too small to provide *special education* programs or serve students with *low-incidence disabilities* pool their resources and develop a service across district boundaries to reach all those in the cooperating districts who are in need of a specific service. Sometimes referred to as *cooperative plans* or *intermediate districts*.

sheltered employment A *structured program* of activities involving *work evaluation*, *work adjustment*, occupational skill training, and remunerative employment designed to prepare individuals either for competitive employment or for continued work in a protective environment.

sheltered English A term that does not correctly connote its meaning. Refers to a method of teaching English to minority children that involves teaching the *language* at an accelerated speed through the use of reading and content-area instruction. Some success of this method over traditional methods has been noted. The method has similarities to many *special education* approaches, such as language experiences.

sheltered workshops Similar to *sheltered employment* except that it exists only in a protective environment. Unlike competitive employment, preference is given to applicants with *severe disabilities*.

shoreline Any continuous physical element that functions as a guide for *blind* persons in *mobility*—e.g., the edge of the sidewalk.

short-term memory A *memory* state that is very short. In research, it usually refers to memory of less than a minute. When a student forgets assignments or directions just given by the teacher, he/she may have a short-term memory problem.

short-term objectives An element of the *individualized education program* that involves a written listing of specific tasks targeted for a child to accomplish in an effort toward achieving the *long-range goals* set for that child for the school term or year.

shunt (shunting) A technique involving the implantation of a tube to drain or provide a bypass for excess *cerebrospinal fluid*, as in individuals with *hydrocephalus*.

SIB See *self-injurious behavior*.

sibilant (sih'-bill-ant) One of the high-*frequency* sounds produced in pronouncing *ch, s, z, j*.

SIBIS See *self-injurious behavior inhibiting system*.

sibling rivalry Competition, resentment, and jealousy that occurs to varying degrees between children of the same parents. A certain amount of sibling rivalry is considered "normal."

sickle cell anemia A blood condition in which the red cells assume a crescent shape and do not function properly in carrying oxygen. The condition is *genetic* and largely limited to African-Americans. It results in low vitality, pain, sloughing of blood cells, and interference with *cerebral* nutrition. If severe enough, it may cause *mental retardation* or death.

sight vocabulary Words basic to formal reading that are memorized or recognized as a whole, rather than by a *blending* of parts.

sighted guide technique A form of assisted travel for *blind* persons in which a seeing person (the **sighted guide**) allows a blind person to lightly hold the inside of his/her arm. This is the most common form of *mobility* for blind children under 11 years of age.

sign language Any form of communication based on the systematic use of physical gestures that can be differentiated by *deaf* individuals. Current educational practice uses the term *total communication* to refer to the combined use of sign language, *fingerspelling*, speech, *speech reading*, and *residual hearing* for communication purposes.

signals Communication designed to *prompt* or remind an individual of what the appropriate behavior is. For example, a teacher may remind a *compulsive* rocker to stop by tugging on his/her ear, thus **signaling** that rocking is inappropriate in this setting; preliminary to a reprimand or further corrective action.

significantly developmentally delayed (SDD) Describes children who are at risk of being *disabled* at a later date.

Signing Exact English (SEE) A *manual method* of communication for *deaf* persons in which the signals follow the English order for basic words. SEE is much more likely to be used in school instruction than *Ameslan*, which is a *language* in itself and is structurally different from English.

simultagnosis (sie-mull-tag-noe'-sis) The ability to recognize when two different parts of the body are touched simultaneously. One's not being able to recognize simultaneous touch may be considered a *"soft" sign* of *minimal brain dysfunction.*

sip and puff chair A type of electric wheelchair with a control device that is activated by the mouth. A short inhaling turns the wheelchair to the left; a long inhaling causes the chair to go in reverse; a short puff or exhaling turns the chair to the right; a continuous puff carries the wheelchair forward.

site-based management An administrative practice common in recent years that emphasizes decentralization in school systems, placing most decisions in the hands of teachers and local administrators.

six-hour retarded A term used in the 1970s to describe disadvantaged and minority children who were *labeled* as *retarded* while at school but who functioned and coped normally in their environment the remainder of the time.

SLA See *semi-independent living arrangement.*

slate and stylus Instruments for writing *braille*. The slate consists of two hinged metal plates, the lower one having rows of indented braille cells and the top one having rows of windows corresponding to the indented braille cells. The braille paper is inserted between the two plates, and the braille dots are impressed with an awl-like stylus into the paper.

sleep disorder Any condition that causes excessive interference with normal sleep.

slow learner A term used to describe students who have *educational retardation* and whose *IQ range* is 70–89. These individuals have some of the same problems in learning and dealing with the environment as students who have *mild mental retardation*, but to a lesser degree.

SLP See *speech and language pathologist.*

smooth muscles The muscles of internal body organs that contract and relax involuntarily and do not fatigue as easily as the voluntary muscles. Reactions to tense, unpleasant emotional situations may have an unfavorable effect on these muscles, and children living under environmental pressures who chronically complain of stomach pain may be suffering this effect.

Snellen chart A white background imprinted with black letters or symbols of graded size that is used to test distant field *visual acuity*. The use of this chart, combined with teacher observation, is one method of *screening* for *visual* problems.

social competence The ability to function adequately in society; more specifically, includes competence in grooming, eating, etiquette, and social graces. Also called *social maturity.*

social inclusion A *concept* emerging from the *inclusion* movement that extends the concept of inclusion beyond the educational framework to promote social friendships and the involvement of the *disabled* and nondisabled in the community.

social learning The process of developing *social competence* in one's interactions with other individuals.

social learning curriculum A program for children with *mild mental retardation*, originated by Herbert Goldstein in 1969, that provides social training through a continuous sequence of experiences that were determined based on the learning characteristics of students with *mental retardation*.

social maturity The ability to behave appropriately in various situations and to accept the obligations of good citizenship. Equivalent in meaning to *social competence*.

social mobility The movement of individuals or groups from one socioeconomic level to another, either upward or downward; greatly influenced by family goals, *educational potential*, level of education, earning power, and sometimes by the birth of a child with a *disability* into the family.

social perception The ability to interpret the social environment, as in being aware of people's moods and realizing the causes and effects of one's own behavior. Persons with *mental retardation* and some individuals with *learning disabilities* have problems in this area.

social promotion The advancement of a pupil to the next higher *grade level* at the time the *peer group* advances, even if the student has not mastered the content taught in the current grade. Although some research supports this practice, it is now being questioned by educational reformers.

social quotient An expression of social development derived from a measurement device such as the Vineland Social Maturity Scale. Social quotient is computed in a manner similar to *IQ*—i.e., social age divided by *chronological age* and multiplied by 100. A term currently in greater use is *adaptive behavior*.

social reinforcement The use of personal *attention*, friendly remarks, a smile, positive comments, etc., to motivate desired responses.

social worker A professional trained to aid individuals with *disabilities* and disadvantaged persons by collecting home and environmental information and coordinating and dispensing services.

socialized delinquency A *syndrome* of *behavior disorders* that includes truancy, gang membership, theft, and *norm* violation.

socialized-aggressive Describes an individual who exhibits his/her *aggression* as a member of a group (gang). (See also *socially maladjusted*.)

socially maladjusted Describes a state of persistent refusal to behave within the minimum standards of conduct required in society. Socially maladjusted children tend to destroy school property, abuse privileges, ignore responsibility, and ridicule teachers, peers, and others with whom they come in contact. (See also *socialized-aggressive*.)

sociodrama A technique involving the simulation of social or vocational situations in which pupils play the roles of individuals as those individuals might be in real life; used to increase *social maturity*. This technique offers an opportunity to explore and have experiences prior to actually being involved in similar situations in real life, thus preparing individuals to select behaviors for life adjustment.

sociogram A graph plotting the structure of *interpersonal relations* in a group or class. Utilizes answers to questions concerning, for example, choices of classmates as partners in order to indicate members of the group who are causing friction, who are isolates, who are looked upon as leaders, etc.

sociopath An individual who has a morbid attitude toward society and lacks conscience in accepting responsibility for unacceptable behavior. Criminals, for example, often reveal **sociopathic** behavior.

soft palate See *palate*.

"soft" sign Refers to mild abnormalities that are more difficult to detect than the obvious or gross problems but indicate the possibility of a disabling condition. "Soft" signs usually are measured by *psychometric* means and are suggestive of *neurological* disorders and mild *learning disabilities*.

somatopsychology (soe-mat-oh-sigh-kahl'-ah-jee) The study of both the body and the mind, specifically of the effect of body deviation on behavior.

somatotype (soe-mat'-oh-tipe) One of three types of bodily configurations. (See *ectomorphic, endomorphic, mesomorphic.*)

SOMPA See *System of Multicultural Pluralistic Assessment.*

sonic glasses Eyeglasses equipped with small disc elements that emit different *pitch* sounds depending on the closeness of objects. These glasses help those with *visual impairments* locate objects by discriminating differences in echoes, similar to the skill used by bats. The same technology has also been embedded in **sonic canes**.

sonogram An *X-ray* type of examination of a pregnant woman in which the *fetus* is outlined by sonar waves; used to identify certain deviations in the size and position of the fetus, as well as physical defects. Another term is *ultrasound*.

Spalding Unified Phonics A system of teaching reading and spelling that emphasizes the 70 phonograms representing the 44 sounds of English. The sounds, rather than the names of the alphabet letters, and their various combinations are taught.

spastic 1. **Spasticity** generally refers to muscular incoordination resulting from muscle spasms, opposing contractions of muscles, and *paralytic* effects. 2. The name for a form of *cerebral palsy* having these characteristics.

spatial (spay'-shul) Anything related to or involving the interpretation of space. Spatial *concepts* are often difficult for individuals with *mental retardation*; individuals with *learning disabilities* sometimes have this difficulty and, as a result, encounter rather severe learning problems.

special class A *self-contained program* in which students spend all or most of their day with others who have similar problems. Special classes were the primary *service delivery system* option for those with *disabilities* prior to 1972.

special day school Any learning *institution* that serves children with exceptionalities during daytime hours. This type of school has no *residential services*.

special education A broad term covering programs and services for students who *deviate* physically, mentally, or emotionally from the norm to an extent that they require unique learning experiences, techniques, or materials in order to be maintained in the general education classroom, or in specialized classes and programs if their problems are more severe. As defined by *Public Law 101–476*, special education is specifically designed instruction, at no cost to the parent, to meet the unique needs of a student with a *disability*, including classroom instruction, physical education, home instruction, and instruction in hospitals and *institutions*.

special education diploma Graduation certification awarded to students with *disabilities* who have met the *objectives* of their *individualized education program*; now given in many states in place of the general diploma.

Special Education Programs (SEP) See *Office of Special Education Programs.*

special health problem Any condition that interferes with an individual's well-being and *educational potential* but is not classified under *orthopedic, sensory,* or mental *disabilities.* Progressive deterioration and low vitality conditions such as *muscular dystrophy, cystic fibrosis, myasthenia gravis, cardiovascular* disorders, *diabetes,* and *arthritis* are examples of special health problems.

Special Olympics An athletic organization for youngsters with *disabilities* that functions at local, state, and international levels for the enhancement of the skills of participants in a way similar to the regular Olympics.

special school districts The same *concept* as *intermediate districts,* but involves smaller school districts. The districts cooperate in servicing students with *low-incidence disabilities.* The St. Louis Special School District is the oldest and largest, servicing 24 districts.

specialized health care needs A term that has come into use with reference to children who require technological health care procedures for life support. Examples are ventilation procedures and kidney dialysis.

specific language disability A condition characterized by a lack of achievement in a particular *language* area.

specific learning disability See *learning disability.*

spectogram A *visual* voiceprint analogous to a fingerprint. An electronic in-strument, a **spectograph**, plots *frequencies* of overtones against time in a sine wave and allows playback of speech and sound patterns for analysis.

speech and language pathologist (SLP) A person approved by the American Speech-Language-Hearing Association to work with children who have speech and *language disorders.* Also known as a *speech clinician.*

speech audiometer An instrument for measuring hearing that is used to determine when the testee can identify words being said, rather than just tones, at controlled levels of *intensity.* (See also *audiometer.*)

speech clinician (pathologist) (therapist) A professional who has special training in speech improvement and correction; works with individuals who have some problem with speech, *language,* or spoken communication that is not expected to improve with maturation alone.

speech correction Refers to a treatment program or service that has the *objective* of improving the abilities of individuals who have a deficiency or difficulty in spoken *language* production.

speech defect (disorder) Any imperfection in an individual's production of the sounds of *language*; caused by problems such as inadequate muscle coordination, faulty *articulation,* poor voice quality, or *organic* defects. The most accepted definition emphasizes that the condition, to be so identified, must interfere with communication, call *attention* to the speaker, or cause the speaker *anxiety* or *maladjustment.*

speech pathology (pathologist) The field of diagnosing and treating speech problems and the lack of speech development; involves *individualized testing* and *instruction,* as well as work with small groups.

speech reading (lip reading) A skill taught to persons who are *deaf* and *hard of hearing* through which they can understand what is said by another person by observing the *context* of the situation and the *visual* cues of speech production, such as movements of lips and facial features.

speech reception threshold (SRT) The *decibel* (loudness) level at which an individual can understand speech.

speech therapy A planned program of speech improvement and correction for individuals who have a *disability* in *language* communication and speech adjustment that is not expected to improve solely through their normal maturation.

sphincter (sfingk'-ter) A ring-like muscle that constricts a passage or closes a natural *orifice* (body opening).

spina bifida A *congenital malformation* of the spine characterized by lack of closure of the vertebral column, which often allows protrusion of the spinal cord into a sac at the base of the spine. The degree of severity may vary, but this condition often causes *paralysis* of the lower *extremities*, changes in *tactile* and thermal sensations, and a lack of bowel and bladder control. Whenever possible, surgery is performed at an early age to reduce the debilitating effects. Spina bifida frequently is associated with *hydrocephalus* and a reduction of *intelligence*, unless *shunting* is done.

spina bifida occulta A form of *spina bifida* in which there is a spinal defect but the spinal cord is not injured or exposed; children with spina bifida occulta do not have the usual *paralysis* and other characteristics associated with *spina bifida*.

spinal meningitis See *meningitis*.

splinter skills Selected activities or abilities that develop to an excessive level in a child with *disabilities* while other skills are at a much lower level; most often observed in students with *mental retardation* or *autism*.

SQ3R A method associated with the *learning strategies approach*; emphasizes *s*urvey (rapid preview of material), *q*uestion (convert each section or subtitle to a question), (1) *r*ead (rapidly read sections), (2) *r*ecite (answer questions), (3) *r*eview (make a written or an *oral* statement of what has been learned).

SRT See *speech reception threshold*.

SSI See *supplemental security income*.

SST See *student support team*.

staff development See *inservice training*.

staffing A meeting of teachers, *therapists*, administrators, and others involved in the planning or *evaluation* of an educational or a *therapeutic* program. The meaning of the term may vary from state to state; in some states it may refer specifically to an *individualized education program* meeting. Also termed *case conference*.

stammer A speech problem in which the speaker makes involuntary stops and repetitions with the effect of jerky, halting speech. (See also *dysfluency, stuttering*.)

standard deviation A measure of expressing the variability of a set of scores or attributes. Small standard deviations mean the scores are distributed close to the *mean*; large standard deviations mean the scores are spread over a wider *range*.

standard practice The professional "method of choice" that can reasonably be expected to be replicated from one area to another.

standard score A general term referring to a transformed or normalized score; used to compare an individual's performance to that of a *norm range*.

standardized test A measure that is administered and scored by uniform *objective* procedures and for which norms have been established so the scores of anyone completing the test can be compared to the norms.

standing table A table-shaped piece of equipment with a half-circle cut out of it and having a gate in the back that allows a person with *physical disabilities* who is otherwise bedridden or in a wheelchair to stand erect for physical relief, to increase strength, and, at times, for social interaction.

Stanford-Binet A widely used, individually administered test for measuring *intelligence*; consists of a number of different types of items. The test has been through a number of revisions and with the Wechsler Scales makes up the most often used measures of intelligence.

stapes The innermost of the three small bones in the middle ear that conduct vibrations from the *tympanic membrane* to the inner ear. Often called the "stirrup" because of its shape. The other two bones are the *incus* and the *malleus*.

staphylococcus (staf-uh-loe-kah'-kus) Ball-shaped bacteria that occur in clusters and give rise to infections such as boils, abscesses, and carbuncles. These are sometimes called "staph" infections.

startle response 1. The reaction of an individual to loud shouts or to bangs on a table, for example, which interrupt behavior. 2. An innate *reflex* that is triggered when one is confronted with a frightening *stimulus*. (See *Moro reflex*.)

state education(al) agency (SEA) Terminology used in federal and state legislation to refer to the department in state government that has primary responsibility for public school education.

state plan The written summary of the projected organization and description of a state program, often required by federal legislation.

status offenders Refers to young people who run away from home, create *discipline* problems, or generally exhibit behaviors that, because of their age, are against the law. (If these persons were adults, these acts would not be against the law.)

status seizure (status epilepticus) A *grand mal seizure* that starts, stops, and repeats itself after 5 minutes, or a *seizure* that lasts longer than 10 minutes. Status seizures, unlike certain other seizures, are viewed as serious enough to warrant calling an ambulance or physician.

statutory right A right based on a statute or law passed by a unit of federal, state, or local government.

Steinut's disease See *myotonic dystrophy*.

stenosis (steh-noe'-sis) Narrowing of any canal or passage, especially one of the *cardiac* valves.

stereognosis (stair-ee-og-noe'-sis) The ability to recognize objects by touch. The inability to do this may be a *"soft" sign* of *minimal brain dysfunction*.

stereotoner An electronic instrument that converts printed images to audible tones; useful for *blind* individuals.

stereotype (adj., **stereotypic**) 1. A fixed or standardized response to specific *stimuli* or situations. This characteristic is often displayed by students with *disabilities* and tends to make certain responses and behaviors predictable. 2. A *label* applied to a person who has characteristics common to and identified with members of a given group.

stereotypic behavior A behavior pattern, such as swaying the body back and forth or moving the head from side to side, that is a characteristic motion of *blind* persons. Such behavior patterns are interpreted to be acts of involuntary *self-stimulatory behavior* resulting from a lack of meaningful activity. Because the *symptoms* are also observed in individuals with *emotional disturbances, brain injuries,* and *mental retardation*, the terminology is changing to stereotypic behavior or *manneristic behaviors.*

stereotypies The rhythmic actions of healthy infants, seen in the arms, legs, and trunk.

stigmata Physical features or markings that are used in *diagnosis*. In *Down syndrome*, the *epicanthal fold* of skin around the eyes, short stubby fingers, and palm crease are identifying stigmata.

Still's disease A *chronic* form of *arthritis* that affects most of the joints of the body and is accompanied by irregular fever and enlargement of the spleen and lymph nodes.

stimulant Anything that temporarily arouses or heightens physiological or *organic* activity.

stimulus (pl., **stimuli**) Any object or happening that excites a response from an organism.

stimulus-based treatments Approaches that focus on events that precede a behavior in contrast with conventional treatments that manipulate consequences of these behaviors.

stoma An external opening created by surgery—on the abdomen, by an *ileostomy* or *colostomy*; on the throat, by *laryngectomy.*

strabismus (strah-bis'-mus) A condition in which a person's eyes do not see on the same plane. The eyes can assume any pattern of faulty *convergence* or divergence. Such a condition may result in a lack of *fusion* (i.e., a lack of *binocular vision*). The basic problem is with balance of the muscles of the eyes. See also *esophoria* and *exophoria.*

Strauss syndrome A condition in children characterized by *hyperactivity*, uncoordinated movements, poor *concentration*, and learning problems. A. A. Strauss connected this set of *symptoms* with *brain damage*. More recently, however, the term has been used to designate a condition characterized by the symptoms that Strauss described but with or without *diagnosed brain injury.*

strephosymbolia (stref-oh-sim-boe'-lee-ah) A disorder in which objects are perceived in reverse, as in a mirror. This condition may affect one's ability to distinguish between letters such as *b* and *d* or *q* and *p*, and it also may cause a tendency to reverse direction in reading. (See also *dyslexia* and *learning disability*.)

streptococcus (strep-toe-kah'-kus) Ball-shaped bacteria that occur in chain-like formations and are found in many *pathological* infections, such as the sore throat that precedes *rheumatic fever*. The shortened term is "strep," as in "strep throat."

stress The condition of being under emotional or physical pressure, usually caused by external influences that may contribute to bodily or mental tension. Positive stress is called *eustress*. Negative stress is called *distress* or in slang use, stress, though this latter use is incorrect.

stretch reflex The tendency for a muscle to contract involuntarily after it is extended quickly.

striated (or **striped**) **muscles** The voluntary muscles that move the body. These are the muscles that are *conditioned* when an individual learns an action.

stroke A sudden or severe bodily attack caused by the rupture of a blood vessel in the brain, too much heat, or injury to the brain or spinal cord. Residual effects may include varying degrees of *paralysis*, *memory* loss, inhibited *language*, and psychological *disorientation*.

structural analysis In reading, the use of *decoding* skills to break a word into its parts (root, suffix, prefix) in order to understand its meaning.

structure of the intellect A model, developed by J. P. Guilford, that postulates that certain *contents of thought* are associated with certain *operations* or thinking functions to produce certain *products of thinking*. This model is one of the most systematic attempts to describe *intellectual* processes.

structured learning A group technique used to teach social skills, employing four components: *modeling*, *role playing*, performance *feedback*, and *transfer (of learning)*. These four elements must be incorporated in the order in which they are listed. Feedback may be in terms of rewards or knowledge of performance.

structured program 1. A *concept* advanced by William Cruickshank in which learning activities and the environment are carefully designed by the teacher. 2. Any systematic, programmed *curriculum* that deemphasizes group or informal instruction.

student support team (SST) A group of educationally related personnel set up in the school system to receive *referrals* before children are screened by *special education* personnel. The SST determines and documents the severity of the problem and which alternative approaches might be used before special education is considered. In many cases, other services are offered in lieu of special education. This practice was initiated in the 1990s. (See also *teacher assistance team*.)

study booth See *carrel*.

stupor A condition of extreme *apathy* with a lack of sense or feeling; results from *stress* or shock.

stuttering Speech characterized by *blocking*, hesitation, or repetition of single sounds, words, and sometimes sentences. (See also *dysfluency*.)

sub nom. A Latin abbreviation in a citation to a case that indicates that the case was decided by another court under a different name (sub meaning "under," and nom. being an abbreviation for the Latin word nomine, meaning "name").

subcutaneous Refers to the area below the skin.

sublimate (n., **sublimation**) To direct energy from its natural course to one that is more socially acceptable or more useful to the person. Sublimation is the result of this action.

subsequent injury clause See *second injury clause*.

substance abuse The inappropriate intake of alcohol or other drugs or chemical substances.

substance right A guaranteed right, such as the right to an education, usually granted by statutes and constitutions.

substitute consent Agreement made by a person on behalf of someone who is considered incapable of making his/her own decisions.

substitution (in speech) An *articulatory* defect of speech in which a correct sound is replaced with an incorrect sound, such as when one says "wed" instead of "red."

subtest A part of a test; items measuring a particular type of skill arranged together.

successive approximation A learning technique in which a student's emitted behavior must improve with each occurrence for the student to receive *reinforcement*. Used by teachers working with children who have *autism* and other *severe disabilities* to guide the students more closely to desired behavior responses.

super phone A telephone communication device that translates a message from a *deaf* person into a speech-*synthesized* message.

superego A term first discussed in Sigmund Freud's writings on *psychoanalytic* theory in the 1890s as the aspect of one's being that contains the conscience and serves as a guide for achieving socially acceptable solutions to problems.

superlearning A *concept* based on the work of Georgi Lazanov that emphasizes the body and mind working in harmony. Techniques involve the use of *music therapy*, relaxation exercises, breathing rhythm, etc., during the learning process.

supine A position of lying on one's back with the face upward. Opposite of *prone*.

supplemental security income (SSI) A federally financed and administered income maintenance support program based upon need. Persons with mental or *physical disabilities* who are unable to support themselves can qualify for this program. The funds often are used to maintain a person in a *group home* or nursing home.

support services Programs that are not of a strictly educational nature but that are essential for the educational development of students with *disabilities* (e.g., *physical therapy*, medical *intervention*). These services must be delineated in an *individualized education program*; *IDEA* refers to them as *related services*.

supported employment A program of the 1980s emphasizing the placement of individuals with *disabilities* in competitive employment under the supervision and training of a *job coach*, who is usually an employee of the company at which the individual is working.

supportive braces Adaptive devices designed to support specific parts of the body. They may be worn temporarily until an injury mends or a muscle strengthens, or they may be needed indefinitely.

suppression The intentional exclusion of thoughts or feelings from consciousness, often to avoid or overcome unacceptable thoughts or desires.

supra A Latin word in a citation to a case indicating that the same case was referred to in an earlier part of the same article, chapter, book, judicial opinion, or other writing. It means the opposite of *infra*.

surrogate parent(s) As stipulated in PL 101–476, a substitute parent who is to be appointed if the real parent cannot be present in *due process* hearings. The surrogate parent is to serve as an *advocate* for the rights of the child.

survival education (camping) See *wilderness education*.

suspension The removal of a student from school for 10 or fewer days. (Under *Honig v. Doe*, limit is 10 days; under Jeffords Amendment, can be up to 45 days under certain circumstances.) Suspensions do not require parental notification or a hearing. However, the suspension of a student with *disabilities* does require an *individualized education program* review and the development of a disciplinary plan that may include suspension.

sweep check A *screening* test, as for *hearing loss*, in which *acuity* at certain representative *frequencies* is checked at a predetermined level (e.g., 30 *db*). The sweep check allows for the administration of a large number of tests in a relatively short time.

symbiotic psychosis A severe *behavior disorder* of childhood marked by *autistic*-like behavior and excessive clinging to parents.

symbolic function Representing one thing with another (e.g., using words to represent people, objects, and ideas).

symbolic material In J. P. Guilford's model (see *structure of the intellect*), elements that have no natural meaning (e.g., numbers, syllables, letters).

symbolization The representation of ideas or tangible objects with words, figures, marks, or signs. Symbolization involves more abstract thinking than does dealing with the tangible objects themselves, and thus may be more difficult for a child to learn.

symptom An outward sign that indicates the possibility of a disease or mental/emotional problem (e.g., a cough may point toward the *diagnosis* of a cold, flu, pneumonia, etc.). If symptoms are treated without removing the cause, the condition may be masked or, in the case of *maladaptive behavior*, other symptoms may replace the original ones; this is called **symptom substitution**.

syndactylism (sin-dak'-til-izm) A *congenital syndrome* characterized by webbed fingers or toes.

syndrome A group or complex of signs that constitute a particular condition. More specifically applied, an accumulation of *symptoms* that jointly characterize a disease.

synkinesis (sin-kih-nee'-sis) A *"soft" sign* of *minimal brain dysfunction* described as "mirror movement"; for example, in testing, the serial touching of the thumb to the fingers may be mirrored by the opposite hand that is not being tested.

synovial (sin-oh'-vee-uhl) **membrane** The sheath that lines the ligamentous surfaces of joint capsules and tendons and secretes **synovia**, a lubricating fluid that facilitates articulation between the tendon and bone.

synovitis (sin-oh-vie'-tiss) A condition in which the *synovial membrane* is *inflamed*, resulting in more limited movement of joints.

syntax (or **grammar**) The *linguistic* rules of word order for meaningful sentences. **Syntactic** is the descriptive term that applies to grammar and rules governing sentence structure and word/phrase sequence.

synthesis (sin'-theh-sis) (v., **synthesize**) The formation of a whole by combining its various components. Children who have difficulty learning often have trouble recognizing and combining individual observations to perceive a total incident or idea.

synthesized (synthetic) speech Mechanically produced sounds that are intelligible and carry meaning.

synthetic touch A *concept* applied to *blind* children in which the *tactile* exploration of small objects is used as the basis for *perception*. If a child feels a baseball, for example, we say his/her concept of it is based on the tactile experiences of feeling the whole ball. (See also *analytic touch*.)

syphilis (sif'-ih-lis) A *venereal disease* progressing in three stages—primary, secondary, and tertiary—that if untreated will lead to *chancres*, *lesions*, general ill health, and eventually death. A pregnant woman with untreated syphilis may deliver a *malformed* baby with active syphilis.

system of least prompts A *prompting* system that is most effectively used with students with *severe disabilities* who know how to perform a task but need to do so faster or in a different environment.

The student is initially given the least amount of assistance possible. If the student does not respond with the least amount of assistance, he/she is gradually given more assistance until a correct response is achieved. (The teacher may, for example, give verbal assistance, then gesture, then demonstrate, and then, if still no response, physically guide the student.)

system of maximum prompts A *prompting* system commonly used with students with *severe disabilities* when they are initially learning a targeted *objective*. The student is given the maximum assistance possible (i.e., full physical assistance) until a certain *criterion* is reached. Then a less intrusive prompt is used (i.e., partial physical assistance) until a certain criterion is reached. This process continues through less intrusive prompts until the student is performing the targeted objective independently.

System of Multicultural Pluralistic Assessment (SOMPA) An approach to *assessment* developed by Jane Mercer that included social and ethnic consideration in judging individuals' potential for learning.

T

tachistoscope (tak-iss'-toe-skope) A simple device that is basically a "window" or frame used to control the number or amount (and sometimes the length of exposure) of words, numbers, pictures, or other *visual stimuli* exposed for reading. The principle behind the use of this device is that it is beneficial for the student to focus on the exact learning desired and to avoid distractors. (See also *typoscope*.)

tactile (tactual) Pertaining to the sense of touch. (See also *haptic*.)

tactile agnosia (ag-noe'-zee-ah) The inability to recognize *stimuli* through the sense of touch.

tactile discrimination The ability to determine the sameness of or the difference between two or more *stimuli* through the sense of touch/feel alone.

tactile perception The ability to interpret (attach meaning to) environmental information, including size, shape, and texture, via the sense of touch.

tactilear (tack'-till-ear) Refers to a watch-like type of electronic device that changes speech into a *tactile* form that is imprinted on the arm.

talented Describes someone showing a natural aptitude or ability in a specific field without the implication of an exceptionally high degree of general *intelligence*. The *concept* of talent is sometimes used in reference to *gifted and talented*.

talking book A record or audiotape of a book or periodical recorded for use by persons who are *blind* or *partially sighted*. Listening to a recording is a faster, more efficient means of receiving information than is reading *braille* or reading print using *low-vision aids*.

tandem gait Walking a line heel to toe in sequential steps. A child who does not do this well or displays loss of control while walking in this way may be exhibiting a *"soft" sign* of *minimal brain dysfunction*.

tantrum A violent fit of bad temper manifested by crying, sudden destructiveness, striking the wall or floor, and the like. Continued tantrums may signal a *behavior disorder* warranting special services.

tardive dyskinesia (tar'-dive dis-kih-nee'-zee-ah) A medical condition resulting as a side effect of long-term use of antipsychotic medications, characterized by involuntary movements of the face, mouth, tongue, trunk, and upper *extremities*. Grimacing, blinking, and lip smacking are among the expressed behaviors.

target behavior A specifically selected action or goal to be attained under *behavior modification* principles and techniques.

task analysis The process of breaking down learning tasks into the smallest elements in the proper sequence. The resulting instruction involves systematically teaching specific elements in sequence or, in the case of *backward (reverse) chaining*, teaching "backward" to the just-previous element.

TAT See *teacher assistance team.*

taxonomy A scheme or system used to categorize or classify, as for *behavior disorders* or *objectives* in education.

Tay-Sachs disease A *hereditary* condition resulting from a *metabolic* error in processing fats, which leads to *severe mental retardation* (also called *amaurotic family idiocy*) and death in early childhood. Often called an "ethnic" disease because it is found mainly in children of Ashkenazi Jewish descent.

TB See *tuberculosis.*

TBI See *traumatic brain injury.*

TDD See *telecommunication device for the deaf.*

teacher aide A subprofessional assigned to a classroom to help with certain tasks and details, usually of a noninstructional nature. The aide's duties generally consist of material preparation, supervision of independent study and activities, record keeping, and errand running. Another term is *paraprofessional*, or *parapro.*

teacher assistance team (TAT) A term equivalent to *student support team*; these individuals provide a *prereferral system* and *intervention* before *special education* services are attempted.

technological aids Telecommunication, *sensory*, and other devices used by persons to help reduce the effects of *disabilities.*

technology-based assessment A term of the 1990s that refers to the use of computers and expert systems to maintain careful checks on what and how much students are learning.

telebinocular Describes optical instruments used to test an individual's *visual efficiency* by measuring how well the testee combines images, perceives depth, and so on.

telecommunication device for the deaf (TDD) An electronic device through which individuals with *hearing impairments* can communicate with other individuals, both *hearing impaired* and *non-hearing impaired.* A telephone number followed by "TDD" means that an agency or company (or another *deaf* person) has a device for communicating electronically with deaf individuals.

teleschool See *school-to-home telephone program.*

telescopic lenses One, two, or three lenses used for each eye, usually in eyeglasses or clip-on glasses, to improve distance vision, especially for those having severe *visual disabilities.*

telescoping A programming option for *gifted* students that means teaching the same amount of material in less than the usual amount of time. A form of *acceleration.*

terminal objectives The *short-term objectives* or *long-range goals* specified by an *individualized education program.*

test item The smallest *unit* of a test (e.g., "How are an apple and a peach alike?").

tetanus (tet'-nus) An *acute* infectious disease commonly called "lockjaw" that is characterized by spasms of voluntary muscles, especially the jaw. This condition is caused by a bacillus usually introduced through a break in the skin.

therapeutic recreation A form of treatment that employs leisure activities of a mildly physical nature as corrective measures.

therapy (adj., **therapeutic**) Any treatment or structuring of the environment to improve an individual's well-being. A person whose work is specifically intended for providing therapy may be called a **therapist**.

therblig This term, which is almost "Gilbreth" spelled backwards, refers to any of the 17 fundamental motions that have been found to be useful in describing all manual operations; Gilbreth is the name of the person who first enumerated these fundamental motions. These operations have been found to be most useful in *task analysis* and in instructing individuals with *severe*/profound *disabilities*. Examples of the therbligs include grasp, reach, hold, and release.

"think-aloud" data protocols Refer to data collection methods in which students *verbalize* the step-by-step processes by which they derive a product.

thinning Gradually presenting reinforcers less frequently as a new, desired behavior is acquired.

threshold Refers to the smallest amount of *stimulus* energy capable of arousing an impulse in a receptor or nerve cell and resulting in a sensation. Stimulus energy below that level is described as "below threshold" or "does not elicit sensation."

threshold vocabulary A core of vocabulary necessary for basic communication. In individuals with *developmental dis-*

abilities the threshold vocabulary would be those words necessary for communication in basic *activities of daily living.*

thyroid An *endocrine* gland, located in the front lower portion of the neck, that secretes *hormones* that regulate the body's rate of *metabolism.*

tibia The larger of the two bones of the lower leg, located to the inside of the smaller bone, the *fibula.*

tic A habitual spasmodic movement or twitching of a muscle or group of muscles, often involving the face.

time and motion study A comparison of the speed at which an individual without a *disability* can do a task and the speed at which an individual with a disability can do the same task, to determine a ratio of *efficiency* in productivity; commonly used in *sheltered workshops* to determine wages and set *piecework* job rates.

time sampling Recording behaviors at specific intermittent periods, as contrasted with recording them continuously for the full time of observation. Time sampling could consist of, for example, recording behaviors during the initial 10 minutes of each 30-minute period during a 3-hour daily program.

time-out A *behavior management* technique that eliminates possible *reinforcing* events for undesirable behaviors for a given time. For example, a child may be moved away from classmates to a corner of the room or to a *carrel.*

tinnitus (tih-nie'-tus) A condition in which one hears an abnormal noise in the ears without external *stimuli.* This noise may be a ringing, buzzing, roaring, clicking, or similar sound.

titmus A test of *visual acuity* in which the subject looks into a viewing instrument and the examiner obtains a measure of his/her visual acuity at near and far points.

TMR See *trainable mentally retarded.*

token An object, to which a value is assigned, that is used in *behavior management* as a reward. Accumulated tokens can be exchanged for desired objects or activities corresponding to the values of the tokens attained.

tone deafness A condition in which an individual is unable to hear or distinguish certain sound *frequencies.*

tongue thrust An undesirable pushing of the tongue forward or between the teeth and the lips. Sometimes seen in children with *Down syndrome*, for example.

tonic Describes the phase of a *seizure* in which the entire body becomes rigid and stiff. The tonic phase is followed by a phase in which the muscles are relaxed.

tonic neck reflex An involuntary movement in which one arm straightens and stiffens and the other bends and stiffens when the head is turned.

tonus Muscle firmness or mild *rigidity* that indicates a muscle is in a state of being ready to respond normally to *stimuli.* A muscle without tonus is said to be *flaccid.*

tool subject An area of learning that involves knowledge and skills that have to be mastered to effectively study other subjects. Reading, writing, and arithmetic are commonly regarded as being tool subjects.

tort A legal term referring to an actionable wrong or injury to another; a civil wrong for which a private citizen may recover money damages.

torticollis (tore-tih-coal'-iss) See *wryneck.*

total communication A system of *expressive/receptive language* in which

manual signs and *fingerspelling* are simultaneously combined with speech, *speech reading*, and listening in the way deemed most beneficial to individuals with *hearing impairments.*

total inclusion Some authors differentiate total inclusion from *full inclusion*, in which "total" means all children with *disabilities* are assigned to general education settings even if only for social benefits. See *full inclusion* and *inclusion.*

total positioning systems The new term for wheelchairs.

total service plan The part of the *individualized education program* that describes *long-term goals* and strategies for both instruction and *related services*, and recommends placement.

tough love A no-holds-barred approach to the treatment of students suffering from drug abuse. Some professionals consider the approach to be too strong in its methods, but its success has been good.

Tourette's (too-rets') **syndrome** A rare disease that manifests itself as multiple *tic*-like movements and *vocalizations.* The condition usually starts in children between 2 and 14 years of age with rapid eye blinks or facial tics, and progresses to other parts of the body. The best control at that time is the use of strong *tranquilizers.*

toxemia (tock-see'-mee-uh) Blood poisoning caused by the absorption of a specific material, chemically related to proteins, during the *metabolism* of a vegetable or an animal organism. Toxemia during pregnancy may increase the risk of birth of a child with a *disability.*

toxic Poisonous, as in having a poisonous substance in the blood.

toxoplasmosis (tock-so-plaz-moe'-sis) A disease caused by the infection of body tissues by a toxoplasma, a parasitic microorganism. If contracted *congenitally*, the condition probably is one of the most damaging of all *prenatal* infections; about 75% of the offspring born of mothers having *acute* toxoplasmosis have some involvement, such as *hydrocephalus*, *seizures*, *spasticity*, *anemia*, *jaundice*, or an enlarged liver and spleen.

trachea (tray'-kee-ah) The *cartilaginous* tube leading from the *larynx* to the lungs that serves as the air passage to and from the lungs. Often referred to as the windpipe.

tracheotomy (tray-kee-ah'-toe-me) An incision of the windpipe through the skin and muscles to improve breathing.

trachoma (trah-koe'-mah) A *chronic inflammation* of the mucous membrane that lines the inner surface of the eyelid; believed to be conveyed to the eye through the common use of washcloths, towels, or handkerchiefs, or by the fingers.

traction A technique used in setting or straightening bones and in treating back problems, in which weights exert a steady pull on the portion of the body being treated.

trailing A technique used by *blind* persons to aid *mobility*, in which they trace lightly over a straight surface with the backs of their fingers, as when they are moving along a wall or down a hallway.

trainable mentally retarded (TMR) A term that was introduced in state educational codes to define children who were thought not to be able to profit suitably from general education classes or classes for students with *mild mental retardation*. Most of the state codes stipulated that the *intellectual* level with moderate retardation, when *assessed* with an individual *intelligence* test, would involve *IQ* scores ranging from 35 to 55, and that the children would have other characteristics indicating their potential for prof-

iting from a program designed to help pupils with social adjustment, *self-help skills*, and controlled work settings. Children with moderate retardation score lower than 3 *standard deviations* below the *mean* on individually administered intelligence tests and generally have an intellectual ability of one-third to one-half that of an average child of comparable *chronological age*. The more acceptable term is *moderate mental retardation*. With *inclusion*, many of these students now are enrolled at least part time in general education classes.

tranquilizer Any drug that quiets and calms but does not have a *hypnotic* effect.

transcendence One of the *concepts* in R. Feuerstein's *mediated learning experience*, which seeks to train *generalization* or the use of principles. The idea is to train students with *mental retardation* so that they are able to learn more than just what they are taught; rather, the goal is that they acquire principles, rules, and functions for application in future situations.

transdisciplinary programming An educational approach that emphasizes communication and shared performance among members of various professional specialties and others on an individual's educational or planning treatment team.

transduce (n., **transduction**) To convey information from one *sensory modality* to another. (Transduction is the conversion of received information from one sensory modality to another.) Some students with *learning disabilities*, for example, may be able to recognize an object when they look at it but not when they touch it; such students have problems in transduction.

transfer (of learning) The application of already learned knowledge and skills in a variety of new and related situations.

transformation 1. A change in the composition or structure of a basic sentence (e.g., You solved those problems. Transformation: You didn't solve those problems.) 2. One of J. P. Guilford's products of thinking in which existing information is changed to be used in another form. (See *structure of the intellect.*)

transition See *transition services.*

transition (transition programming) Services that provide a bridge between school and employment, stemming from a concern in the 1980s about students graduating from high school without being prepared for employment.

transition services A provision of *IDEA* that requires the planning and implementation of a coordinated set of activities for students with *disabilities* that promotes their successful movement from school to postschool activities including postsecondary education, vocational training, employment (including *supported employment*), *adult education/* services, and independent living/community participation. The law basically requires that such a plan, which outlines the responsibilities of the school and other agencies to accomplish the student's successful movement into the community, be in place for students with *disabilities* from age 16 on.

transitional time-limited employment A type of supported work designed to meet the needs of persons with *chronic mental illness.*

translocation The attachment of a portion of a *chromosome* of one group to another group, thereby resulting in an excess of *genetic* material in one cell and a deficiency in another.

transposition The interchanging of positions of two words or of two letters or sounds in a word, or the pronunciation of a word out of *context* when reading aloud. May indicate a *language disorder* or *learning disability.*

trauma An undesirable, abrupt physical or emotional change in an organism, caused by violence, shock, or force.

traumatic brain injury (TBI) Injury to the head that produces a severe *memory* disorder with a poor carryover of new learning. Individuals who experience such injuries will express some characteristics similar to those of individuals with *learning disabilities* and may be placed in learning disability programs, but this placement may not be the most appropriate. The term traumatic brain injury refers to open or *closed head injuries* resulting in *impairments* that are immediate or delayed but that affect *cognition, language,* memory, *attention,* reasoning, abstract thinking, judgment, problem solving, *sensory* and *motor* abilities, psychosocial behavior, physical function, speech, and information *processing.* Although some of these behaviors may be characteristic of individuals with *mental retardation* or other *disabilities,* traumatic brain injury is considered a distinctly different classification. Although it may be permanent, in most cases the resulting condition may exist for only a few months to several years.

Treacher-Collins syndrome A *genetic mutation* involving facial bone abnormalities and defects of the *auditory canal, ossicles,* and *palate. Mental retardation* and *deafness* are usually present.

tremor 1. A quivering or vibratory motion of any part of the body. 2. A *symptom* of a form of *cerebral palsy* characterized by shaking motions or involuntary alternate movements.

triplegia (try-plee'-juh) A form of *paralysis* in which three limbs are affected.

trisomy (try'-suh-mee) The presence of three *chromosomes* rather than the normal two in a set. **Trisomy 21** is a technical term for the most common form of *Down syndrome*. In trisomy 21, the 21st chromosome pair is actually a triplet; thus, the individual cell contains 47 chromosomes rather than the normal 46.

TTY An abbreviation for a telecommunication system (Telephone TYpewriter) in which *deaf* persons use a portable keyboard to communicate with other deaf individuals or with agencies that have corresponding equipment. (See also *TDD*, which is the most acceptable term.)

tubal ligation (lie-gay'-shun) Sterilization of a female by tying, severing, or crushing the *uterine* (fallopian) tubes to prevent the passage of eggs that otherwise could be fertilized.

tuberculosis (TB) A *chronic communicable disease* caused by the tubercle bacillus, which destroys tissues of body organs and bones. The lungs are most often affected.

tuberous sclerosis (too'-burr-us skleroh'-sis) A *neurological* disorder characterized by one or more of the following: *epileptic seizures*, *mental retardation*, tumors, skin *lesions*. A common skin manifestation is a reddish/bluish "birthmark" area on the cheeks, nose, and chin.

tuning fork A metal instrument with two prongs that, when caused to vibrate, produces a tone of a certain *pitch*. Tuning forks are used for testing hearing through both *air conduction* and *bone conduction*.

tunnel vision A defect in which the *visual field* is contracted to a degree at which only central *visual acuity* is functioning. The resulting sight is similar to the effect of looking through a tunnel.

Turner syndrome A disorder in females, resulting from an absence of one of the sex *chromosomes*, that affects secondary sex characteristics and may include *mental retardation* or learning problems.

turtle technique A behavioral approach taught to children in which they learn to use *cognitive* processes to retard responses, delay anger, or neutralize *aggressive* behavior. The term implies slowing behavior like a turtle.

tutorial plan A teaching program sometimes used with *gifted* children in which the students remain assigned to their general education classes but are released at specific times during the day to work individually or in small groups with a *special education* teacher. The intent is to assist the students in more fully exploring their fields of interest and in expanding their opportunities for experiences.

tympanic membrane The *eardrum*, or thin membranous structure between the outer and middle ear. The eardrum's vibrations, caused by sound waves striking it through the *auditory canal* of the outer ear, are conveyed to the *ossicles*, which transmit the vibratory movement to the fluid in the inner ear.

tympanogram A recording produced by a **tympanometer**, a device used to measure the internal pressure of the middle ear to determine if abnormalities exist that could impair *hearing acuity* or *accuracy*. (See *tympanometry*.)

tympanometry (tim-pan-ah'-meh-tree) An audiometric measurement involving a device (a *tympanometer*) inserted in the ear to apply air pressure against the *eardrum* so that the internal pressure of the middle ear can be determined. The device provides physical measurements in the form of a *tympanogram*, a recording that can indicate abnormalities of the eardrum, middle ear cavity, and bones of the middle ear *(ossicles)*. (See also *impedance audiometry*.)

tympanostomy (tim-pan-oss'-toe-mee) **tubes** Polyurethane devices inserted in the *eardrum* to reduce pressure on the middle ear; colloquially called "tubes in the ears."

type-token Refers to the ratio of the total number of different words (types) to the total number of words (tokens). This measure is frequently used in studies of *language development* as an indication of *language* complexity.

typoscope A simple device used to isolate single words or a row of words in a reading passage; used with students who have difficulty seeing words separately and distinctly. Usually consists of poster paper, construction paper, or any heavy paper into which a slit is cut that is the size of a word or line of words. (See also *tachistoscope.*)

U

UAF See *University Affiliated Program.*

UAP See *University Affiliated Program.*

ulna The larger of the two bones in the forearm, located on the little finger side of the arm. The other bone is the *radius.*

ultrasonography A medical testing procedure in which high-*frequency* vibrations are used to produce an image of an unborn *fetus* without producing potential danger, as in *X-ray* testing. Referred to generally as *ultrasound.* (See also *sonogram.*)

ultrasound See *sonogram; ultrasonography.*

unconditioned reflex A natural, innate reaction to an external *stimulus* that is not learned or acquired by *conditioning*; for example, when air is blown into the face, the eyes will blink.

underachiever An individual who produces at a level below that predicted by general testing; indicates that the individual is functioning significantly below his/her capability.

ungraded class A structure in which students work at their own rate with the assistance of individual instruction and without assignment to *grade level.*

unified sports activities Three programs started by *Special Olympics* to counteract the exclusionary activities of organized sports. The three programs are called Sports Partnership, Partners Club, and Unified Sports. All emphasize *inclusionary* principles and allow individuals with *disabilities* to compete in sports with individuals without disabilities.

unilateral On one side only; used to refer to conditions on only one side of the body.

unit 1. One of a series of learning activities organized around a central topic or problem area; these activities span several subject matter areas, although one area may be emphasized more than another. 2. The simplest *product of thinking* in J. P. Guilford's model, represented by *figural* or symbolic structures. (See *structure of the intellect.*)

University Affiliated Program (UAP) Name given to the *interdisciplinary* training centers sponsored by the federal government. Purposes were to demonstrate innovative methods of delivering services, training specialists, and conducting research on *developmental disabilities.* Also abbreviated *UAF.*

uremia (you-ree'-mee-ah) A condition marked by an excess of chemical urea and nitrogenous waste in the blood, causing a *toxic* condition.

urinalysis A chemical analysis of urine, taken routinely during medical examinations, to determine any abnormal excretion of substances into the urine caused by physiological conditions.

U.S. An abbreviation, in a citation to a decision of the U.S. Supreme Court, that indicates that a judgment of that Court is reported in a certain volume of the *United States Reports*, which contain only the judgments and other orders of the U.S. Supreme Court. The volume number precedes the U.S. designation, the page number follows it, and the date of the judgment is set out in parentheses after the page reference.

U.S.C. An abbreviation for *United States Code*, an official publication of the U.S. government that contains the codified acts of Congress.

U.S.C.A. An abbreviation for *United States Code Annotated*, a commercial publication that contains the codified acts of Congress.

Usher's syndrome A condition in which the individual has *retinitis pigmentosa* plus *hearing impairment*.

USLW An abbreviation for *United States Law Week*, a commercial publication that reports the judgments of various courts during a particular week. The volume of *USLW* precedes the *USLW* designation, and the page number in the report follows it, with the identity of the court and date of judgment set out in parentheses after the page number.

uterus (adj., **uterine**) The organ of the female body that contains and nurtures the fertilized egg and developing *fetus*.

uvula (you'-vyuh-luh) The flap of connective tissue that extends downward at the back of the soft *palate* in the throat area. The uvula assists the individual in closing the *nasal* cavity; thus, problems with the uvula or its absence produces nasal speech sounds.

V

vacated In a citation to a case, indicates that a higher court has set aside the judgment of a lower court.

VAKT An *acronym* for *visual, auditory, kinesthetic*, and *tactile*. Refers to a *multisensory* approach to teaching reading developed by Grace Fernald to assist children with severe *reading disabilities*. The approach employs the tracing of letters and auditory responses to supplement a weak visual channel. Also called the *Fernald method*.

validity A term referring to how well an instrument or method measures what it is supposed to measure.

valproic acid A drug approved for use in the United States during the 1980s for the control of *seizures*. The drug was effectively used in Europe before becoming approved in this country.

variable interval A term applied to *reinforcement* based on non-set times.

variable ratio A term applied to *reinforcement* based on a non-set number of performances.

vasectomy The surgical removal of the tube, or a portion of the tube (vas deferens), that carries sperm. This procedure is generally considered a permanent form of sterilization, just as *tubal ligation* in females is considered permanent.

VD See *venereal disease*.

velum The small structure at the end or back of the soft *palate* that closes the *nasal* cavity during the production of most words in English. When it is missing or nonfunctional, a person's speech becomes *hypernasal*. Also called the *uvula*.

venereal disease (VD) Any of several contagious diseases usually transmitted by genital contact or sexual intercourse.

Untreated venereal disease during pregnancy may contribute to the birth of a child with *disabilities*.

verbal test An *intelligence* test or *subtest* that requires spoken *language* and the use of words to measure *intellectual* potential.

verbal unreality (or **verbalism**) Usually refers to *blind* persons' use of terms that are not within their *sensory* experience, as in describing blood as "red" rather than "sticky and warm."

verbalize (n., **verbalization**) To express something in spoken *language*. The verbalization of conscious emotions and thought often is helpful in bringing about psychological adjustment.

verbo-tonal method An approach to developing the speaking and listening skills of persons with *hearing impairments* that was developed at the University of Zagreb in the former Yugoslavia. This method emphasizes the training or retraining of the *auditory perceptual* areas of the brain to assist the individual in perceiving speech sounds and making the best use of *residual hearing*.

verdict A decision by a judge or jury in favor of one side or the other in a case.

vertex Refers to the normal, headfirst position of a *fetus* during birth. For comparison, see *breech birth*.

vertigo A disorder of the sense of balance, or equilibrium, which causes dizziness or giddiness.

vestibule (ves'-tih-bule) A space or cavity at the entrance of a body canal, as in the **vestibular** mechanism of the inner ear.

vicarious (vie-care'-ee-us) **learning** Knowledge that is attained as an unexpected or unplanned outcome of experiences. This type of learning results from watching others or *modeling* their behavior. Sometimes this type of modeling may be done to the extreme that a person "lives through" another.

video self-modeling A technique for facilitating a student's self-*evaluation* skills that involves the student's viewing videotaped samples of his/her appropriate and inappropriate behavior. After the student views the tapes for a while, the teacher elicits his/her views about the behaviors seen.

video-based modeling A technology employed since the 1980s with increased frequency wherein students with *disabilities* view videotapes that show model behaviors and then discuss and role-play the desired behaviors.

vigilance The ability to maintain *attention* on a task despite challenges. In the case of some students with *disabilities*, the ability of the student to marshal his/her attention to initially focus on a task.

virtual reality A term coined by Jason Lanier in 1985 that has come to be used to convey the use of technology in place of senses in body functions or processes of persons with *disabilities*. One example is a temperature-sensing device for prostheses that in essence replaces the body's function in this regard or at least provides the equivalent. Also describes a computer-generated environment that can simulate real-life experiences.

virus (adj., **viral**) Any of a large group of tiny infectious agents that can replicate only within living host cells.

visual (adj., **visually**) Pertaining to the sense of sight.

visual acuity One's ability to see things and to accurately distinguish their characteristics; how well one sees.

visual agnosia See *agnosia*.

visual closure Being able to perceive wholes from seeing only parts of them, as in recognizing that a picture of part of a face represents a face or identifying a word after seeing only a part of that word. Training in visual closure is beneficial to children who have difficulty relating parts to the whole.

visual discrimination The ability to use the sense of sight to determine whether things one sees are the same or different.

visual efficiency The effectiveness with which an individual uses his/her eyesight. Two persons with equal *visual acuity* may not use their vision equally; the person who makes better use of vision would be said to have greater visual efficiency. Visual efficiency can be trained, according to Natalie Barraga and others.

visual field See *field of vision.*

visual impairment In education, defined as a deficiency in eyesight that is great enough that the student requires special provisions. The student may be *blind* or *partially sighted.* (See also *blindness; legal blindness.*)

visual memory The ability to recall images after a lapse of time. Visual memory is important in *academic achievement,* and *impairment* in this ability results in *learning disorders.*

visual perception The ability to interpret what is seen.

visual reception The ability to receive information through the seeing channel.

visual screening 1. A *time-out* procedure in which a *therapist* or teacher screens his/her face or turns it away from a child as a form of removal without removing the child from the environment. 2. The preliminary *assessment* of the vision of a group of children to determine those who may have problems with eyesight and need further testing.

visual tracking An early developmental *visual* ability in which an infant's eyes follow a person or object moving across

his/her *field of vision.* In work with individuals with *severe* and *profound mental retardation,* the development of this ability may be an *objective* for instruction.

visualization (v., **visualize**) The act of interpreting in *visual* terms or describing in visible form.

visual-motor coordination The ability to combine vision with movement of the body or its parts. This skill is necessary in many academic areas including handwriting, mathematics, and physical education.

visual-motor memory The ability to accurately remember previously seen experiences involving movement.

visual-motor perception The formation of an idea or *concept* through the use of vision and physical activity. In *visual perception,* only *visual* processes are involved; in visual-motor perception, the acts of physically creating (e.g., drawing) and perceiving an object are combined.

vitreous (vih'-tree-us) **humor** The fluid in the back chamber of the eye that fills the space between the *retina* and the *lens.*

vocal nodules Callous-like growths that form on the vocal folds, resulting in harshness or *hoarseness* of the voice.

vocalize (n., **vocalization**; adv., **vocally**) To make sounds with the voice.

vocational counseling The help provided by a specially trained person in selecting an occupation (including discussions about the education or training needed to prepare for the occupation selected) and in seeking, applying for, and obtaining employment. This term is similar to, but less formal than, *vocational guidance.*

vocational education A formalized program with the goal of preparing individuals to work in a chosen occupation or upgrading employed workers in their existing work situations.

vocational (work) evaluator An individual skilled in the administration and interpretation of vocational *assessment* tests and other types of vocationally oriented *evaluation* procedures.

vocational guidance Refers to an organized program to assist pupils in choosing, securing training for, and becoming successfully employed in an occupation for which their abilities qualify them. *Vocational counseling* is a less formalized approach having the same general *objectives*.

vocational rehabilitation The service of providing *diagnosis*, guidance, training, physical restoration, and placement to persons with *disabilities* for the purpose of preparing them for and involving them in employment that can help them to live with greater independence. The preferred term is now *rehabilitative services*.

vocational workshop program A specific educational offering that is work-oriented and is carried out in a controlled environment.

vocoder (voe-koe'-der) An electronic device that allows persons who are *deaf* to make fine speech *discriminations* by use of the *tactual* mode. Vocoder is a shortened form for "voice coder."

voice disorder A condition marked by abnormal spoken *language* production. May involve unusual *pitch*, volume, or quality of sounds.

vowel An alphabet letter representing the sounds of *a, e, i, o, u* and sometimes *y*. Spoken English has 12 vowel *phonemes*.

W

walker A framework designed with handgrips or rails that is used to support

an individual with *physical disabilities* in an upright position and in walking.

Warkany's syndrome See *intrauterine growth retardation*.

watch-tick test An informal *screening* measure of hearing in which the tester holds a watch or clock that has a loud tick near the pupil's ear and asks the pupil to indicate when he/she ceases to hear the ticks as the tester moves away. The tester should use the same watch or clock for each test and should know the approximate distance at which a person with normal hearing ceases to hear the tick in order to recognize *hearing losses* in the population being tested. This test is, of course, an unreliable measure and provides only a rough *screening*.

weighted designation system A means of determining *class sizes* in which students having *disabilities* are counted differentially. Thus, a child with *mild mental retardation* who is included in a general education class may be counted twice, with the assumption being that the student requires twice the *attention* and time from the teacher.

whole language The philosophy and perspective that guide the simultaneous teaching of the four *language* arts: reading, writing, speaking, and listening. The key to whole language instruction is that children learn to read and write while participating in social situations that are natural. Thus, reading, writing, speaking, and listening are taught simultaneously rather than in isolation.

Wild Boy of Aveyron Appellation for the 12-year-old male found abandoned and living in a forest in France, who was taught by Jean Itard around 1800. Itard named him Victor and used a *sensory* training program to make him more social and knowledgeable. Because of his work with Victor, Itard has often been referred to as the "Father of Special Education."

wilderness education (camping) An approach to the treatment of students with *emotional/behavior disorders.* that involves immersing them in a wilderness experience with a counselor(s) in which survival and progress are synonymous with group involvement. Sometimes called wilderness *therapy.*

Wilson's disease The *generic* term for a *hereditary syndrome* characterized by *mental retardation* and the accumulation of copper deposits in some body organs.

word-finding problem A term used by *speech and language pathologists* to characterize the speech of children who have difficulty in mentally locating the word they want to use and thus will have difficulty in labeling and will substitute a similar word (e.g., boot for sock).

words in color Name given to an innovation in *language* instruction introduced to make the 26-letter English alphabet more *phonetic.* In this system, each *phoneme* is consistently represented by a different color.

work activity center A sheltered setting for persons with *severe disabilities* in which they are taught work and daily activities of life. The areas of instruction can include, among others, cooking, cleaning, dressing, and caring for clothes.

work adjustment Hershenson's theory in career development, which provides a *conceptual* framework that can be used in *transition* planning. Takes into account (a) work personality (self-concept and personal *motivation* for work); (b) work competencies (job-related habits and skills); and (c) work goals (personal career time and specific *objectives*).

work evaluation The selective analysis of simulated or real *job samples* for the purpose of *assessing* a client's aptitude and skills for a specific application.

work experience Describes a program that helps students acquire desirable job skills, aptitudes, and habits and has as its purpose supervised part-time or full-time employment.

work-study program A *curriculum* in which high-school-level students work at a job part-time and attend class the remainder of the time. The intent is to give the pupils actual *work experiences* that they can relate to class work, so that it will be more practical. Such programs may be referred to as *on-the-job training.*

workmen's compensation An insurance program carried by an employer and required by all states that covers employees for time lost as a result of injuries or certain occupational diseases. This insurance includes liability coverage to protect the employer against most damage suits brought by employees or their survivors. (See also *second injury clause.*)

writ of certiorari (rit of cert'-i-or-are-i) The process used by lawyers to request that the supreme court of a state or the United States review the transcript of a lower court's decision. If the higher court decides to review a case, it is said that the court "grants *certiorari*"; if it does not request a transcript, it is said to have "denied *certiorari.*" If *certiorari* is granted, a decision can be expected at the next session of the court. See also *cert. den* and *granted cert.*

wryneck A spasmodic condition in which the neck draws the head to one side; observed in young children and those with certain forms of *cerebral palsy.* Same as *torticollis.*

Wyatt v. Stickney A significant piece of litigation (1971) that affirmed the *right* *to treatment* of residents with *mental illness* and *mental retardation* in two Alabama state *institutions*. Set a *precedent* for courts to grant the right to adequate treatment and education for involuntarily committed residents within state facilities.

X

X ray A form of radiation that has wavelengths much shorter than those of light, has the property of penetrating various thicknesses of solids, and acts on photographic plates and fluorescent screens like light. X rays are used in medical *diagnosis* and *assessment* for the medical treatment of selected conditions.

xerophthalmia (zee-rof-thal'-mee-ah) A condition marked by dryness of the *cornea* and *conjunctiva* of the eye resulting from a vitamin A deficiency. Individuals with this condition experience *night blindness* as an early *symptom*.

Y

Yerkish A communication system originally used in the Yerkes Primate Laboratory in Atlanta, Georgia, to teach a chimpanzee to communicate. The system utilizes a large symbol board that the chimpanzee touches to relay commands. Recently the system has been used with individuals who have *severe disabilities*.

Ypsilanti project See *Perry project*.

Z

zero reject One of the principles upon which *PL 94–142*, *IDEA*, and numerous court cases have been based. Essentially, it says that no child, regardless of the degree of *disability*, may be refused a *free appropriate public education* if other children of the same age are served.

zone of proximal development One of the *constructs* in Leo Vygotsky's learning theory that is the equivalent of saying a child has a zone of *readiness* for instruction and that teachers must be aware of the child's available zone and instruct within it.

Abbreviations and Acronyms

A

AAMR	American Association on Mental Retardation
AD	assistive device
ADA	average daily attendance
ADD	attention deficit disorder
ADHD	attention deficit hyperactivity disorder
ADL	activities of daily living
ADM	average daily membership
AFI	amaurotic family (familial) idiocy
AIDS	acquired immune deficiency syndrome
ALT	academic learning time
ANOVA	analysis of variance
AP	advanced placement
APGAR	appearance or coloring, pulse,
(Apgar Test)	grimace, activity, and respiration
ARC	AIDS-related complex; Association for Retarded Citizens; Association for Retired Citizens
ART	aggression replacement training
ASL	American Sign Language
ATD	assistive technological device

B

BASIC	Beginners All-purpose Symbolic Instruction Code
BCS	battered child syndrome
BD	behavior disorder
BEH	Bureau of Education for the Handicapped

C

CA	chronological age
CAI	computer-assisted instruction
CBA	curriculum-based assessment
CBM	curriculum-based measurement
CBI	competency-based instruction
CF	cystic fibrosis
CFR	*Code of Federal Regulations*
CHI	closed head injury
CIC	clean intermittent catheterization
CMV	cytomegalovirus
CODA	certified occupational disability assistant
COHI	crippled and other health impaired
CP	cerebral palsy
CPR	cardiopulmonary resuscitation
CR	conditioned reflex (response)

CRT   criterion-referenced testing

CT   consultant (consulting teacher)

CWPT   classwide peer tutoring

D

DAP   developmentally appropriate practice

db   decibel

DD   developmental disability

DISTAR   Direct Instruction System for Teaching Arithmetic and Reading

DLO   desired learner outcome

DNA   deoxyribonucleic acid

DNR   do not resuscitate

DOT   *Dictionary of Occupational Titles*

DPT   diagnostic-prescriptive teaching

DSM   *Diagnostic and Statistical Manual of Mental Disorders*

DTH   developmental training home

E

E/BD   emotional/behavior disorder

ED   refers to the U.S. Department of Education; emotional disturbance

EDA   electrodermal audiometry

EDGAR   Education Department General Administrative Relations

EEG   electroencephalogram

EH   educationally handicapped

EHA   Education for All Handicapped Act of 1975 (now known as the Individuals with Disabilities Education Act)

EHLR   *Education for the Handicapped Law Reporter*

EKG   electrocardiogram

ELP   estimated learning potential

EMH   educable mentally handicapped

EMR   educable mentally retarded

ENCOR   Eastern Nebraska Community Office of Retardation

ESEA   Elementary and Secondary Education Act

ESY   extended school year

F

FAC   facilitative communication

FAPE   free appropriate public education

FAS   fetal alcohol syndrome

FERPA   Family Education Rights and Privacy Act

504   refers to Section 504 of the Rehabilitation Act of 1973

FTE   full-time equivalent

G

GLD   general learning disability

H

HIV   human immunodeficiency virus

Hz   hertz

I

IDEA   Individuals with Disabilities Education Act

IEP   individualized education program

IFSP   individual family service plan

IHSS   in-home support services

IIP   individual implementation plan

ILS   independent living skills

IMC   instructional materials center

IPA   international phonetic alphabet

IPI   individually prescribed instruction

IPP   individualized program plan; individualized progress plan

IQ   intelligence quotient

IRI   individual reading inventory

ISAAC   International Society for Augmentative and Alternative Communication

ISO   International Standards Organization

ISP   individual services plan

ISS   in-school suspension

ITA   initial teaching alphabet

ITP   interservice transition plan

ITR   intensive training residence

J

JND   just noticeable differences

JRA   juvenile rheumatoid arthritis

L

LD   learning disability/learning disabled

LEA   local education(al) agency

LRE   least restrictive environment

LSS   local school system

M

MA   mental age

MBD   minimal brain dysfunction

MCE   Manually Coded English

MCT   minimum competency testing

MD   muscular dystrophy

MI,
MIMH   mild disabilities; mild mental retardation; mildly mentally handicapped

MID   mild intellectual disability

MIT   melodic intonation therapy

MLE   mediated learning experience

MO,
MOMH   moderate mental retardation; moderately mentally handicapped

MR   mental retardation/mentally retarded

MS   multiple sclerosis

M-team   multidisciplinary team

N

94–142   refers to Public Law 94–142, the Education for All Handicapped Children Act of 1975

O

OCR   Office for Civil Rights

OHI   other health impaired

OJT   on-the-job training

OSEP   Office for Special Education Programs, U.S. Department of Education

OSERS   Office of Special Education and Rehabilitative Services, U.S. Department of Education

OT   occupational therapy

P

PARC   Pennsylvania Association for Retarded Children

PC   politically correct; personal computer

PCMR   President's Committee on Mental Retardation

PET   Parent Effectiveness Training

PIP prescriptive instructional plan

PKU phenylketonuria

PL Public Law

PRN *pro re nata,* Latin for "to use as needed or required"

PT physical therapy

PVT prevocational teacher

Q

qid *quarter in die,* Latin for "four times daily"

R

RAID rules, approval, ignoring, and disapproval

REI regular education initiative

RLF retrolental fibroplasia

RNA ribonucleic acid

RT recreational therapy

RVI related vocational instructor

S

SDD significantly developmentally delayed

SEA state education(al) agency

SED seriously emotionally disturbed

SEE Signing Exact English

SEP (Office of) Special Education Programs

SIB self-injurious behavior

SIBIS self-injurious behavior inhibiting system

SLA semi-independent living arrangement

SLP speech and language pathologist

SOMPA System of Multicultural Pluralistic Assessment

SQ3R survey, question, read, recite, and review

SRT speech reception threshold

SSI supplemental security income

SST student support team

T

TAT teacher assistance team

TB tuberculosis

TBI traumatic brain injury

TDD telecommunication device for the deaf

TMR trainable mentally retarded

TTY telephone typewriter

U

UAF, UAP University Affiliated Program

U.S. United States (in reference to the *United States Reports*)

U.S.C. *United States Code*

U.S.C.A. *United States Code Annotated*

USLW *United States Law Week*

V

VAKT visual, auditory, kinesthetic, and tactile

VD venereal disease

Associations and National Centers

AASK: Adopt a Special Kid
2201 Broadway, Ste 702
Oakland, CA 94610

Abledata
8455 Colesville Rd., Ste 935
Silver Spring, MD 20910-3319

Access Unlimited
3535 Briarpark Dr., Ste 102
Houston, TX 77042

Activating Children Through
Technology
27 Horrabin Hall
Western Illinois University
Macomb, IL 61455

Alexander Graham Bell Association
for the Deaf
3417 Volta Pl. NW
Washington, DC 20007-2778

American Association of the Deaf-Blind
814 Thayer Ave., Ste 302
Silver Spring, MD 20910

American Association on Mental
Retardation (AAMR)
444 N. Capitol St. NW, Ste 846
Washington, DC 20001-1512

American Association of University
Affiliated Programs for Persons
with Developmental Disabilities
8630 Fenton St., Ste 410
Silver Spring, MD 20910

American Bar Association
1800 M. St. NW, Ste 200
Washington, DC 20036

American Epilepsy Society
638 Prospect Ave.
Hartford, CT 06105-4298

American Foundation for the Blind
11 Penn Plaza, Ste 300
New York, NY 10001

American Occupational Therapy
Association (AOTA)
4720 Montgomery Ln.
P.O. Box 311220
Bethesda, MD 20824-1220

American Orthotic and Prosthetic
Association
1650 King St., Ste 500
Alexandria, VA 22314

American Physical Therapy
Association
1111 N. Fairfax St.
Alexandria, VA 22314

American Printing House for the Blind
1839 Frankfort Ave.
P.O. Box 6085
Louisville, KY 40206-0085

American Psychological Association
(APA)
1200 17th St. NW
Washington, DC 20036

American Group Psychotherapy
Association, Inc.
25 E. 21st St., 6th Floor
New York, NY 10010

American Rehabilitation Counseling
Association
5999 Stevenson Ave.
Alexandria, VA 22304

American School Counselor
Association (ASCA)
5999 Stevenson Ave.
Alexandria, VA 22304

American Society for Deaf Children
2848 Arden Way, Ste 210
Sacramento, CA 95825-1373

American Speech-Language-Hearing
Association (ASHA)
10801 Rockville Pike
Rockville, MD 20852

American Vocational Association
Special Needs Division
1410 King St.
Alexandria, VA 22314

Amyotrophic Lateral Sclerosis
Association
21021 Ventura Blvd., Ste 321
Woodland Hills, CA 91364

ARCH National Resource Center
800 Eastowne Dr., Ste 105
Chapel Hill, NC 27514

Association for Children with Down
Syndrome
2616 Martin Ave.
Bellmore, NY 11710

Association for Driver Educators for
the Disabled
P.O. Box 49
Edgerton, WI 53534

Association for Neurometabolic
Disorders
c/o Cheryl Volk
5223 Brookfield Ln.
Sylvania, OH 43560-1809

Association for Persons with Severe
Handicaps
11210 Greenwood Ave. N.
Seattle, WA 98133

Association for Retarded Citizens
(ARC) of the United States
500 E. Border, Ste 300
Arlington, TX 76010

Association for the Blind
and Visually Impaired
206 N. Washington St., Ste 320
Alexandria, VA 22314

Association for the Gifted
A Division of the Council
for Exceptional Children (CEC)
1920 Association Dr.
Reston, VA 22091-1589

Association of Birth Defect Children
827 Irma Ave.
Orlando, FL 32803

Association of Canadian Educators
of the Hearing Impaired
58 Portugal Cove Rd.
St. Johns, NF, Canada A1B 2L9

Association of Educational Therapists
14852 Ventura Blvd., Ste 207
Sherman Oaks, CA 91403

Association on Higher Education
and Disability (AHEAD)
P.O. Box 21192
Columbus, OH 43221

Asthma and Allergy Foundation
of America
1125 15th St. NW, Ste 502
Washington, DC 20005

Attention Deficit Disorder
AD-IN (Attention Deficit
Information Network)
475 Hillside Ave.
Needham, MA 02194

Augmentative and Alternative
Communication
One James St. S
Hamilton, Ontario, Canada L8N 3K7

Australia Society for the Study of
Intellectual Disability and the
New Zealand Association for the
Scientific Study of Mental Deficiency
School of Education
Macquarie University
N.S.W. 2109 Australia

Autism Society of America
7910 Woodmont Ave., Ste 650
Bethesda, MD 20814

Autism Society of Canada
129 Yorkville Ave., Ste 202
Toronto, Ontario, Canada M5R 1C4

Canadian Association for Community
Living
4700 Keele St.
Kinsman Bldg., York University
North York, Ontario, Canada M3J 1P3

Canadian Cystic Fibrosis Foundation
2221 Yonge St., Ste 601
Toronto, Ontario, Canada M4S 2B4

Canadian Down Syndrome Society
12837 76th Ave., Ste 206
Surrey, British Columbia, Canada
V3W 2V3

Canadian Hard of Hearing Association
2435 Holly Ln., Ste 205
Ottawa, Ontario, Canada K1V 7P2

Canadian Hearing Society
271 Spadina Rd.
Toronto, Ontario, Canada M5R 2V3

Canadian National Institute
for the Blind
1929 Bayview Ave.
Toronto, Ontario, Canada M4G 3E8

Canadian Osteogenesis Imperfecta Society
128 Thornhill Crescent
Chatham, Ontario, Canada N7L 4M3

Canadian Rehabilitation Council
for the Disabled
45 Sheppard Ave. E, Ste 801
North York, Ontario, Canada M2N 5W9

Canadian Rett Syndrome Association
555 Fairway Rd.
Kitchener, Ontario, Canada N2C 1X4

CEC Pioneers Division (CEC-PD)
A Division of the Council
for Exceptional Children
1920 Association Dr.
Reston, VA 22091-1589

Center for Special Education Finance
(CSEF)
American Institutes for Research
1791 Arastradero Rd.
P.O. Box 1113
Palo Alto, CA 94302

Center for Universal Design
North Carolina State University
School of Design
Box 8613
Raleigh, NC 27695-8613

Children and Adults with Attention
Deficit Disorders (CHADD)
1859 North Pine Island Rd., Ste 185
Plantation, FL 33317

Children and Adults with Attention
Deficit Disorders (CHADD)—Canada
P.O. Box 23007
Ottawa, Ontario, Canada K2A 4E2

Clearinghouse on Child Abuse
and Neglect Information
P.O. Box 1182
Washington, DC 20013

Clearinghouse on Disability
Information
Office of Special Education and
Rehabilitation Services
U.S. Dept. of Education
330 C St. SW
Switzer Bldg., Rm. 3132
Washington, DC 20202-2524

Cleft Palate Foundation
1218 Grandview Ave.
Pittsburgh, PA 15211

Commission on Rehabilitation
Counselor Certification
162 N. State St., Ste 317
Chicago, IL 60601

Conference of Educational
Administrators Serving the Deaf
and Convention of American
Instructors of the Deaf
800 Florida Ave. NE
Washington, DC 20002

Conferences Inc.
c/o James F. Neils
516 26 Davis St., Stes 211 & 212
Evanston, IL 60201-4644

Council for Children with Behavioral
Disorders (CCBD)
A Division of the Council for
Exceptional Children
1920 Association Dr.
Reston, VA 22091-1589

Council for Educational Diagnostic
Services (CEDS)
A Division of the Council for
Exceptional Children
1920 Association Dr.
Reston, VA 22091-1589

Council for Exceptional Children (CEC)
1920 Association Dr.
Reston, VA 22091-1589

Council of Administrators of Special
Education (CASE)
A Division of the Council for
Exceptional Children
1920 Association Dr.
Reston, VA 22091-1589

Cystic Fibrosis Foundation
6931 Arlington Rd.
Bethesda, MD 20814

DIRECT LINK for the disABLED
P.O. Box 1036
Solvang, CA 93464

Division for Children's
Communication Development (DCCD)
A Division of the Council for
Exceptional Children
1920 Association Dr.
Reston, VA 22091-1589

Division for Culturally and Linquistically Diverse Exceptional Learners (IDEAL)
A Division of the Council for Exceptional Children
1920 Association Dr.
Reston, VA 22091-1589

Division for Early Childhood (DEC)
A Division of the Council for Exceptional Children
1920 Association Dr.
Reston, VA 22091-1589

Division for Learning Disabilities (DLD)
A Division of the Council for Exceptional Children
1920 Association Dr.
Reston, VA 22091-1589

Division for Research (DR)
A Division of the Council for Exceptional Children
1920 Association Dr.
Reston, VA 22091-1589

Division of International Special Education and Services (DISES)
A Division of the Council for Exceptional Children
1920 Association Dr.
Reston, VA 22091-1589

Division of the Physical and Health Disabilities (DPHD)
A Division of the Council for Exceptional Children
1920 Association Dr.
Reston, VA 22091-1589

Division on Career Development and Transition (DCDT)
A Division of the Council for Exceptional Children
1920 Association Dr.
Reston, VA 22091-1589

Division on Mental Retardation and Developmental Disabilities (MRDD)
A Division of the Council for Exceptional Children
1920 Association Dr.
Reston, VA 22091-1589

Division on Visual Impairment (DVI)
A Division of the Council for Exceptional Children
1920 Association Dr.
Reston, VA 22091-1589

Epilepsy Canada
1470 Peel St., Ste 745
Montreal, Canada H3A 1T1

Epilepsy Foundation of America
4351 Garden City Dr.
Landover, MD 20785-2267

ERIC Clearinghouse on Adult, Career and Vocational Education
Ohio State University
1960 Kenny Rd.
Columbus, OH 43210

ERIC Clearinghouse on Disabilities and Gifted Education
Council for Exceptional Children
1920 Association Dr.
Reston, VA 22091-1589

Foundation for Education and Research in Vision (FERV)
P.O. Box 14170
Houston, TX 77211

Georgia Society to Prevent Blindness, Inc.
455 E. Paces Ferry Rd., Ste 222
Atlanta, GA 30305

International Association of Special
Education (IASE)
c/o Nomsa Gwalla-Ogisi
University of Wisconsin
Whitewater, WI 53190

International Rett Syndrome
Association
9121 Piscataway Rd., Ste 2B
Clinton, MD 20735

International Society for Augmentative
and Alternative Communication
(ISAAC)
P.O. Box 1762, Station R
Toronto, Ontario, Canada M4G 4A3

International Society for Prevention
of Child Abuse and Neglect
1205 Oneid St.
Denver, CO 80220

Jewish Association for ADD
1416 Avenue M., Ste 202
Brooklyn, NY 11223

Job Opportunities for the Blind
National Center for the Blind
1800 Johnson St.
Baltimore, MD 21230

Learning Disabilities Association
(LDA) of America
4156 Library Rd.
Pittsburgh, PA 15234

Learning Disabilities Association
(LDA) of Canada
323 Chapel St., Ste 200
Ottawa, Ontario, Canada K1N 7Z2

March of Dimes Birth Defects
Foundation
1275 Mamaroneck Ave.
White Plains, NY 10605

Mobility International USA
P.O. Box 10767
Eugene, OR 97440

Muscular Dystrophy Association (MDA)
3300 E. Sunrise Dr.
Tucson, AZ 85718-3208

Muscular Dystrophy Association
(MDA) of Canada
150 Eglinton Ave. E, Ste 400
Toronto, Ontario, Canada M4P 1E8

National Academy for Certified
Clinical Mental Health Counselors
801 N. Fairfax St., Ste 304
Alexandria, VA 22314

National Association for Creative
Child and Adult
8080 Spring Valley Dr.
Cincinnati, OH 45236

National Association for Music
Therapy
8455 Colesville Rd.
Silver Spring, MD 20910

National Association for Parents
of the Visually Impaired
P.O. Box 317
Watertown, MA 02272-0317

National Association for the Gifted
5100 N. Edgewood Dr.
St. Paul, MN 55112

National Association for Visually
Handicapped (NAVH)
22 W. 21st St., 6th floor
New York, NY 10010

National Association of Developmental
Disabilities Councils
1234 Massachusetts Ave. NW, Ste 103
Washington, DC 20005

National Association of Parents
of Blind Children
1800 Johnson St.
Baltimore, MD 21230

National Association of Private
Schools for Exceptional Children
1522 K St. NW, Ste 1032
Washington, DC 20005

National Association of
Rehabilitation Facilities
1920 Association Dr.
Reston, VA 22091-1589

National Association of School
Psychologists (NASP)
8455 Colesville Rd., Ste 1000
Silver Spring, MD 20910

National Association of State Directors
of Developmental Disabilities Services
113 Oronoco St.
Alexandria, VA 22314

National Association of State Directors
of Special Education
1800 Diagonal Rd., Ste 320
Alexandria, VA 22314

National Association of the Deaf
814 Thayer Ave.
Silver Spring, MD 20910-4500

National Association for the Visually
Handicapped (NAVH)
22 W. 21st St.
New York, NY 10010

National Ataxia Foundation
750 Twelve Oaks Ctr.
15500 Wayzata Blvd.
Wayzata, MN 55391

National Attention Deficit Disorder
Association (NADDA)
P.O. Box 488
42 Way to the River
West Newbury, MA 01985

National Board for Certified
Counselors (NBCC)
3D Terrace Way
Greensboro, NC 27403

National Center for Learning
Disabilities
381 Park Ave. St., Ste 1420
New York, NY 10016

National Center for Stuttering
200 E. 33rd St.
New York, NY 10016

National Center for Youth
with Disabilities
University of Minnesota
Box 721
420 Delaware St. SE
Minneapolis, MN 55455

National Clearing House of
Rehabilitation Training Materials
816 W. 6th St., OSU
Stillwater, OK 74078-0435

National Clearinghouse on
Postsecondary Education for
Individuals with Disabilities
Heath Resource Center
1 Dupont Cir. NW, Ste 800
Washington, DC 20036-1193

National Council on Disability
1331 F St. NW, Ste 1050
Washington, DC 20004-1107

National Cued Speech Association
P.O. Box 31345
Raleigh, NC 27622

National Down Syndrome Congress
1605 Chantilly Dr., Ste 250
Atlanta, GA 30324

National Down Syndrome Society
666 Broadway, 8th floor
New York, NY 10012-2317

National Easter Seal Society (NESS)
230 W. Monroe St., Ste 1800
Chicago, IL 60606-4802

National Fibrous Sclerosis Association
8000 Corporate Dr., Ste 102
Washington, DC 20036

National Fragile X Foundation
1441 York St., Ste 215
Denver, CO 80206

National Head Injury Foundation
1776 Massachusetts Ave. NW, Ste 102
Washington, DC 20036-1904

National Hemophilia Foundation
110 Greene St., Ste 303
New York, NY 10012

National Industries for the Severely
Handicapped
2235 Cedar Ln.
Vienna, VA 22182

National Information Center for
Children and Youth with Disabilities
(NICHCY)
P.O. Box 1492
Washington, DC 20013

National Information Center
on Deafness (NICD)
Gallaudet University
800 Florida Ave. NE
Washington, DC 20002-3695

National Information Clearinghouse
on Children Who Are Deaf-Blind
345 N. Monmouth Ave.
Monmouth, OR 97361

National Legal Resource Center
for Child Advocacy and Protection
American Bar Association
1800 M St. NW
Washington, DC 20036

National Library Service for the Blind
and Physically Handicapped
Library of Congress
1291 Taylor St. NW
Washington, DC 20542

National Mental Health Association
1021 Prince St.
Alexandria, VA 22314-2971

National Multiple Sclerosis Society
733 3rd Ave., 6th floor
New York, NY 10017

National Organization of Parents
of Blind Children
1800 Johnson St.
Baltimore, MD 21230

National Organization on Disability
910 16th St. NW, Ste 600
Washington, DC 20006

National Organization on Fetal
Alcohol Syndrome
1815 H St. NW, Ste 710
Washington, DC 20006

National Parent Network on
Disabilities (NPND)
1600 Prince St., Ste 115
Alexandria, VA 22314

National Parent-to-Parent Support
and Information System
c/o Kathleen Judd
P.O. Box 907
Blue Ridge, GA 30513

National Rehabilitation Association
633 S. Washington St.
Alexandria, VA 22314

National Rehabilitation Information
Center (NARIC)
8455 Colesville Rd., Ste 935
Silver Spring, MD 20910

National Resource Center
for Paraprofessionals in Education
and Related Services
CASE/CUNY, Rm. 620
25 W. 43rd St.
New York, NY 10036

National Resource Center for Special
Needs Adoption
16250 Northland Dr., Ste 120
Southfield, MI 48075

National Scoliosis Foundation
72 Mount Auburn St.
Watertown, MA 02172

National Society to Prevent Blindness
500 E. Remington Rd.
Schaumburg, IL 60173

National Spinal Cord Injury
Association
545 Concord Ave., Ste 29
Cambridge, MA 02138

National Therapeutic Recreation
Society
2775 S. Quincy St., Ste 300
Arlington, VA 22206

National Transition Network
University of Minnesota
6 Pattee Hall
150 Pillsbury Dr. SE
Minneapolis, MN 55455

National Tuberous Sclerosis
Association
8000 Corporate Dr. Ste 120
Landover, MD 20785

Neurofibromatosis, Inc.
8855 Annapolis, Ste 110
Lanham, MD 20706-2924

Orton Dyslexia Society
Chester Bldg., Ste 382
8600 LaSalle Rd.
Baltimore, MD 21286-2044

Osteogenesis Imperfecta Foundation
5005 W. Laurel St., Ste 210
Tampa, FL 33607

President's Committee on Mental
Retardation
Wilbur J. Cohen Bldg., Rm. 5325
330 Independence Ave. SW
Washington, DC 20201

Recordings for the Blind (RFB)
20 Roszel Rd.
Princeton, NJ 08540

Registry of Interpreters for the Deaf
8719 Colesville Rd., Ste 310
Silver Spring, MD 20910

Rehabilitation Services Administration
Department of Education
330 C St.
Washington, DC 20202-2531

Respite Care
National Resource Center
800 Eastowne Dr., Ste 105
Chapel Hill, NC 27514

Retinitis Pigmentosa International
Society for Degenerative Eye Diseases
P.O. Box 900
Woodland Hills, CA 91365

Rural Institute on Disabilities
52 Corbin Hall
University of Montana
Missoula, MT 59812

Signing Exact English (SEE)
Center for the Advancement
of Deaf Children
P.O. Box 1181
Los Alamitos, CA 90720

Specialized Training of Military
Parents (STOMP)
c/o Washington PAVE
12208 Pacific Highway SW
Tacoma, WA 98499

SpecialLink
186 Prince St.
Sydney, Nova Scotia, Canada B1P 5K5

Spina Bifida Association of America
4590 MacArthur Blvd. NW, Ste 250
Washington, DC 20007-4226

Spina Bifida Association of Canada
220-388 Donald St.
Winnipeg, Manitoba, Canada R3B 2J4

Stuttering Foundation of America
P.O. Box 11749
Memphis, TN 38111-0749

Stuttering Resource Foundation
123 Oxford Rd.
New Rochelle, NY 10804

Teacher Education Division (TED)
A Division of the Council for
Exceptional Children
1920 Association Dr.
Reston, VA 22091-1589

Technology and Media Division
(TAM)
A Division of the Council for
Exceptional Children
1920 Association Dr.
Reston, VA 22091-1589

Tourette's Syndrome Association
42-40 Bell Blvd.
Bayside, NY 11361-2861

Tourette's Syndrome Foundation
of Canada
238 Davenport Rd., Box 343
Toronto, Ontario, Canada M5R 1J6

Turner Syndrome Society
of the United States
15500 Wayzata Blvd.
Wayzata, MN 55391

United Cerebral Palsy Association
Community Service Division
1522 K St. NW, Ste 1112
Washington, DC 20005

United Ostomy Association
36 Executive Pk., Ste 120
Irvine, CA 92714-6744

U.S. Office of Special Education and
Rehabilitative Services
Switzer Bldg., 330 C St. SW
Washington, DC 20202

World Institute on Disability
510 16th St., Ste 100
Oakland, CA 94612-1502

Legal Terms

amicus curiae A Latin term meaning, literally, "friend of the court." Used in discussions of a case to indicate an individual or organization that is neither *plaintiff* nor *defendant* in a *civil case* but, because of special expertise or interest, is allowed by a court to become involved in the case. The involvement usually consists of submitting a "brief" (written presentation) containing supporting legal arguments and special facts to the court.

cert. den. An abbreviation for *certiorari* denied. In a citation to a case, indicates that a higher court (usually, the Supreme Court) has declined to order a lower court to send the case to it for review. By contrast, *cert. granted* means the higher court has ordered a lower court to send a case to it for review.

cert. granted An abbreviation for *"certiorari granted,"* which indicates that a higher court agrees to review a case; *"cert. den."* means that it will not. If *certiorari* is denied, the lower court ruling stands and continues to apply in the U.S. Circuit in which it was issued. In practice, other courts often use such rulings as a *precedent.*

certiorari A Latin term (abbreviated **cert.**) that indicates in a citation to a case that an order from an appeals court (usually, the Supreme Court) to a lower court has been entered to either require or decline to require the lower court to send up a case for review. The right-to-education cases decided by the U.S. Supreme Court usually go to that court on a petition (request) for certiorari by one of the parties (and the court sometimes grants the request and orders the lower court to send the case to it for review).

CFR See *Code of Federal Regulations.*

civil case A lawsuit brought by one or more individuals to seek redress of some legal injury (or aspect of an injury) for which there are civil (noncriminal) remedies. In right-to-education cases, these remedies are based on the federal or state constitutions, federal or state statutes, or federal or state agency regulations, or a combination of federal and state constitutions, statutes, and regulations. Right-to-education cases are always civil suits.

class action A *civil case* brought on behalf of the *plaintiffs* who are named in the suit as well as on behalf of all other persons similarly situated to vindicate their legally protected interests. *Mills v. Board of Education* was brought on behalf of 12-year-old Peter Mills and six other school-age children who were named in the complaint, as well as on behalf of all other *exceptional children* in the District of Columbia. By contrast, *Board v. Rowley* was not a class action lawsuit because it was brought on behalf of only one person, who sued to protect only her rights, not the rights of other people.

Code of Federal Regulations (CFR) A publication of the U.S. government that contains the regulations of the executive agencies of the government (e.g., U.S. Department of Education) that have been instated to implement laws (statutes) passed by Congress (e.g., *PL 94–142*).

competing equities A term describing a situation in which two or more people or groups of people have rights or privileges that cannot be fully satisfied without infringing on the rights or privileges of one another. For example, children with *disabilities* have some rights to be integrated with nondisabled children, but nondisabled children also have rights to an education that is not disrupted by children with disabilities. In such a case, the competing equities of both groups of children must be weighted against each other and a decision made by a court or other policymakers as to which claims prevail. Another way of thinking about competing equities is to ask: Whose rights or privileges are to be reduced for the benefit of other people?

consent agreement 1. An out-of-court agreement, formally approved by the court, that is reached by the parties to a lawsuit. In *Pennsylvania Association for Retarded Children (PARC) v. Commonwealth of Pennsylvania*, a court entered an order that it adopted pursuant to a consent agreement between the *plaintiffs* and *defendants*. 2. A legal term denoting an agreed-upon stipulation regarding an individual's treatment, involvement in research, or other action, based on that person's capacity to make decisions, having adequate information, and in the absence of force or coercion. *Informed consent* means that the individual is apprised of all rights and the consequences of consent.

de facto A Latin term that means, literally, "by reason of the fact." The follow-

ing is an example of its use: *Integration* by race and *disability* now is required by law (*de jure* integration), but may not actually occur in some schools or among some students (de facto *segregation*).

defendant The party in a lawsuit against whom legal action is taken. For example, if a parent sues a school system, the school system is the defendant.

de jure A Latin term that means, literally, "by law." In the past, *segregation* of the schools by race or *disability* was required by the laws of some states; thus, de jure segregation was enforced. Present law requires de jure *integration*.

dicta A Latin term describing *language* in a judicial opinion that is not essential to the disposition of the case or to the court's reasoning and that is regarded as gratuitous. Dicta are persuasive but not binding on other courts, whereas the court's holding and reasoning are.

discovery The process by which a party to a civil suit can find out about matters relevant to the case, including information about what evidence the other side has, what witnesses will be called, and so on. Discovery processes for obtaining information include depositions and interrogatories to obtain testimony, requests for documents or other tangibles, and requests for physical or mental examinations.

due process of law A right to have any applicable federal or state law applied reasonably and with sufficient safeguards, such as hearings and notice, to ensure that an individual is dealt with fairly; protects the rights of children and parents in identification, *evaluation* , and placement; provides for prior notice, parental consent, impartial hearing, appeals, written decision, and *surrogate parents*. Due process of law is guaranteed under the Fifth and Fourteenth Amendments to the federal Constitution.

EHLR An abbreviation for *Education for the Handicapped Law Reporter*; used in the works of a commercial publisher that report the opinions and judgments of many of the *special education* cases decided by state and federal courts.

en banc A French term meaning, literally, "on the bench." Refers to a situation in which a court consisting of more than one member (such as a federal appeals court) hears a case with all of its members present at the hearing and participating in the decision. Usually, federal courts of appeals are divided into panels (or groups) of judges, and only one panel hears a case and makes the judgment of the court, without the participation of the other members of the court. Sometimes, however, a case is so difficult or important that all members of the court hear the case and decide the outcome. The court then sits en banc— all together on the bench.

et seq. A Latin abbreviation for "and following" (et means "and"; seq. is an abbreviation for sequens, which means "following"). It is used in citations, where it always follows a noun (e.g., Vol. 20, *United States Code*, Sections 1401 et seq.—hence, "and following sections").

ex rel. A Latin abbreviation for ex relationale that indicates a lawsuit is brought on behalf of one person by another (e.g., the attorney general of a state may sue on behalf of an individual; thus, the case is captioned "State of Kansas, ex rel. Jane Doe, an incompetent, v. Superintendent, State Hospital"). The lawsuit normally is one in which the state attorney general seeks to vindicate a legal position that is favorable to the state and its citizens on behalf of a person not able to bring a lawsuit directly.

expert witness A person called to testify in a case because he/she has a recognized competence in an area. For ex-

ample, experts in the right-to-education cases had doctoral degrees in the field of *special education*, were authors of numerous professional publications pertaining to *exceptional children*, and were *consultants* to *advisory committees* on education.

F. Supp. An abbreviation for *Federal Supplement*; used in citations to a lawsuit's reported judgment and order. Indicates that the case was decided by a federal trial court (a "district" court) and is reported in a certain volume of the reports of the federal trial courts. The volume of the reports precedes the F. Supp. designation; and the identity of the court and the date of the judgment are set out in parentheses after the page number. Thus, in *PARC v. Commonwealth of Pennsylvania*, 343 F. Supp. 279 (E.D. Pa. 1972), the case is reported in volume 343 of the *Federal Supplement*, beginning at page 279, and was the decision of the federal district court for the Eastern District (section) of Pennsylvania in 1972.

F.2d An abbreviation for *Federal Report, 2d Series*; used in citations to a lawsuit's reported judgment and order. Indicates that the case was decided by a federal court of appeals and is reported in a certain volume of the reports of the federal courts of appeals. The volume of the reports precedes the F.2d designation; the page at which the report begins follows the F.2d designation; and the identity of the court and the date of the judgment are set out in parentheses after the page number. Thus, *Smuck v. Hobson*, 408 F.2d 175 (D.C. Cir. 1969), shows that the appellate judgment (in the case involving school classification practices of the District of Columbia Board of Education) is reported in volume 408 of the *Federal Report, 2d Series* , beginning at page 175, and was a decision of the federal court of appeals (D.C. Circuit Court of Appeals) in 1969.

Fed. Reg. An abbreviation for *Federal Register*, a daily publication of Congress, that contains the text of new laws and regulations and comments by members of Congress on matters of public policy.

in re A Latin term in the title of a law case that indicates "in the matter of." It is always followed by the name of a party to the lawsuit (e.g., In Re: John Doe, a minor; here, the title to the lawsuit means, "In the matter of John Doe, a minor/ child").

infra A Latin word in a discussion of a case indicating that the same case is referred to in a later part of the same article, chapter, book, judicial opinion, or other writing (e.g., the court may refer to the *Rowley* case, infra, meaning that it is discussed later in its opinion or, literally, within its opinion). Opposite of *supra*.

injunctive relief A remedy granted by a court forbidding or requiring some action by the *defendant*. Injunctive relief includes temporary restraining orders and preliminary and final injunctions. These types of relief differ from one another in that they are issued for different lengths of time, at different stages of the litigation process, and on the basis of different degrees of proof.

on remand A reference in a citation to a case that indicates that a lower court entered a judgment, for at least a second time, when it received the case from a higher court with a judgment and order to act in a particular way (e.g., the court's initial judgment is appealed, the appeals court enters a judgment to reverse in part and affirm in part and directs the lower court to change its original order; the lower court does so when the case is "on remand" to it from the higher court).

parens patriae A Latin term that means, literally, "father of the country," and that refers today to the doctrine that a state may act in a paternalistic way on behalf of its citizens, especially those who are children or who have *mental disabilities* and therefore are less effective than other people in protecting themselves. The parens patriae doctrine justifies, for example, compulsory education, which the state requires of all children for their own good.

per curiam A Latin term in a citation to a case that refers to the judgment of a court entered "by the court" (rather than by a judge who writes the opinion for the court). A per curiam judgment normally does not include the opinion of the judge, only the court's disposition of the case (e.g., affirmed, petition denied, etc.).

PL An abbreviation for "Public Law," referring to a statute passed by Congress as a public law. Every public law has a number that follows the PL designation; thus, *PL 94–142* refers to Public Law 142 of the 94th Congress.

plaintiff A person who brings a lawsuit to redress a violation of one or more of his/her legal rights.

precedent A previous decision by a judge or court that serves as a rule or guide to support other judges in deciding cases involving similar or analogous legal questions. In the early right-to-education cases, courts cited some famous education decisions as precedents, including *Brown v. Board of Education*, outlawing *segregated* schools, and *Gobson v. Hansen*, outlawing the track system in the District of Columbia. Just as *PARC* and *Mills* were cited as precedent by other courts for finding a constitutional right to education, so *Rowley* is now cited on various legal issues.

private action A case brought on behalf of one or more individuals to vindicate violation of their own legally protected interests. As distinguished from a *class* *action*, where the *relief* applies to all persons similarly situated or within the class represented by the *plaintiffs* (e.g., *PARC*), any relief granted in private action applies only to those plaintiffs actually before the court (e.g., *Rowley*).

procedural right A right that relates to the process of enforcing substantive rights or to obtaining *relief*, such as the right to a hearing, the right to present evidence in one's defense, and the right to counsel.

quid pro quo A Latin term that means, literally, "something for something" and indicates an exchange of money and/or goods (e.g., a school district provides *inservice training* in exchange for—as a quid pro quo for—state aid to defray expenses).

relief A remedy for some legal wrong. Relief is requested by a *plaintiff* and is granted by a court against a *defendant*.

reversed (rev'd) A word in a citation to a case that indicates that a higher court has overturned the result, and usually the reasoning, of a lower court and entered (or ordered the lower court to enter) a different judgment. Sometimes a higher court can reverse part of a lower court's judgment and affirm part of it; whether that is possible depends on the nature of the judgment.

settlement An out-of-court agreement among parties to a lawsuit, which resolves some or all of the issues involved in a case.

statutory right A right based on a statute or law passed by a unit of federal, state, or local government.

sub nom. A Latin abbreviation in a citation to a case that indicates that the case was decided by another court under a different name (sub meaning "under," and

nom. being an abbreviation for the Latin word nomine, meaning "name").

substance right A guaranteed right, such as the right to an education, usually granted by statutes and constitutions.

supra A Latin word in a citation to a case indicating that the same case was referred to in an earlier part of the same article, chapter, book, judicial opinion, or other writing. It means the opposite of *infra*.

U.S. An abbreviation, in a citation to a decision of the U.S. Supreme Court, that indicates that a judgment of that Court is reported in a certain volume of the *United States Reports*, which contain only the judgments and other orders of the U.S. Supreme Court. The volume number precedes the U.S. designation, the page number follows it, and the date of the judgment is set out in parentheses after the page reference.

U.S.C. An abbreviation for *United States Code*, an official publication of the U.S. government that contains the codified acts of Congress.

U.S.C.A. An abbreviation for *United States Code Annotated*, a commercial publication that contains the codified acts of Congress.

USLW An abbreviation for *United States Law Week*, a commercial publication that reports the judgments of various courts during a particular week. The volume of *USLW* precedes the *USLW* designation, and the page number in the report follows it, with the identity of the court and date of judgment set out in parentheses after the page number.

vacated In a citation to a case, indicates that a higher court has set aside the judgment of a lower court.

verdict A decision by a judge or jury in favor of one side or the other in a case.

Periodicals and Journals

AAC: Augmentative and Alternative
Communication
Decker Periodicals
P.O. Box 620, L.C.D.1
Hamilton, Ontario
Canada L8N 3K7

Academic Therapy (see *Intervention in*
School and Clinic)

ACEHI Journal
Association of the Canadian
Educators of the Hearing Impaired
4–116 Education N.
University of Alberta, Edmonton
Alberta, Canada T6G 2G5
or
58 Portugal Cove Rd.
St. Johns, Newfoundland
Canada A1B 2L9

Adapted Physical Activity Quarterly,
Human Kinetics Publishers, P.O.
Box 5076, Champaign, IL 61825

Adult Residential Care Journal, ACSW
720 Ottawa St., Ste 100
Leavenworth, KS 66048

Advanced Development (A Journal on
Adult Giftedness)
1452 Marion
Denver, CO 80218

American Annals of the Deaf
Gallaudet, KDES, PAS-6
800 Florida Ave. NE
Washington, DC 20002

American Archives of Rehabilitation
Therapy
36 Pine Valley Rd.
Conway, AR 72032
(publication discontinued with
completion of vol. 35, no. 3,
Winter 1987)

American Deafness and Rehabilitation
Association Journal
P.O. Box 251554
Little Rock, AR 72228
(formerly *Journal of*
Rehabilitation of the Deaf)

American Journal of Art Therapy
Vermont College
Norwich University
Montpelier, VT 05602

American Journal of Diseases of
Children (see *Archives of*
Pediatrics and Adolescent
Medicine)

American Journal of Mental Retardation
American Association on Mental
Retardation
444 N. Capitol St. NW, Ste 846
Washington, DC 20001-1512

*American Journal of Occupational
    Therapy*
    1383 Piccard Dr.
    P.O. Box 1725
    Rockville, MD 20850

American Journal of Orthopsychiatry
    American Orthopsychiatric
    Association
    49 Sheridan Ave.
    Albany, NY 12210

*American Journal of Speech-Language
    Pathology*
    10801 Rockville Pike
    Rockville, MD 20852-3279

American Rehabilitation
    Superintendent of Documents
    U.S. Government Printing Office
    Washington, DC 20402

AMP
    National Amputation Foundation
    73 Church St.
    Malverne, NY 11565

*Analysis and Intervention in
    Developmental Disabilities* (see
    *Research in Developmental
    Disabilities*)

Annals of Dyslexia
    The Orton Dyslexia Society
    8600 LaSalle Rd.
    Chester Bldg., Ste 382
    Baltimore, MD 21286-2044
    (formerly *Orton Society Bulletin*)

Applied Linguistics
    Oxford University Press
    Walton St.
    Oxford, England OX2 6DP

Archives of Disease in Childhood
    B.M.A. House
    Tavistock Sq.
    London, England WCIH 9JR

*Archives of Otolaryngology—Head
    and Neck Surgery*
    American Medical Association
    515 N. State St.
    Chicago, IL 60610

*Archives of Pediatrics and Adolescent
    Medicine*
    American Medical Association
    515 N. State St.
    Chicago, IL 60610
    (formerly *American Journal of
    Diseases of Children*)

Art Therapy
    The American Art Therapy
    Association
    1202 Allanson Rd.
    Murdelein, IL 60060

Arts in Psychotherapy
    Elsevier Science, Ltd.
    Oxford Fulfillment Ctr.
    P.O. Box 800
    Kidlington, Oxford
    England OX5 1DX

*ASHA (American Speech-Language-
    Hearing Association Journal)*
    10801 Rockville Pike
    Rockville, MD 20852-3279

Audecibel
    20361 Middlebelt
    Livonia, MI 48152

*Augmentative and Alternative
    Communication (AAC)*
    Decker Periodicals
    P.O. Box 620, Station A
    One James St. S
    Hamilton, Ontario, Canada L8N 3K7

Augmentative and Alternative Communication
    International Society of
    Augmentative and Alternative
    Communication
    Williams and Wilkins
    428 E. Preston
    Baltimore, MD 21202

Australasian Journal of Special Education
    Business Mgr.
    3 Ocean View Crescent
    Mt. Osmond 5064
    S. Australia

Australia and New Zealand Journal of Developmental Disabilities
    P.O. Box 255
    Carlton, S. Victoria 3053
    Australia
    or
    Special Education Centre
    University of Newcastle
    New South Wales 2308
    Australia

Australian Teacher of the Deaf
    P.O. Box 4120
    Parrematta, NSW 2124
    Australia

B. C. Journal of Special Education
    c/o Dr. Margaret Csapo
    Dept. of Educational Psychology
    and Special Education
    University of British Columbia
    2125 Main Mall
    Vancouver, Canada BC V6T 1Z4

Behavior Disorders
    Council for Children with
    Behavior Disorders (CCBD)
    A Division of the Council for
    Exceptional Children
    1920 Association Dr.
    Reston, VA 22091-1589

Behavior in Our Schools, Buena Vista
    College, Fourth and College Sts.,
    Storm Lake, IA 50588

Behavior Modification
    Sage Publications
    2455 Teller Rd.
    Newbury Park, CA 91320

Behavior Problems Bulletin
    Victoria College—Burwood
    Campus
    221 Burwood Highway
    Burwood, Victoria 3125
    Australia

Beyond Behavior
    Council for Children with
    Behavior Disorders
    c/o Reece Peterson
    202A Barkley Center
    University of Nebraska—Lincoln
    Lincoln, NE 68582-0732

Braille Monitor
    National Federation of the Blind
    1800 Johnson St.
    Baltimore, MD 21230

Breakthrough
    National Tay-Sachs
    and Allied Disease Association
    385 Elliot St.
    Newton, MA 02164

Bridge, The
    Beecher House
    P.O. Box 11
    Guilford, CT 06437

British Association of Teachers of the Deaf Journal
    Attn: G.F.E. Clark, ACP
    Gaters Gardens, Sandford,
    Crediton, Devon
    England EX17 4LU
    (formerly *Teacher of the Deaf*)

British Journal of Disorders of Communication (see *European Journal of Disorders of Communication*)

British Journal of Physical Education
Ling House
162 King's Cross Rd.
London, England WCIX 9DH

British Journal of Special Education
Basil Blackwell Ltd.
P.O. Box 87
Oxford, England OX2 ODT
or
National Council for Special
Education
1 Wood St.
Stratford-Upon-Avon
Warwickshire, England CV37 6JE

British Journal of Visual Impairment
c/o South Regional Association
for the Blind
55 Eton Ave.
London, England NW3 3ET

Bulletin
American Association for
Rehabilitation Therapy
P.O. Box 93
North Little Rock, AR 72116

*Canadian Journal of Special
Education*
Simon Fraser University
c/o Dr. Bernice Wong
Faculty of Education
Burnaby, British Columbia
Canada V5A 1F6

*Career Development for Exceptional
Individuals*
Division on Career Development
and Transition
Council for Exceptional Children
1920 Association Dr.
Reston, VA 22091-1589

CASE Newsletter
Council for Administrators of
Special Education
615 16th St. NW
Albuquerque, NM 87104

CASE in POINT
Council for Administrators of
Special Education
615 16th St. NW
Albuquerque, NM 87104

*Challenge, Reaching and Teaching the
Gifted Child*
Good Apple
Box 299
Carthage, IL 62321-0299

Challenging Times
National Professional Resources
Dept. 6
25 South Regent St.
Port Chester, NY 10573

Child: Care, Health and Development
Blackwell Scientific Publications,
Ltd.
P.O. Box 87
Oxford, England OX2 ODT

Child Abuse and Neglect
Pergamon Press
Elsevier Science, Ltd.
Oxford Fulfillment Centre
P.O. Box 800, Kidlington
Oxford, England OX5 1DX
or
600 White Plains Rd.
Tarrytown, NY 10591
(Editor: Richard D. Krugman.
Kempenat Center, 1205 Oneid St.,
Denver, CO 80220)

Child and Family Behavior Therapy
Haworth Press
10 Alice St.
Binghamton, NY 13904

Child and Youth Care Forum
　Human Sciences Press
　233 Spring St.
　New York, NY 10013-1578

Child and Youth Services
　Haworth Press
　10 Alice St.
　Binghamton, NY 13904

Children and Youth Services Review
　Pergamon Press
　Elsevier Science, Ltd.
　Oxford Fulfillment Centre
　P.O. Box 800, Kidlington
　Oxford, England OX5 1DX

Children's Health Care
　Lawrence Erlbaum Associates
　365 Broadway, Ste 102
　Hillsdale, NJ 07642

Children's Legal Rights Journal
　William S. Heir & Co.
　1285 Main St.
　Buffalo, NY 14209

Clearing House Memo
　National Clearing House of
　Rehabilitation Training Materials
　1816 W. 6th St.
　Stillwater, OK 74078

Clinical Neuropsychologist
　SWETS & Zeitlinger BV
　Heereweg, 347-B
　2161 CA Lisse
　Netherlands

Cognitive Rehabilitation
　Neuroscience Publishers
　6555 Carrollton Ave.
　Indianapolis, IN 46220

Counseling and Human Development
　Love Publishing Co.
　P.O. Box 22353
　Denver, CO 80222

Counterpoint
　LRP Publications
　747 Dresher Rd.
　P.O. Box 980
　Horsham, PA 19004

Creative Child and Adult Quarterly
　National Association of Creative
　Children and Adults
　8080 Spring Valley Dr.
　Cincinnati, OH 45236

Creativity Research Journal
　Lawrence Erlbaum Associates
　365 Broadway, Ste 102
　Hillsdale, NJ 07642

Deaf American (see *Deaf American Monograph*)

Deaf American Monograph
　National Association of the Deaf
　814 Thayer Ave.
　Silver Spring, MD 20910
　(formerly *Deaf American*)

Deficience Mentale/Mental Retardation
　York University
　4700 Keele St.
　North York, Ontario
　Canada M3J 1P3

Developmental Disabilities Bulletin
　Developmental Disabilities Centre
　6-123d Education North
　University of Alberta, Edmonton
　Alberta, Canada T6G 2G5
　(formerly *Mental Retardation and Learning Disability Bulletin*)

*Developmental Medicine and Child
    Neurology*
    Blackwell Scientific Publishers
    P.O. Box 87
    Oxford, England OX2 ODT

Diagnostique
    Council for Educational
    Diagnostic Services (CEDS)
    1920 Association Dr.
    Reston, VA 22091-1589

Disability and Society
    P.O. Box 25, Arlington
    Oxfordshire, OX14 3UE
    United Kingdom
    (formerly *Disability, Handicap
    and Society*)

Disability, Handicap and Society (see
    Disability and Society)

Disabled U.S.A. (see *Worklife*)

*Division for Children's Communication
    Development (DCCD)*
    Council for Exceptional Children
    1920 Association Dr.
    Reston, VA 22091-1589

*Division of the Physical and Health
    Disabilities (DPHD)*
    Council for Exceptional Children
    1920 Association Dr.
    Reston, VA 22091-1589

Division on Visual Disabilities (DVD)
    Council for Exceptional Children
    1920 Association Dr.
    Reston, VA 22091-1589

DPH Journal
    Division on Physical and Health
    Disabilities
    Council for Exceptional Children
    1920 Association Dr.
    Reston, VA 22091-1589

Dyslexia Review
    Dyslexia Institute
    133 Gresham Rd.
    Starnes, England TW18 2AJ

Educating Able Learners (EAL)
    Gifted Student Institute
    P.O. Box 11388
    Ft. Worth, TX 76110-0388

*Education and Training in Mental
    Retardation*
    Division on Mental Retardation
    and Developmental Disabilities
    Council for Exceptional Children
    1920 Association Dr.
    Reston, VA 22091-1589

Education and Treatment of Children
    Pressley Ridge School
    530 Marshall Ave.
    Pittsburgh, PA 15214

*Education for the Handicapped Law
    Report* (see *Individuals with
    Disabilities Education Law Report*)

*Education for the Hearing Impaired
    Bulletin*
    1537 35th St. NW
    Washington, DC 20007

Educator, The
    International Council for Education
    of the Visually Handicapped
    Perkins School for the Blind
    175 N. Beacon St.
    Watertown, MA 02172

Education of the Visually Handicapped
    (see *Re:View*)

*Emotionally Handicapped Children's
    Bulletin*
    Southern Connecticut
    State College
    New Haven, CT 06515

Entourage
G. Allen Roehr Institute
Kinsmen Bldg.
York University Campus
4700 Keele St.
Downview, Ontario
Canada M3J 1P3

European Journal of Disorders of
Communication
Allen Press
P.O. Box 1897
Lawrence, KS 66044-8897
(formerly *British Journal of*
Disorders of Communication)

European Journal of Special Needs
Education
International Thomson
Publishing Services
Cheriton House, Dept. J
North Way, Andover
Hampshire, England SP10 5BE

Exceptional Child (see *International*
Journal of Disabilities:
Development and Education)

Exceptional Child Education
Resources
Council for Exceptional Children
1920 Association Dr.
Reston, VA 22091-1589

Exceptional Children
Council for Exceptional Children
1920 Association Dr.
Reston, VA 22091-1589

Exceptional Education Quarterly (see
Remedial and Special Education)

Exceptional Parent
Fulco Company
P.O. Box 3000, Dept. E.P.
Denville, NJ 07834-9919

Exceptionality
Division for Research of the
Council for Exceptional Children
1920 Association Dr.
Reston, VA 22091-1589

Focus
National Technical Institute for
the Deaf
One Lomb Memorial Dr.
P.O. Box 9887
Rochester, NY 14623-0887

Focus on Autism and Other
Developmental Disabilities
Pro-Ed
8700 Shoal Creek Blvd.
Austin, TX 78758-6897

Focus on Exceptional Children
Love Publishing Co.
P.O. Box 22353
Denver, CO 80222

Fountainhead
American Association for
Education of the Visually
Handicapped
919 Walnut St.
Philadelphia, PA 19107
(publication discontinued with the
Spring 1982 issue)

Future Reflections
National Federation of the Blind
1800 Johnson St.
Baltimore, MD 21230

Gallaudet Today
Office of Alumni and Public
Relations
800 Florida Ave. NE
Kendall Green NW
Washington, DC 20002

G/C/T (see *Gifted Child Today*)

Gifted Child Quarterly
National Association
for Gifted Children
1155 15th St. NW, Ste 1002
Washington, DC 20005

Gifted Child Today (GCT)
Prufrock Press
P.O. Box 8813
Waco, TX 76714-8813
(formerly *G/C/T*)

Gifted Children Monthly
213 Hollydell Dr.
Sewell, NJ 08080

Gifted Education International
AB Academic Publishers
P.O. Box 42
Bicester, Oxon
England OX6 7NW

Habilitative Mental Health Care
Newsletter
P.O. Box 57
Bear Creek, NC 27207

Hearing Journal
Williams & Williams Co.
P.O. Box 64025
Baltimore, MD 21264

Hearing Rehabilitation Quarterly
New York League for the
Hard of Hearing
71 W. 23rd St.
New York, NY 10010

Hospice Journal
National Hospice Organization
1901 N. Moore St., Ste 901
Arlington, VA 22209

In the Mainstream
Mainstream, Inc.
3 Bethesda Metro Ctr., Ste 830
Bethesda, MD 20814-5330

Inclusion Times
National Professional Resources
25 South Regent St.
Port Chester, NY 10573

Inclusive Education Programs
747 Presher Rd.
P.O. Box 980
Horsham, PA 19044-0980

Individuals with Disabilities Education
Law Report (IDELR)
747 Dresher Rd.
P.O. Box 980
Horsham, PA 19044-0980
(formerly *Education for the*
Handicapped Law Report)

Infants and Young Children
Aspen Publications
7201 McKinney Cir.
Frederick, MD 21701

Infant-Toddler Intervention: The
Transdisciplinary Journal
Singular Publishing Group
4284 41st St.
San Diego, CA 92105-1197

Innotek Newsletter
National Lekotek Center
2100 Ridge Ave.
Evanston, IL 60201

Interaction
National Council on
Intellectual Disability
Action House
Edinburgh Ave., GPO Box 647
Canberra Act 2601, Australia

International Journal of Disabilities:
Development and Education
University of Queensland, St. Lucia
Queensland 4067
Australia
(formerly *Exceptional Child*)

International Journal of Rehabilitation Research
Chapman & Hall
North Way, Andover
Hampshire, England SPIO 5BE

International Journal of Special Education
University of British Columbia
Educational Psychology and Special Education
2125 Main Mall
Vancouver, British Columbia
Canada V6T 125

International Journal of Special Education and Disability
Eleanor Schonell Special Education Research Center
University of Queensland, St. Lucia
Queensland 4067, Australia

Intervention in School and Clinic
Pro-Ed Journals
8700 Shoal Creek Blvd.
Austin, TX 78758-6897
(formerly *Academic Therapy*)

Issues in Law and Medicine
Office of Publication
P.O. Box 1586
Terre Haute, IN 47808-1586

Issues in Special Education and Rehabilitation (ISER)
Shunit Reiter, Editor
University of Haifa
Mount Carmel, Haifa 31905
Israel

Japanese Journal of Special Education
c/o Institute of Special Education
University of Tsukuba
Sakwa-Mura
Nii Hari-Gun
Ibaraki-Ken 305
Japan

JCD, Journal of Counseling and Development
American Counseling Association
5999 Stevenson Ave.
Alexandria, VA 22304
(formerly *Personnel and Guidance Journal*)

John Tracy Clinic Bulletin
John Tracy Clinic
806 W. Adams Blvd.
Los Angeles, CA 90007

Journal for Culturally and Linguistically Diverse Exceptional Learners
Division for Culturally and Linguistically Diverse Exceptional Learners
University of Akron
Akron, OH 44325-5007

Journal for the Education of the Gifted
Association for the Gifted
University of North Carolina Press
P.O. Box 2288
Chapel Hill, NC 27514
or
1920 Association Dr.
Reston, VA 22091-1589

Journal for Vocational Special Needs Education
c/o Dr. Clide D. Classity
Managing Editor
PTEC Clearwater
6100 N. 154th Ave.
Clearwater, FL 34620
or
Department of Vocational Education
624 Aderhold Hall
University of Georgia
Athens, GA 30602

Journal of Abnormal Child Psychology
Plenum Publishing Corp.
233 Spring St.
New York, NY 10013

Journal of Abnormal Psychology
American Psychological
Association
750 1st St. NW
Washington, DC 20002-4242

*Journal of Adolescent Chemical
Dependency* (see *Journal of Child
and Adolescent Substance Abuse*)

*Journal of Applied Rehabilitation
Counseling*
National Rehabilitation
Counseling Association
8807 Sudley Rd., Ste 102
Manassas, VA 22110

Journal of Auditory Research
Box N
Groton, CT 06340

*Journal of Autism and Childhood
Schizophrenia* (see *Journal of
Autism and Developmental
Disorders*)

*Journal of Autism and Developmental
Disabilities*
Plenum Publishing Co.
Eric Shopler, Editor
233 Spring St.
New York, NY 10013
(formerly *Journal of Autism and
Childhood Schizophrenia*)

*Journal of Behavior Therapy and
Experimental Psychiatry*
Elsevier Science, Ltd.
Oxford Fulfillment Centre
P.O. Box 800, Kidlington
Oxford, England OX5 1DX

*Journal of Child and Adolescent
Substance Abuse*
Haworth Press
10 Alice St.
Binghamton, NY 13904-1580
(formerly *Journal of Adolescent
Chemical Dependency*)

Journal of Child Language
Cambridge University Press
110 Midland Ave.
Port Chester, NY 10573

Journal of Child Sexual Abuse
Haworth Press
10 Alice St.
Binghamton, NY 13904-1580

*Journal of Childhood Communication
Disorders*
Division for Children's
Communication Development
(DCCD)
Council for Exceptional Children
1920 Association Dr.
Reston, VA 22091-1589

*Journal of Clinical and Experimental
Neuropsychology*
SWETS North America
P.O. Box 517
Berwyn, PA 19312

Journal of Clinical Child Psychology
Lawrence Erlbaum Associates
365 Broadway, Ste 102
Hillsdale, NJ 07642

Journal of Communication Disorders
Elsevier Science
655 Avenue of the Americas
New York, NY 10010

Journal of Counseling and Development
American Counseling Association
5999 Stevenson Ave.
Alexandria, VA 22304

Journal of Creative Behavior
Creative Education Foundation
1050 Union Rd., Ste 4
Buffalo, NY 14224

Journal of Developmental and
Physical Disabilities
Plenum Publishing Co.
Vincent B. Van Hassett, Editor
233 Spring St.
New York, NY 10013

Journal of Disability Policy Studies
University of Arkansas Press
Fayetteville, AR 72701

Journal of Dyslexia
Chester Bldg.
8600 LaSalle Rd., Ste 382
Baltimore, MD 21204

Journal of Early Intervention
Council for Exceptional Children,
1920 Association Dr.
Reston, VA 22091-1589
(formerly *Journal of the Division*
for Early Childhood)

Journal of Educational and
Psychological Consultation
Lawrence Erlbaum Associates
365 Broadway, Ste 102
Hillsdale, NJ 07642

Journal of Emotional and Behavioral
Disorders
Pro-Ed Journals
8700 Shoal Creek Blvd.
Austin, TX 78758-6897

Journal of Experimental Analysis of
Behavior
Department of Psychology
Indiana University
Bloomington, IN 47405

Journal of Experimental Education
Heldref Publications
1319 18th St. NW
Washington, DC 20036-1802

Journal of Genetic Psychology
Heldref Publications
1319 18th St. NW
Washington, DC 20036-1802

Journal of Head Trauma Rehabilitation
Aspen Publications
1600 Research Blvd.
Rockville, MD 20850

Journal of Intellectual Disability
Research
Blackwell Scientific Publishers
P.O. Box 87
Oxford, England OX2 ODT
(formerly *Journal of Mental*
Deficiency Research)

Journal of Learning Disabilities
Pro-Ed
8700 Shoal Creek Blvd.
Austin, TX 78758

Journal of Mental Deficiency Research
(see *Journal of Intellectual*
Disability Research)

Journal of Motor Behavior
Heldref Publications
1319 18th Street NW
Washington, DC 20036-1802

Journal of Music Therapy
National Association
of Music Therapy
8455 Colesville Rd., Ste 930
Silver Spring, MD 20910

*Journal of Optometric Vision
   Development*
      College of Optometrists
      in Vision Development
      P.O. Box 285
      Chula Vista, CA 92012

Journal of Pediatric Psychology
      Plenum Publishing Corp.
      227 W. 17th St.
      New York, NY 10011

Journal of Pediatrics
      11830 Westline Industrial Dr.
      St. Louis, MO 63141

Journal of Physical Therapy
      American Physical Therapy
      Association
      1156 15th St. NW
      Washington, DC 20005

*Journal of Practical Approaches to
   Developmental Handicap*
      c/o Rehabilitation
      Studies Program
      4th floor, Education Tower
      University of Calgary
      2500 University Drive NW
      Calgary, Alberta
      Canada T2N 1N4

Journal of Prosthetics and Orthotics
      American Academy of Orthotists
      and Prosthetists
      1650 King St., Ste 500
      Alexandria, VA 22314-2747
      (formerly *Orthotics and
      Prosthetics*)

*Journal of Reading, Writing and
   Learning Disabilities International*
      (see *Reading and Writing
      Quarterly*)

Journal of Rehabilitation
      National Rehabilitation
      Association
      633 S. Washington St.
      Alexandria, VA 22134-4193

Journal of Rehabilitation of the Deaf
      (see *American Deafness and
      Rehabilitation Association Journal*)

Journal of Special Education
      Pro-Ed
      8700 Shoal Creek Blvd.
      Austin, TX 78758

*Journal of Special Education
   Technology*
      Peabody College
      Box 328
      Vanderbilt University
      Nashville, TN 37203

*Journal of Speech and Hearing
   Disorders (JSHD)*
      10801 Rockville Pike
      Rockville, MD 20852

*Journal of Speech and Hearing
   Research*
      American Speech-Language-
      Hearing Association
      10801 Rockville Pike
      Rockville, MD 20852

*Journal of the Academy of
   Rehabilitation Audiology,
   Communicative Disorders*
      Communication Arts Center 229
      University of Northern Iowa
      Cedar Falls, IA 50614

*Journal of the Acoustical Society of
   America*
      American Institute of Physics
      Attn: Paula Schein
      500 Sunnyside Blvd.
      Woodbury, NY 11797

*Journal of the American Optometric
    Association*
    243 N. Lindburgh Blvd.
    St. Louis, MO 63141

*Journal of the Association for Persons
    with Severe Handicaps (JASH)*
    11202 Greenwood Ave. S
    Seattle, WA 98133-8612

*Journal of the British Association of
    Teachers of the Deaf*
    Britain Association of Teachers
    of the Deaf
    Attn: G.F.E. Clark, ACP
    2 Gaters Gardens, Sandford
    Crediton, Devon
    England EX17 4LU

*Journal of the Division for Early
    Childhood* (see *Journal of Early
    Intervention*)

*Journal of Visual Impairment and
    Blindness*
    15 W. 16th St.
    New York, NY 10011
    (formerly *New Outlook for the
    Blind*)

Juvenile and Family Court Journal
    National Council of Juvenile and
    Family Court Judges
    University of Nevada—Reno
    Box 8978
    Reno, NV 89507

*Juvenile Diabetes Foundation
    International*
    432 Park Avenue S, 16th floor
    New York, NY 10016

*Language, Speech and Hearing
    Services in Schools*
    ASHA
    10801 Rockville Pike
    Rockville, MD 20852

*Leadership Times for Special Service
    Personnel*
    National Professional Resources
    35 Regents St.
    Port Chester, NY 10515

Learning Disabilities Focus (see
    *Learning Disabilities Research and
    Practice*)

*Learning Disabilities Research and
    Practice*
    Division for Learning Disabilities
    Council for Exceptional Children
    1920 Association Dr.
    Reston, VA 22091-1589
    (formerly *Learning Disabilities
    Focus*)

Learning Disabilities Quarterly
    Council for Learning
    Disabilities (CLD)
    P.O. Box 40303
    Overland Park, KS 66204

*Mental and Physical Disability Law
    Reporter*
    Commission on the Mental and
    Physical Disability Law
    1800 M St. NW
    Washington, DC 20036

Mental Retardation
    American Association
    on Mental Retardation
    444 N. Capitol St. NW, Ste 846
    Washington, DC 20001-1512

*Mental Retardation and
    Developmental Disabilities
    Research Reviews*
    Society for Developmental
    Pediatrics
    Wiley-Liss Publications
    665 3rd Ave.
    New York, NY 10158

*Mental Retardation and Learning
Disability Bulletin* (see
Developmental Disabilities Bulletin)

Mental Retardation Bulletin (see
Developmental Disabilities Bulletin)

M S Canada
Multiple Sclerosis Society
of Canada
250 Bloor St. E, Ste 820
Toronto, Ontario
Canada M4W 3P9

*National Clearinghouse of
Rehabilitation Training Materials*
816 W. 6th St.
Oklahoma State University
Stillwater, OK 74078-0435

National Disability Law Reporter
747 Dresher Rd.
P.O. Box 980
Horsham, PA 19044-0980

National Rural Project Newsletter (see
Rural Special Education Quarterly)

New Outlook for the Blind (see *Journal
of Visual Impairment and
Blindness*)

Network Magazine
Promoting Inclusive Communities
Private Bag 4004
Kimberly Road
Levin, New Zealand

NTID Focus
One Lomb Memorial Dr.
Rochester, NY 14623

Occupational Therapy Newsletter
1382 Piccard Dr.
Rockville, MD 20850
(publication discontinued as of
January 1990)

Orthotics and Prosthetics (see *Journal
of Prosthetics and Orthotics*)

Orton Society Bulletin (see *Annals of
Dyslexia*)

Otolaryngology
Lippincott/Harper Journals
Loose Leaf Division
100 Insurance Way
Hagerstown, MD 21740

Paraplegic News
5201 N. 19th Ave., Ste 111
Phoenix, AZ 85015

Personnel and Guidance Journal (see
*JCD, Journal of Counseling and
Development*)

*Perspectives for Teachers of the
Hearing Impaired* (see *Perspectives
in Education and Deafness*)

Perspectives in Education and Deafness
Gallaudet College
800 Florida Ave. NE
Washington, DC 20002
(formerly *Perspectives for
Teachers of the Hearing Impaired*)

Physical Medicine and Rehabilitation
Hanley & Belfus
210 S. 13th St.
Philadelphia, PA 19107

Physical Therapy
1111 N. Fairfax St.
Alexandria, VA 22314

Reading and Writing Quarterly
Taylor & Francis
Rankin Rd., Basingstone Hants
England RG24 OPR
(formerly *Journal of Reading,
Writing and Learning Disabilities
International*)

Rehabilitation Gazette
    5100 Oakland Ave., Ste 206
    St. Louis, MO 63110-1406

*Remedial and Special Education
    (RASE)*
    Pro-Ed
    8700 Shoal Creek Blvd.
    Austin, TX 78758-6897
    (formerly *Exceptional Education
    Quarterly*)

*Research in Developmental
    Disabilities*
    Elsevier Science, Ltd.
    Oxford Fulfillment Centre
    P.O. Box 800, Kidlington
    Oxford, England OX5 1DX
    (incorporated the journal *Analysis
    and Intervention in Developmental
    Disabilities* in January 1987)

Re:View
    Heldref Publications
    4000 Albermarle St. NW
    Washington, DC 20016
    (formerly *Education of the
    Visually Handicapped*)

*Roeper Review: A Journal on Gifted
    Child Education*
    P.O. Box 329
    Bloomfield Hills, MI 48013

Rural Special Education Quarterly
    American Council on Rural
    Special Education
    Department of Special Education
    University of Utah
    221 Milton Bennion Hall
    Salt Lake City, UT 84112
    (formerly *National Rural Project
    Newsletter*)

Schizophrenia Bulletin
    National Institute of
    Mental Health
    Superintendent of Documents
    U.S. Government Printing Office
    Washington, DC 20402

Seeing Eye Guide
    P.O. Box 375
    Morristown, NJ 07960

Sexuality and Disability
    Human Sciences Press
    233 Spring St.
    New York, NY 10013-1578

Sign Language Studies
    Linstock Press
    4020 Blackburn Lane
    Burtonsville, MD 20866-1167

Special Children
    American Association
    of Special Educators
    P.O. Box 168
    Fryeburg, ME 04037

Special Education Forward Friends
    National Council
    for Special Education
    12 Hollycroft Ave.
    London, England NN3 72L

Special Education Report
    Capital Publications
    P.O. Box 1453
    Alexandria, VA 22313

Special Educator
    CRR Publishing Co.
    LRP Publications
    1035 Camphill Rd.
    Ft. Washington, PA 19034

Special Educator, The
  747 Dresher Rd.
  P.O. Box 980
  Horsham, PA 19044

Special Services in the Schools
  Haworth Press
  10 Alice St.
  Binghamton, NY 13904

Sports 'n Spokes
  2111 E. Highland Ave., Ste 180
  Phoenix, AZ 85016-4741

Talent Tabloid
  Talent Identification Program
  Duke University
  Box 40077
  W. Duke Bldg.
  Durham, NC 27708

Talents and Gifts
  Association for the Gifted
  Frank Porter Graham Child
  Development Center
  c/o Dr. J. Gallagher
  Hwy. 54 Bypass West
  Chapel Hill, NC 27514

*Teacher Education and Special
  Education (TESE)*
  Teacher Education Division
  Council for Exceptional Children
  1920 Association Dr.
  Reston, VA 22091-1589

Teacher of the Deaf (see *British
  Association of Teachers of the Deaf
  Journal*)

Teaching Exceptional Children
  Council for Exceptional Children
  1920 Association Dr.
  Reston, VA 22091-1589

Their World
  National Center for Learning
  Disabilities
  381 Park Ave., Ste 1420
  New York, NY 10016-8806

*Topics in Early Childhood Special
  Education*
  Pro-Ed
  8700 Shoal Creek Blvd.
  Austin, TX 78758-6897

Topics in Language Disorders
  Aspen Publications
  P.O. Box 990
  Frederick, MD 21701

*Topics in Learning and Learning
  Disabilities*
  Pro-Ed
  8700 Shoal Creek Blvd.
  Austin, TX 78758-6897

Understanding Our Gifted
  Open Space Communications
  P.O. Box 18268
  Boulder, CO 80308-8268

Visually Handicapped
  Heldref Publications
  4000 Albermarle St. NW
  Washington, DC 20016

Volta Review
  3417 Volta Pl. NW
  Washington, DC 20007

Worklife
  President's Committee on
  Employment of People with
  Disabilities
  1111 20th St. NW, Ste 636
  Washington, DC 20036
  (formerly *Disabled U.S.A.*)

Sources of Legal Assistance

American Bar Association
1800 M St. NW, Ste 200
Washington, DC 20036

American Civil Liberties Union
132 W. 43rd St.
New York, NY 10036

Architectural and Transportation
Barriers Compliance Board
1331 F St. NW, Ste 1000
Washington, DC 20004

Association for Retarded Citizens (ARC)
500 E. Border St., Ste 300
Arlington, TX 76010

Center on Human Policy
Syracuse University
200 Huntington Hall
Syracuse, NY 13244-2340

Children's Defense Fund
25 E St. NW
Washington, DC 20036

Commission on the Mentally Disabled
1800 M St. NW
Washington, DC 20036

Council for Exceptional Children
Governmental Relations Unit
1920 Association Dr.
Reston, VA 22091-1589

Disability Rights Center
2500 Q St. NW, Ste 121
Washington, DC 20007

Disability Rights Education and
Defense Fund, Inc. (DREDF)
2212 6th St.
Berkeley, CA 94710

Education Law Center, Inc.
155 Washington St., Rm. 205
Newark, NJ 07102

Mainstream, Inc.
3 Bethesda Metro Ctr., Ste 830
Bethesda, MD 20814

Mental Disability Legal
Resource Center
1800 M St. NW
Washington, DC 20036

Mental Health Law Project
1101 15th St. NW, Ste 1212
Washington, DC 20005

National Association of
Coordinators of State Programs
for the Mentally Retarded
113 Oronoco St.
Alexandria, VA 22314

National Association on Legal
Problems of Education
3601 Southwest 29th, Ste 223
Topeka, KS 66614

National Center for Law and Deafness
800 Florida Ave. NE
Washington, DC 20002

Public Interest Law Center
125 S. 9th St.
Philadelphia, PA 19107

U.S. Department of Justice
Civil Rights Division
Special Litigation Section
10 Pennsylvania Ave. NW
Washington, DC 20530

Washington Legal Foundation
Court-watch
2009 Massachusetts Ave. NW
Washington, DC 20036